Such
Good Girls

SUCH GOOD GIRLS

THE JOURNEY OF THE HOLOCAUST'S
HIDDEN CHILD SURVIVORS

R. D. ROSEN

HARPER PERENNIAL

NEW YORK • LONDON • TORONTO • SYDNEY • NEW DELHI • AUCKLAND

A hardcover edition of this book was published in 2014 by Harper, an imprint of HarperCollins Publishers.

SUCH GOOD GIRLS. Copyright © 2014 by R. D. Rosen. All rights reserved. Printed in the United States of America. No part of this book may be used or reproduced in any manner whatsoever without written permission except in the case of brief quotations embodied in critical articles and reviews. For information, address HarperCollins Publishers, 195 Broadway, New York, NY 10007.

HarperCollins books may be purchased for educational, business, or sales promotional use. For information, please e-mail the Special Markets Department at SPsales@harpercollins.com.

FIRST HARPER PERENNIAL EDITION PUBLISHED 2015.

Designed by Michael P. Correy

The Library of Congress Cataloging-in-Publication Data has catalogued the hardcover edition as follows:

Rosen, Richard Dean.
Such good girls : the journey of the Holocaust's hidden child survivors / R. D. Rosen.
pages   cm
ISBN 978-0-06-229710-5
1. Schwarzwald, Selma, 1937– 2. Hillel, Flora, 1936– 3. Heijmans, Carla, 1931– 4. Jewish children in the Holocaust—Biography. 5. Holocaust survivors—New York—Biography. I. Title.
D804.48.R67   2014
940.53′18083—dc23   2014014200

ISBN 978-0-06-229711-2 (pbk.)

18 19   ov/LSC   10 9 8 7 6 5 4

In memory of my mom and dad,
always with me.

*Everyone knows of course the story of Anne Frank, but
Anne Frank did not survive the war, whereas we, luckily,
did. One could say that we were fortunate, and for that
reason we have remained more or less silent to this day.*

—Ed van Thijn, then Mayor of Amsterdam, speaking at the
Hidden Child Congress in Amsterdam, 1992

It would be easier to live without remembering all the time.

—a Holocaust survivor in the
documentary *Four Seasons Lodge*

CONTENTS

AUTHOR'S NOTE
ON NONFICTION

The personal histories at the heart of this book are based entirely on the words of the subjects themselves—whether preserved in correspondence, family documents, other written memorabilia, or recollected in present-day interviews conducted by the author. There is, of course, no such thing as perfect recall; the passage of time alone wreaks havoc on benign memories, let alone on memories so singularly traumatic, so beyond comprehension even now. The people who experienced hiding firsthand and somehow lived to tell the tale—the three women in this book, for example—inevitably stumbled at times in the telling. On such occasions, I've turned to the historical record for additional details or clarification. Some actual events have been enhanced with likely details and dialogue based on the recollections of my subjects and in consultation with them. Otherwise, the events, details, and emotions described herein have been neither invented nor embellished.

A Note on Names

This book concerns three women who were forced to adopt new names in order to survive the Holocaust. I've tried to identify them by their original names whenever possible, but since that was not always possible to do and still maintain the integrity of their stories, I've provided below a brief key to the names of the book's major characters.

SOPHIE was born Selma Schwarzwald in 1937 in Lvov, Poland, the only child of Laura and Daniel Schwarzwald. In 1942, Selma escaped the Lvov ghetto with her mother, bearing papers identifying Selma as Zofia Tymejko and Laura as Bronislawa Tymejko, a fatherless Catholic girl and her widowed mother. In the pages that follow, I've continued to call the mother Laura (although she was considered Bronislawa to the world), but refer to her daughter Selma by her new name, Zofia. Laura and Zofia settled first in Kraków and then in Busko-Zdrój, Poland. In 1944, they were joined by Laura's younger sister, known as Putzi, but who had been living under the name Ksenia Osoba, with the nickname of Nusia.

In 1953, Laura and Zofia, now living in London, still under their false Catholic names, obtained British citizenship. Laura chose Turner as their new family surname, and Zofia Anglicized her name to Sophie Turner until she later married David Zaretsky and became (and remains to this day) Sophie Turner Zaretzky.

FLORA was born Flora Hillel in San Remo, Italy, in 1935, the only child of parents from Czechoslovakia. After her father's death from tuberculosis in 1937, she and her mother, Stefanie, moved to Nice, France, in 1939 to escape Mussolini. Shortly before her mother was deported by the Nazis in 1943, Flora was handed over to convent nuns, who gave her the Christian name Marie Hamon, which she retained until reverting to Flora and taking the permanent name of Hogman, the name of the couple who hid her in 1943 in southern France and adopted her after the war. After the deaths of her adopted mother in 1956 and adopted father in 1958, she moved to New York and has remained Flora Hogman to this day.

CARLA was born Carla Heijmans in 1929 and kept her birth name until she married Ed Lessing in 1949. At that point she became, and remains, Carla Lessing.

Introduction: Why Is This Seder Different from All Other Seders?

At the end of March 2010, a friend invited me to a Passover seder in Greenwich Village. It was one of those seders common among Manhattan types who over the years have stripped their Judaism down to a proud cultural core. We were Jews who had drifted far from regular Shabbat dinners, synagogues, and bar and bat mitzvahs, but we clung to the Passover seder as the one unsinkable ritual of our Jewish upbringings. It was a time to relive the raucous seders of our childhoods and celebrate the emancipation of the Jews from Egyptian bondage, as well as the freedoms that we all took for granted in the most Jewish big city in the freest country in the world.

The trees were just budding outside the apartment's casement windows on West Twelfth Street when the ten of us sat down at the long table. I didn't know all of the people, but we were a familiar assortment of savvy, secular, casually dressed types: a cable TV executive, a novelist, an editor, a lawyer, a real estate agent, a doctor. We ranged in age from our thirties to our seventies.

There was just one person at the table who didn't quite fit: an affable woman in her seventies with a cherubic face and close-cropped blond hair who had come alone and was seated directly across from me with a colorful scarf loosely knotted around her neck. She had the appealing air of someone perpetually on the verge of laughing. Among the darker-haired guests, she didn't look Jewish, but she seemed well enough acquainted with the feast's rituals and laughed with everyone else when we complained of the interminable wait for each installment of the meal, stole pieces of matzoh and sips of wine, and interrupted our reading of the Haggadah to complain of its historical inaccuracies and improbabilities.

But her fair coloring and faint European accent, which was hard to place, made her stand out from the rest of us irreverent Reform Jews at the table. At the first real break in the proceedings—somewhere between the gefilte fish and the chicken soup—I asked her about herself. For all I knew, this was her first seder and I didn't want her to feel uncomfortable. She said her name was Sophie Turner Zaretsky, that she was a retired radiation oncologist and was distantly related to the host.

"I can't place your accent," I said. "Where did you grow up?"

"Poland."

"Oh, I'm half Polish," I said, glad to have something in common. "On my father's side. Warsaw. So you were in Poland during the war?"

"Yes," she said.

"What were you doing?"

"Hiding," she replied softly and with no more emotion than if she had been telling me what movie she had seen the night before.

With that one word, of course, all my assumptions about her collapsed. She was a Jew after all, and one whose childhood put the rest of ours in stark perspective. I quickly calculated that, if she were in her seventies, then she had been a little girl during the war.

I felt that uncomfortable twinge of privilege that I often experience when confronted with those less fortunate—let alone someone who really happened to wake up on the wrong side of history's bed. I didn't know quite what to say. Had her parents been murdered? How many European Jewish children had survived the Holocaust? I had no idea. All I knew was that Sophie had grown up in one of the very worst places in history to be a Jew.

On the other hand, I had grown up in one of the safest places ever, a lakefront suburb of Chicago that had been hospitable to Jews since at least the 1920s. My four grandparents had found their way from Shkud, Lithuania; Chvanik, Belorussia; and Warsaw to Chicago in the early part of the twentieth century—a quarter century before the Nazis invaded Poland. My parents, born here, grew up in the urbanized shtetls of Chicago's west side, enveloped by family, before joining the new diaspora to the suburbs in the 1950s. Highland Park, twenty-odd miles north of the city, had actually become famous for its overprotected, entitled children. In 1960, when I was in sixth grade, the town was singled out in a *Saturday Evening Post* feature story—later a book—called "Suburbia's Coddled Kids." The article portrayed a few of my wealthier sixth-grade classmates as absurdly sheltered, including a boy who had allegedly tried to pay for his thirty-five-cent school lunch with a fifty-dollar bill.

Ever since I could remember, I had been troubled by the seder service's most punitive passage, when the Haggadah takes up the issue of the "wicked child," one of the four types of children to whom the story of the Exodus must be explained. The wicked child asks "What does it all mean to you?"—excluding himself from the community. To him, it is said that God brought the Jews out of slavery, but not him; the wicked child would not be redeemed. While all four children—the wise, the simple, the one who's unable to ask about it at all, and the wicked—may represent aspects of a single self, the wicked child spoke to my anxiety about my good fortune and a fear that, raised in my suburban bubble, I was insufficiently connected to the history of my own people.

Sixteen or more Polish relatives on my father's side had perished in the Holocaust, but these family ghosts—at once too remote and too numerous—were rarely even mentioned at home. Beyond that, as far as I knew, the family's only personal connection to the Holocaust, and it was a distant one, was a letter my grandmother had sent to my father from Warsaw when she returned there to visit her mother after twenty-two years in America. He probably first showed it to us when I was in my twenties. "I stayed in Berlin with my aunt four days," my grandmother wrote. "I saw Hitler on a parade last Sunday. Things are not so hot in Berlin, but I'm glad I saw everything." Her letter is dated July 18, 1934, barely two weeks after Hitler's "Night of the Long Knives," the ruthless, murderous purge of political opponents, left-wingers, anti-Nazis, and other undesirables that cemented his power.

Growing up, I didn't know any survivors. The Nazis' Final Solution was like a dark cloud that had passed overhead long ago—not a handful of years before—but could still be seen in the distance, if you cared to glance in that direction. America couldn't seem to put enough distance between it and the Holocaust. Among children, the Holocaust was mostly the subject of nervous jokes ("Eat—you look like someone from Auschwitz") and ditties like the one sung to the tune of the "Colonel Bogey March," variations of which made the rounds of countless American playgrounds in the 1950s:

Hitler had only one big ball
Göring had two but they were small
Himmler had something sim'lar
And poor Goebbels had no balls at all

The attempt to emasculate these monsters after the fact was a bizarre expression of our impotence in the face of the Nazis' atrocities. Recasting Nazism as comedy in the 1960s—from *Hogan's Heroes* to *The Producers*—helped to hide our own government's inaction during the war and its sinister expediency after it. Without informing the public, the United States' OSS recruited the Nazis' Eastern Front intelligence chief, Reinhard Gehlen, and thousands of Nazi spies—some of them war criminals—for their intelligence—often unreliable and fabricated—on the Soviet Union. Nazi scientists Wernher von Braun and Arthur Rudolph were repackaged for the burgeoning U.S. space program as harmlessly apolitical scientists, although during the war their V-2 rocket had been built at Nordhausen at a cost of more than 10,000 dead slave laborers.

General Dwight D. Eisenhower released film of concentration camp atrocities made right after liberation. The footage, shot by Hollywood directors recruited for the purpose, had a brief run as newsreels in American movie theaters in 1945, but for the next decade most Americans were shielded from the worst images of the Final Solution. Orson Welles's 1946 poorly reviewed movie *The Stranger* featured some very brief atrocity footage, and Alain Resnais's remarkable 1955 art house documentary *Night and Fog* wasn't released in America until the 1960s. The Holocaust wouldn't become real for many of us children until 1961, when we at last saw the footage of bulldozed Jewish corpses in *Judgment at Nuremberg*, the movie that introduced much of the world to the incontrovertible proof of what the Nazis had done. (The 1959 live TV version of *Judgment* on *Playhouse 90* didn't include documentary footage and had been stripped of any references to gas chambers in deference to its sponsor, the American Gas Association.)

To my embarrassment, I had never talked to a survivor, and now here was Sophie sitting three feet from me, an emissary from a disaster I hadn't emotionally confronted in my life. Here was my chance, but questions don't come easily in the presence of another's tragedy. In any case, I'll never know what I would have asked Sophie next because her cousin Alice Herb, our host, suddenly called to her.

"Sophie, tell him about the bear. Tell him about the bear."

"All right," Sophie said to Alice, then turned to me. "Alice loves the story of the bear. All right. When I was hiding in a small town in Poland with my mother, of course I didn't have many toys. In fact, I had only two—a doll and a little bear I later named Refugee. He was one of those Steiff bears, but he stayed with me after the war and into adulthood and now he's in the Holocaust Memorial Museum in Washington. The copy they made of him to sell in the gift shop is one of their most popular items."

"Amazing," I said.

"Tell him about the space shuttle," Alice said.

"All right, all right," she said with mock irritation, putting up her hand, as if to prevent her cousin from making any more demands. Sophie explained to me that every American astronaut who goes up in the space shuttle can take a couple of personal items along, and that the commander of *Discovery*, Mark Polansky, who's half Jewish and wanted to draw attention to genocide, took a photo of a Darfurian child in a refugee camp and a facsimile of Refugee on a twelve-day mission to the International Space Station in 2006.

"Wow," I said, wincing at how dumb I must have sounded. "That's an amazing story. And you said Refugee was a Steiff bear?"

"A little one." Sophie held her thumb and forefinger three inches apart.

"That's funny, I had the same one," I said, probably more excitably than the coincidence called for. "Actually, I still have it in my closet with a bunch of other Steiff animals my parents got me when I was a kid." What was I doing, inserting my own toys into her narrative? Was I trying to maneuver the conversation onto safer ground? "Unfortunately," I insisted on adding, "he's lost an arm. And I think his head came off. You obviously took better care of yours."

And it was true that the small bear, whom I named Beauregard, had been one of my most beloved toys in a childhood which, unlike Sophie's, was full of them. That Sophie and I were connected not only by our Judaism and our Polish origins, but also by the very same make of German teddy bear, felt eerily providential.

I left the seder that evening with Sophie's e-mail address and found myself a couple of months later sitting at the glass-topped dining room table in her Upper West Side high-rise apartment, sipping tea and asking her questions about her childhood hiding from the Nazis with her mother and her bear. I could sense that Sophie was ambivalent about reconstructing a past that had been packed away. When she fished documents and photos out of her file cabinet or boxes in her closet, I felt I was imposing. That my demands on her were in the service of what I hoped would be a charming, inspirational children's book seemed to make the ordeal more palatable, but even so, Sophie's occasional protests—"It was so long ago," "I really can't remember," "Does it really matter when my mother gave me the bear?"—made me feel that I was picking at the margins of a thick scab that had formed over an old and grievous wound. Sophie could have put an end to my literary endeavor with just a word, but she didn't, and I sensed in her, buried beneath her suppression of the past, a faintly beating desire to confront it. (She would tell me much later that she felt a "responsibility" to talk to me.)

I drafted the text of a children's story called *Refugee: The True Story of a Girl, a Bear, and the Holocaust*, and kept meeting periodically with Sophie to clarify events and chronology. When we got together, sometimes at a café near her apartment, I tried not to overstay my welcome, since I continued to feel that I had subtly pressured her into sharing the details of a story she otherwise would have been content to relate only sparingly, and in passing.

As time went on, however, the adventures of Sophie's bear became inseparable from an infinitely more complex and tragic story that could hardly be contained by a few hundred words aimed at six-year-olds. A year and a half after I left my friends' seder with an idea for a children's book, I realized that I was actually on a longer and more intense serendipitous journey toward a book for grown-ups, one that would eventually embrace the stories of three other hidden child survivors. Sophie, it turned out, was my portal into the world of the very few and very lucky Jewish children who emerged from World War II, our last living witnesses to the Holocaust. Between 1 and 1.5 million Jewish children were living in Europe before the war, but only 6 to 11 percent survived, compared to a third of Jewish adults. Of these child survivors, who numbered between 60,000 and 165,000 children, some had survived the death and work camps, while the rest survived by hiding or being hidden.

Only later still, well into the writing of this book, did I become conscious of the most obvious reason I felt so strongly drawn to Sophie and her history. At the time of the seder both of my parents, now in their feeble nineties after long, productive, and healthy lives, were suffering through their final months. They weren't murdered or starved to death, but died at home within a month of each other, surrounded by state-of-the-art end-of-life care. Nonetheless, I was dealing with the loss of my mom and dad, the most important links to my past and my Jewish heritage. The situation—the expensive and hopeful interventions, the shuttling back and forth between Florida and Chicago, the difficulties of coordinating emotional decisions with my siblings—was full of new fears. I was clinging more tightly than ever to the past, lamenting not only unfinished business, but also unasked questions, and trying to take in the vast unexplored landscape of my family and the ultimate unknowableness of those I loved. In the midst of this period of loss and mourning, whom should fate seat across from me at a seder but a combination of surrogate parent and history tutor, someone who could connect me to the very cataclysm that had been at an inescapable remove in my parents' lives and so conspicuously absent from mine.

Sophie told me what she could remember about her childhood—with the help of some old photos, documents, and an earlier interview she had done with her cousin Alice Herb—and from these elements I could write a credible version of the story from her childlike point of view of events between 1942 and 1948. But how was I going to tell the story from the viewpoint of her late mother, with whom Sophie spent those years and more? Given the peculiarity of their relationship during those years, I longed to capture the discrepancy between their respective realities.

The answer came one day when I was sitting with Sophie in her apartment. As usual Sophie was patiently correcting my mistakes and filling in gaps in my latest draft of her story with new bits of information that, since our last meeting, had been jarred loose from the greater mass of her suppressed memories. Suddenly Sophie pulled a sheaf of typescript pages from a box and said, "I don't know if this will help, but it's something my mother wrote for a class she was taking late in life."

I fanned through the seventeen-page manuscript with a surge of joy. Sophie had just handed me the equivalent of the Rosetta Stone—the means by which I could finally translate Sophie's speculations about her mother's state of mind during and after the war into the hard currency of her mother's own memories. With her mother's essay, I could at last begin to connect the desperate parallel universes in which the two of them lived.

The story of Sophie's bear, her generation, and of the momentous event in 1991 that finally broke the hidden child survivors' adult silence, starts in 1942 in the city of Lvov, Poland, where a girl named Selma Schwarzwald and her mother, Laura, were about to start living side by side in two utterly different lies.

PART ONE
THE CHILDREN

SOPHIE

In late August 1942, when the knock came on the door of the Schwarzwalds' hovel in the Lvov ghetto, it was as if the Messiah himself had arrived. Laura Schwarzwald rose wearily to her feet. With time running out, whoever didn't have the money to buy Christian documents—forged or real baptismal certificates and marriage documents—would almost certainly receive a death sentence instead. Having deported the bulk of Lvov's remaining Jews from the ghetto, the Nazis were now hunting down the last of its inhabitants. Every Jew still alive in the ghetto was standing on the precipice of death. All they had to do was look down and see everyone who had gone before them.

Laura's husband, Daniel, who was at his unpaid job as a security guard for the Third Reich's military engineering organization, had made the arrangements, and here, at last, were the papers that were the family's only remaining hope. Laura pressed her hand against her breast to feel the wad of money safely hidden in her brassiere and opened the door.

The gaunt man who pushed his way past her had circles under his eyes as dark as a panda bear's and a shirt so grimy that its original color could only be inferred. His belt, though pulled tightly around his narrow waist, barely kept his soiled pants up. Was *this* the paperman? she thought. A scrawny, doomed fellow no better off than the rest of them?

"Where is he?" he demanded, scowling.

Bewildered, she asked, "Who?"

"Don't play dumb. The paperman. I was told to come here to buy the papers. For my wife and child."

Laura could barely catch her breath. So the Pole had promised the papers to two separate families? What was he trying to do—get paid twice for the same ones? Weren't the Poles and Ukrainians already making a killing off the Jews' desperation for new identities? Laura's heart sank even more quickly than it had risen at the sound of his knocking.

"They belong to us, the papers!" she screamed at him.

"No need to get excited," the man said arrogantly, looking around the room with its scraps of furniture and its air of death. "I'll sit and wait."

She could hardly bear to look at this withered Jew as he sat in the chair, arms folded, with a pathetic sense of entitlement—entitlement, that is, to go on living too, for another day.

"They aren't your papers," she said to him.

"We'll see about that."

She begged him to leave, not even trying to hold back her tears, but he ignored her and waited in defiant silence as the afternoon dragged on. What had he been just a few months before—a doctor or a lawyer or a businessman like her husband? Who could tell? Now they were like two hungry animals eyeing each other over a meal that hadn't arrived yet.

If her husband were at home, he wouldn't stand for it; he would have thrown this other buyer out, no questions asked. However, something better than her husband intervened: fate. As the ghetto curfew for Jews approached, the paperman still hadn't arrived. The man in her kitchen kept jiggling his leg and checking his wristwatch with increasing anxiety, knowing that to be seen on the street after curfew was to risk being shot like a rabid dog.

"You'd better go," she said, "or the dogs will be eating your corpse in the street tomorrow morning."

He said he'd give the paperman five more minutes.

"Then what?"

"Then I'll leave and come back for them in the morning."

"They're not yours. If they were yours, you'd be in your house waiting for him, not mine."

He consulted his watch yet again. "*Goniff!*" he spat. Finally he could stand it no more and stood up. "Anybody tell you what a good-looking woman you are?"

"Go," Laura said.

He jerked his chin at something over Laura's shoulder, and she turned to see her daughter, Selma, who had wandered in from the other room. She was blond, not yet five.

"Your little girl is pretty too," the man said. "Very fair. You're lucky."

"Not as long as you're here. Go. Go before you get a bullet in the head."

He asked her for a piece of bread.

Thankful that he was leaving, she went to the cupboard and broke off a piece of days-old bread.

Twenty minutes after he left, there was another knock on Laura's door. She hesitated, wondering if the Jew was not giving up that easily. But a different voice was whispering to her through the door. She opened it and a ruddy Pole stumbled in. If history had made the Jews one of the unluckiest people in the world, and now unluckier than ever, Laura was not above solemn gratitude for the fortunate timing of the man's appearance. The round-faced man was very drunk, the only explanation needed for his late arrival. He slumped in the chair recently vacated by her rival and demanded to see the money. From her blouse Laura removed the agreed-upon amount and asked to see the documents.

The man slid the precious papers out of his inside jacket pocket and flourished them for a second before putting them back. Then he wagged his index finger in her face, like a metronome.

"Not until I have a drink," he slurred. "I have to drink in order to stand the sight of all you *żyds*." He drew a circle in the air to indicate the ghetto. "Then we will close the deal."

Every chance to live a little longer had to be bargained for. Laura happened to have half a bottle in the room in the cupboard—how much luck could one woman have!—which she put down before him. He sloshed some into the dirty glass she provided, tossed it back, then poured another and drank that, all the while smacking his lips. Nothing would prevent him from just getting up and stumbling out. Laura's relief turned to anxiety, but her *mazel* held; the Pole couldn't hold his vodka. Laura sat and watched him drink himself into semi-consciousness, then pulled the papers from his pocket and replaced them with the money and waited for him to stir. At that point she was able to maneuver him back into the street. For the rest of her life, she would be as grateful for her good fortune as haunted by it—her family saved at another family's expense.

That night, Laura read the documents over and over again by candlelight. A real Christian birth certificate for Selma and a marriage license for her, both from the same family, with birth dates enough like their own. From that moment, and for the unforeseeable future, Laura and Selma Schwarzwald ceased to exist. Bronislawa Tymejko and her little daughter Zofia Tymejko had taken their place, just as this life in the ghetto—too precarious, really, to be called "life" at all—had replaced the prosperous, cultured existence she and her family had enjoyed until almost exactly three years before.

She'd grown up with her parents, Mina and Josef Litwak, and four siblings in a grand three-story house with French windows, scrollwork, and a courtyard. The home was owned by her wealthy paternal grandfather Moses, who also lived there with his wife, Sarah. In *their* sprawling apartment, the walls were covered in silk, the parquet floors were lined with Persian rugs, the ceiling dripped with chandeliers, and Laura's grandmother favored Parisian dresses and stylish *sheitels*—the wigs worn by Orthodox married women. The crowning achievement of Laura's parents' Judaism was the fact that her father, a banker, and grandfather had organized their own synagogue.

Laura and her husband, Daniel Schwarzwald, who worked in his family's successful timber export business, lived elsewhere in Lvov in a smaller apartment in the Christian section of the city with their two-year-old daughter, Selma. They were all among the highly cultured citizens of Lvov, which until 1918 had been the capital of Galicia, part of the Austrian Empire. Much of the Litwak family spoke German fluently as well as Polish and Yiddish. After the collapse of the Hapsburg monarchy in 1918, Lvov became the third largest city in Poland, and its second most important cultural and intellectual center—a city with well over 100,000 Jews—a third of the city's entire population.

On September 24, 1939, the life that Lvov had known for the past twenty years was shattered as suddenly and easily as one of Moses and Sarah Litwak's Venetian wineglasses. Just two weeks after the Nazis invaded Poland from the west, Russia invaded from the east, where it overwhelmed Polish resistance and took a quarter of a million Poles as prisoners. The Russians occupied Lvov—whose Jewish population began to swell rapidly as it absorbed Jews fleeing the area occupied by Germany in the west—and soon began to deport the city's anti-Communists, "bourgeois bloodsuckers," even Polish Communists, and other "untrustworthy elements" to Siberia. The well-to-do merchants and professionals were relieved of their livelihoods, then retrained as laborers. The Soviets immediately emptied the stores of all food and merchandise and appropriated it for their own use. The citizens of Lvov were ordered to change their zlotys for rubles at the banks, only to be told after standing on line the whole night that there would be no exchange after all. Suddenly the Poles were paupers.

The Soviets had barged into Lvov without much ceremony, and a commissar and his family took over the apartment of Laura's grandparents—moved right in—and forced them to retreat to a single room. The elderly couple cowered in their bedroom, inmates in the ornate prison of their home. The man who had his own synagogue now had barely two kopeks to rub together. The commissar and his family made themselves comfortable, helping themselves to the Litwaks' food and possessions while denying Moses his kosher food.

The commissar then announced that Moses, being a bourgeois, would have to leave Lvov and live at least thirty kilometers away to avoid contaminating the new Communist regime. Preferring starvation to eating *treif*, and death to ceding his home to the intruders, Moses's heart gave out.

That night his little great-granddaughter Selma happened to glimpse, through a bedroom doorway, Moses laid out on his bed in a black suit. To circumvent the Russian Communists' prohibition against any kind of religious ceremony, before dawn the next morning everyone in the family walked separately to the Jewish cemetery to meet his casket and give him a Jewish burial. Many from the Litwak and Schwarzwald family who were there that morning would themselves soon be dead, with neither burial nor family around to say good-bye.

For the moment, though, thirty-year-old Laura, her husband, Daniel, and their Selma seemed safe enough. The Russians retrained Daniel as a road worker, then a baker's apprentice, and, finally, after he hurriedly learned Russian, he was given a job as a timber specialist in a factory. Laura was allowed to remain at home with Selma.

At least on the surface, life in Lvov actually improved for a while. The Russians set about beautifying Lvov, keeping the streets spotless and requiring all tenants to sweep in front of their buildings daily—while wearing white aprons, no less! The Russians quickly organized schools and promoted Russian culture, reopened theaters, and produced ballets the likes of which the Poles had never seen. Moreover, tickets prices were kept low enough so that all workers, including the newly minted laborers, could afford them, the better to expose the locals to Russia's "superior" culture.

But the citizens of Lvov were getting a taste of the worse terror to come. One evening, the Russians cut off electricity, a trick that forced everyone to stay home while the Soviet secret police—the NKVD—went door to door, selecting Polish Communists—who had their own ideas about socialism—for deportation to forced labor camps in Siberia and the Far East, and in some cases immediate death. The ballet tickets may have been cheap, but the towering portraits of Lenin and Stalin left no doubt that life in Lvov would never be the same. Between February and June 1940, the Soviets deported almost 400,000 people from the newly acquired territories, 200,000 Jews among them.

By June 1941, the Germans and the Russians were no longer merely sharing poor Poland. They were now at war with each other, and the Germans were winning. After less than two years of Soviet occupation, the Germans arrived in Lvov in the summer of 1941, routing their former allies—but not before the Soviet secret police murdered thousands of civilian prisoners they had been holding in Lvov prisons. The Germans compounded the violence by promptly blaming the massacre on the Jews, inciting a pogrom organized by the Ukrainian Nationalists that lasted four days and left more than 2,000 Jews dead in the streets of Lvov while the Germans filmed the atrocities.

The Nazis brought to Poland a killing machine the likes of which the human imagination had not yet been able to conjure. The *Einsatzgruppen* were special mobile killing squads, the leading edge of the Final Solution that would not be made official until a few months later. As the German army advanced eastward, the job of the *Einsatzgruppen*, 3,000 executioners divided into four groups, was to follow close behind the *Wehrmacht*, gathering and disposing of the Jewish people as they went.

Between June 30 and July 3, the *Einsatzgruppen* murdered at least 4,000 more Jews with help from Ukrainian Nationalists—herding them to secluded killing grounds, where they were relieved of their watches, jewelry, money, and clothes, then shot to death in the back of the skull, one by one, and piled in mass graves, many of which the victims had dug themselves. Others were gassed in groups after being piled into olive green trucks and vans that had been outfitted and sealed airtight for the purpose.

On July 15, all Jews were ordered to wear a yellow Star of David. On July 25, Ukrainian Nationalists organized another pogrom in which 2,000 more Jews were slaughtered. By the end of 1941, the *Einsatzgruppen* had murdered more than half a million Jews, more than 3,000 a day. Before it was all over, they would murder well over a million Jews. The work was done mostly by professional men—including doctors, lawyers, even clergymen—men whose work ethic and deep sense of duty to the Third Reich, if not an inherited hatred of the Jewish people, made them excellent executioners. To keep up both their strength and morale for this arduous labor, they were well fed and provided with copious amounts of alcohol, but even some Nazis had their limit, could finally take no more of the daily grind of extermination, and were relieved without prejudice by an understanding Führer. Those with sturdier constitutions just kept at it, learning quickly that, once they had negotiated certain moral obstacles, less stubborn than one would have thought, they became accustomed to almost anything, especially if the music blaring over loudspeakers distracted them from the sounds of their own pistol shots and the begging and shrieking of their victims.

But killing Jews one by one could accomplish only so much. By

October 1941, the first Jews were taken as forced labor, and a month later all remaining Jews in Lvov were forced into a ghetto. Laura's family—her parents and her three remaining siblings (a fourth, Edek, had immigrated to Palestine)—were all German-speaking Polish believers in Teutonic culture, but they too awaited their turn. Before long, a group of storm troopers and German soldiers invaded the apartment, where Laura and her husband had hidden her grandfather's gold and silver religious objects. The SS men found everything, including the Torah with its magnificent silver crown and pointer. When Laura refused to tell them what the objects were for, one of them smacked her across the face with the back of his hand.

Laura's brother Manek was soon caught in the street without his Star of David and taken to an SS camp, but at least he was given a pass to return to the apartment at night. One evening he told the adults of watching two German soldiers beat two men for stealing a bar of soap, then bash their skulls against each other until their brains splashed against the wall. Another time, he reported that a soldier took a child by the ankles and swung him as hard as he could against a brick wall. The German was laughing. Atrocities Laura never before imagined had become her daily reality, like the potatoes and cabbage the family now subsisted on.

The Schwarzwalds were told to pack the few belongings that the Soviets and Germans hadn't already taken, and they joined the rest of the city's Jews in the Lvov ghetto in the Zamarstynow borough. Their new home was a single room that the family—Laura, her husband and daughter, her parents, her father's parents, and her aunts and uncles—had to share with another Jew, a total stranger. Not a mile away, the Germans had already established, in a former factory, the Janowska forced labor and concentration camp for Jews destined for Belzec, the extermination camp near Lublin. In fact, Janowska itself became an extermination camp, where killing often took the form of entertainment. The SS officials there organized a prisoner band, instructed them to compose "The Death Tango," and ordered them to play it during executions.

In a matter of weeks, the family's comfortable life had been reduced to a meager existence of fear and chaos. Their only hope was to obtain false documents in the bustling market of Poles and Ukrainians who were getting rich selling their identification papers to the doomed.

Daniel started work as a security guard at a hostel for construction workers of the German military engineering group, Organisation Todt. At least it was a job that paid him in increasingly scarce food and work passes for him and Laura, who was permitted to remain in the apartment with their daughter, as his hausfrau. Laura's two unmarried younger sisters, Adela (whom everyone called Putzi) and Fryda, were given jobs in a factory making military uniforms.

"Selections" continued, now right under their noses. One night Laura heard unfamiliar noises outside and got out of bed to see thousands of Jews, denied transportation, trudging to work on foot before dawn, many near collapse, a column of human despair shuffling along between lines of German soldiers prodding them with their rifles.

After a few weeks, the noise changed to the rumbling sounds of trucks carrying deportees to the concentration camps. The frightened Jews stood tightly packed in the open trucks, staring at the sky, searching for God, hoping for a miracle. Laura heard one man cry out loud, "Sh'ma Yisrael Adonai Eloheinu Adonai Ehad. . . ." Then a woman took up the words that are supposed to be the last ones uttered by a Jew before death. Then the others joined in, like a demented congregation, their voices rising, unheard, into the gray sky.

In exchange for her diamond ring, Laura temporarily rescued her own parents from the Germans and arranged to hide them at her husband's place of work. Life was now a lethal game of musical chairs, in which those who couldn't find one of the diminishing number of places to hide were taken away, almost surely to their deaths.

The Schwarzwalds clung to each other on Janowska Street in the Lvov ghetto as the Germans shot 5,000 Jews who were elderly and sick, and therefore useless to them. In early spring 1942, 15,000 more Jews—mostly women, children, and the elderly—were deported to the extermination camp in Belzec, not far from Lvov. In August, tens of thousands more were sent there. Another thousand orphans and sick Jews were shot dead. By September 1942, of the 100,000 Jews who lived in Lvov before the war, there were approximately 65,000 left, and they could only imagine what was happening elsewhere. Every morning the Jews of Lvov awoke to horrible news—that the nightmare was still real.

Laura learned that in the nearby town of Gorlice, Laura's great-uncle had been made head of that ghetto's Judenrat, or Jewish Council, the administrative organization made up of the community leaders, that the Nazis forced the Jews to form in every ghetto, under penalty of death, to facilitate their own deportation and extermination. This policy, used in the camps as well, put the decision of which Jews would live and which would die not in the hands of God, or even the Nazis, but of the Jews themselves. If the Nazis ordered the head of the Judenrat to produce 5,000 Jews at six in the morning to be deported, he had three choices. He could comply, comforting himself with the Nazis' reassurance that deciding which Jews would live and which would die was preferable to all of them dying. He could refuse and be executed, along with who knows how many others for good measure. Or he could do what Laura's great-uncle did. In Gorlice, the Nazis asked him to prepare lists of Jews to be "resettled." He told them such an assignment would require serious thought, so that he could make sure the Jews left would be of the utmost use to them. "Come tomorrow morning," Laura's great-uncle said, "and I will have for you exactly what you want." When the Nazis returned, they found him dead at his desk, a suicide.

Daniel was able to visit his family in the ghetto only occasionally, leaving Laura and Selma alone and at the mercy of the German soldiers, who three times came to their room and ordered them to be deported to the gas chambers at Belzec. Each time, Laura used her fluent German to persuade them to leave her and Selma alone.

On a fourth visit, the soldiers insisted she come with them, then changed their mind and asked for Selma only, saying that the Führer loved little children and would take good care of her. Laura knew full well how much the Führer loved Jewish children. She had heard Manek's story, and she had already seen the piles of children's corpses behind the fence at the Janowska camp, their blood having been taken for transfusions for soldiers at the Eastern Front. Incredible—the Nazis committing in reality the atrocity that Christians had been falsely accusing Jews of for centuries. Somehow she prevailed again, shooing Selma away, and the soldier softened. He even returned later, warning her that the roundup of Jews was finished for the time being, and that the next day it would be safe for her to go out and forage for food.

But how many times would she be so lucky? It was already too late for her grandfather Moses and her invalid grandmother Sarah, who had been carried off in a chair, loaded onto a truck, then thrown off it, and shot. A friend reported seeing her tiny corpse, like a dog's, on the pavement. It was too late for her own parents, who had been discovered and deported to Belzec, where they too would be murdered. When the soldiers had come for them, her father hid, but as soon as he heard the cries of his wife he came out of hiding, saying he didn't want to be separated, and so he too began the journey to the gas chambers. When Laura and her sister came home to an empty apartment, the building's concierge told them, "The Nazis came for a cleaning." Daniel's family was now also gone. Laura's family and her siblings were among the last of the clan in the ghetto, now a pitiful city populated mostly by ghosts, both living and dead.

The Schwarzwalds knew it wouldn't be much longer before the Nazis closed in on them. The SS were clearing one ghetto block at a time—from the window Laura could see them herding Jews, friends and acquaintances among them—and soon it would be their turn. Laura found a platform under the roof of an adjacent house where they could hide at night, packed in like herrings with fifteen others, including an epileptic girl of thirteen who started to howl at the sound of German boots in the empty apartments below and had to be silenced with a pillow. Laura would toss Selma across a ventilation shaft to someone who caught her on the other side, then leap from a top-floor window of their building to the window of the next with a bag of food and a change of clothes for her daughter.

Meanwhile, her husband hid *on* the roof at work, pressed all night against the drainpipe.

The competition for Christian identification papers that roughly matched the Jews' ages was intense and the price always climbing, but somehow Daniel succeeded first in purchasing authentic Christian birth certificates for his wife's two younger sisters, Fryda and Putzi, who would now become Zofia Wolenska and Ksenia Osoba. Then he was able to purchase a marriage certificate for Laura and a birth certificate for Selma from a family named Tymejko.

The papers for her and her daughter were going to be delivered in two days. By now, Laura could barely summon an ounce of hope. She had become like a stone. She felt as if suffering no longer touched her. A human, apparently, could adapt to anything. In late August, while Daniel was at work, the paperman actually came, and the documents were hers—but only after, by sheer luck, she had gotten rid of an unexpected visitor who claimed that *he* had been promised them as well.

When her husband begged her to leave with Selma, she agreed. He would try his best to follow.

The family's good fortune had run out, though; on the eve of their escape, Daniel found himself in the right place, but at the wrong time.

On September 1, 1942, the Germans ordered all remaining Jews to consolidate their living quarters in one section of the ghetto, and Daniel went to the Jewish Community House to see one of the Jewish Council members, his friend Dr. Katz, to ask him about finding a new place to live. The game of musical chairs was coming to an end.

Unknown to Daniel, a Jew had killed a drunken German soldier the day before, and the Nazis wasted little time retaliating with their customary brutality. While Daniel conferred with Dr. Katz on the second floor, the Nazis surrounded the council building with MG-42 machine guns, a weapon so effective—it could shoot a fifty-round belt in a matter of a few seconds—that it would still be in use seventy years later. SS men stormed the Jewish Council building and forced dozens of Jews outside, where they were instantly mowed down. The SS men then stomped up the stairs and cornered the members of the Jewish Council and the other Jews with them.

Word of the *Aktion* spread quickly inside the ghetto. Laura left Selma with her sister Fryda and headed immediately to the Jewish Community House. Laura wouldn't tell anyone for many, many years what she saw that afternoon, although by then a grisly photograph of it had begun to appear in photographic histories of the Holocaust. There were no signs of life around the building, but six perfectly spaced corpses hung from the second-floor balcony, dangling like a row of marionettes in a toy store.

When Laura saw the dead council members, some of whom she knew, twisting slowly in their nooses, she clutched her stomach and turned away. When she turned back, she didn't see Dr. Katz or her husband among them, and this gave her hope. But she didn't dare advance any farther to investigate. To associate herself with any of the dead men would be suicide. The corpses would remain hanging there for weeks.

Before the day was over, she learned that Dr. Katz had managed to jump out of a second-story window and hide in a cobbler's workshop nearby. He was still alive and reunited with his wife. But Daniel? No one knew for sure.

That night, still hopeful, Laura waited for her husband's return. By morning, her hope had evaporated. If he were alive, she knew, surely he would have gotten word to her. Unless he had been captured, or was hiding in the forest. But false hope was something she couldn't afford. She resigned herself to the likelihood that her husband was gone, Daniel, the man about whom Laura had once written her cousin Tonka in Tel Aviv, "Danek is sweet, loving; I love him with all my heart as a husband, a lover, a friend. Everybody at home is very attached to him and he to them. Grandma never takes her eyes from him. They made out fine with such a son-in-law."

Laura still had her daughter and siblings; the others were gone.

The day after the *Aktion*, September 2, 1942, was Selma's fifth birthday, but there was no party, and no presents, unless her mother's soothing lie counted; she had quickly concocted the fiction that her father was working for the Russians for a while and would return someday.

But Selma wasn't soothed. After listening to the sound of German boots like gunfire on the cobblestones outside and sometimes on the stairwell, she had felt safe only when her father got home from his job in the evening and she could run to him and hug his legs—even when he still worked in the bakery and would be covered in flour. He was blond and had gray-green eyes, just like she did, and she wanted him back. Now.

Selma curled up on a makeshift cot and sobbed into her pillow as Laura watched, berating herself for saying the Russians had taken him. Had there not been a softer lie to tell her, something that promised her father's quicker return, something to get the little girl through these days? Did it even matter, anyway, since they would all be dead soon? Laura comforted her daughter as best she could, but who would comfort *her*? Only her daughter stood between her and serious thoughts of suicide, which would be so much easier than living another day.

Only God knew what was going on in her daughter's head, but her mother saw how quiet she had become, how she endured each new terror in silence. Every once in a while, bright images of their old life peeked through the darkness to torture Laura—her grandparents' Shabbos dinners, the sight of Daniel working on timber-export numbers late at night, how Selma reacted to her first taste of orange—but she would shoulder them away. Look, she thought, look what history has done to us. Would her little girl ever know that not far away Jews were digging their own graves and waiting for the bullet to the base of the skull?

Later that night, the night of Selma's fifth birthday, Laura met with her brother Manek and her two sisters, Putzi and Fryda, and they decided to escape with the false papers that had been Daniel's last gifts to all of them. They decided that Putzi and Fryda would leave first for Kraków by train, after which Laura and Selma would follow a few days later, and finally Manek. There was nothing to lose.

That Putzi was even still alive to make a run for it was itself a miracle. Group by group, the young Jewish women she worked with making military uniforms for the Germans had been taken away and deported until there was only one group left—Putzi's. When the SS men came for them, Putzi ducked down behind her machine, slid to the floor, and held her breath. Somehow the Germans didn't notice. After they marched the other women away, Putzi remained on the floor, alone and trembling, waiting all night for them to come back for her, but they never did. In the morning, she snuck out of the factory and made her way home. For the rest of her life, she would suffer from guilt that she alone had survived.

Even before the papers had arrived, when acquiring Catholic identities looked like it was going to be their only hope, Laura had started reading the catechism to Selma. Before they had been moved to the ghetto, Laura's Christian landlady, the wife of a university professor who had been taken by the Russians, had given her a Polish Catholic catechism and a New Testament and tried to convince her to leave Lvov as soon as possible. She even suggested the family move to a resort town, a place where people were always coming and going anyway, where the locals were accustomed to strangers. She assured Laura that becoming a Catholic would be relatively effortless. She would have to go to church, but only occasionally, and merely watch what the others were doing. She might even see its many advantages over Judaism.

"My children are not happy with me for wanting to help you," her landlady had told her. "What can I do? I can't take a chance that they would report me to the Germans. But, you see, that is what it is like now, Laura. I cannot protect you, but I can give you advice on how to protect yourself. So take this Bible and the catechism"—she made the sign of the cross on Laura's forehead—"and may Jesus Christ be your savior."

She had not taken the woman's advice, but she had taken the books and, thinking ahead, had been quietly preparing her five-year-old daughter for Catholicism. Laura's greatest fear now, on the eve of their attempted escape, was no longer death—what was death to a stone?—but that Selma would inadvertently betray them all if she raised the slightest suspicion that she was a Jew.

"Tell me the five church commandments," Laura would whisper to Selma at bedtime in their ghetto room.

"I don't know, Mama."

"You do know. The first commandment begins, 'On Sundays and holy days of obligation . . .'"

"Please, Mama."

"'On Sundays and holy days of obligation,' you must what?"

Her daughter sighed. "Attend Mass and re—and re—"

"Refrain."

"—refrain from unnecessary work."

"Good girl. Now the next one: 'At least once a year'—what?"

"I'm hungry, Mama."

"Zula," her mother said, using her pet name.

"At least once a year, the sacrament of penance."

"Now the third commandment, the one about the Easter season."

"At least once a year during the Easter season, I must take the Holy Communion."

Laura kissed her hard on the forehead. "You're such a good girl! What about the fourth commandment?"

In the last couple of days before the two of them were to set out into the world as Bronislawa and Zofia Tymejko, Laura's drilling intensified—and that wasn't all.

"I'm giving you a special name today," she told her. "To be safe, so that nothing bad happens to me and you, I will call you Zofia. Zofia Tymejko. That is your new name. My new name is Bronislawa Tymejko."

"That's not a very nice name."

"Which one?"

"Yours is not as nice as Laura."

"That's all right, Zula, because you call me Mama. You must always call me Mama, do you understand? But if someone asks you my name, what do you say?"

"I say your name is Bronislawa."

"Very good. Bronislawa what?"

"I don't know."

"Tymejko. Tymejko."

"Tymejko."

"So what is my name now?"

"Bronislawa Tymejko."

"Very good. Who is Laura Schwarzwald?"

"That's you too."

"No!"

Selma flinched.

"That is no longer my name! That person doesn't exist anymore. You mustn't ever say that again. When someone asks you who your mother is, or what her name is, what do you say?"

"Bronislawa Tymejko."

"Bravo! It's like a game we're playing, but if we break the rules and you accidentally call me Laura, or say that your name is Selma, then the game is over and people will hurt us, or take us away. You don't want that to happen, do you, Zofia?" Laura said.

"No, Mama."

"What's your name, little girl? What do you say from now on when anybody asks you? What do you say?"

"I'm Zofia."

"Zofia who?"

"Zofia Tymejko."

"That's right. And your birthday is July twenty-seventh."

"It's September second, Mama."

"No, that was Selma's birthday. Zofia's birthday is July twenty-seventh. See?" She showed her the birth certificate. "See? And what is my name?"

"I don't like this game."

"It doesn't matter, Zofia."

"I want to be Selma."

"We must play it all the time now or something bad will surely happen to us."

"Why? Why does everyone want to hurt us?"

"That I will explain to you when you are a little older, Zofia. But just now they want to hurt people named Schwarzwald and Litwak, so you are never to say those names. What's your name, little girl?"

"My name is Zofia Tymejko and I was born on July twenty-seventh and I am five years old."

"How old will you be next July twenty-seventh?"

"I don't know."

"Of course you do, Zofia. You're five years old, so on your next birthday on July twenty-seventh, you will be how old?"

"Six."

"Excellent. Now, Zosia, what are the three divine virtues?"

"Faith, hope, and love."

She kissed Zofia's forehead again. "You're so smart, Zosia. And don't talk to anyone. You understand?"

"Yes, Bronislawa Tymejko."

Laura smiled. "But to you, it's still Mama."

"Yes, Mama."

Poor Zula, Laura thought. Her daughter was a blessing and a curse. She was the only reason to live, but for her to survive she was going to have to erase her only child's identity, and destroy who knows what else?

On September 6, 1942, Laura washed and brushed Selma's blond hair and fixed it with a white bow. They both put on their best clothes. With only one small suitcase each and their false documents, they set out on foot for the train station. Just before they walked out of the ghetto, Laura removed her and her daughter's armbands with the Star of David. The trick was to look like they'd just been visiting the ghetto, doing business. Once through the gate, they strode into Christian Lvov, trying to look as little like Jews as possible. This meant walking past the German guards as if it were the most natural thing in the world. She had hired a Pole named Julek to have the rest of their luggage shipped ahead to Kraków, to escort them there, and to collect their luggage in Kraków and help them find a room. He joined them at the appointed street corner and walked silently next to them to the train station, smoking a cigarette. Most of the way there, Laura held her breath.

To everyone in the world but themselves, they were now Bronislawa and Zofia Tymejko.

Once they were settled on the horsehair seats and the train was moving, Laura repeated her strict instructions that Zofia not talk to strangers, to let her answer all questions. When it was necessary to speak, she told Zofia to speak only Polish. Her mother sometimes spoke German too, and Zofia knew many German words.

Once out of the ghetto, Laura felt an unfamiliar surge of hope and permitted herself the thought that maybe her daughter might even go on to have children of her own one day to say Kaddish for all of them. But the hope didn't last long. On the train Julek sat in another row and pretended not to know her and Zofia, and Laura wondered—why not wonder in a world where children could betray their own parents?—if he was planning to turn them in. After all, he already had their money.

The trip ended without incident. Julek didn't denounce them. However, he disappeared with the tickets for their luggage, and presumably the luggage too, leaving Laura and Zofia to find lodging for themselves. Laura looked around for him frantically. Not wanting to call attention to themselves by looking lost near the German policeman patrolling the Glowny station, mother and daughter, with even fewer possessions to their name, then set off in the rain across the plaza to find a room.

Kraków was the capital of the General Government, the name that Germans had given to the occupied region of what had been eastern Poland, and it was swarming with Germans. To avoid prying eyes, Laura moved Zofia and herself frequently, five times in the first month. Zofia was undernourished and constantly sniffling. Laura worried about her health but worried even more that she would make a mistake answering inquisitive neighbors' endless questions while she was out looking for work. But Zofia passed the first tests with flying colors.

Laura had attended university and once wanted to be a doctor, but her ambition even before the war had been moot in a country where Jews weren't allowed to attend Polish medical schools. Her brilliant brother Edek had had to go to engineering school in Italy before immigrating to Palestine in the early 1930s. Now any job at all would have to do; without a job considered "essential" by the Nazis, she couldn't feed Zofia and they couldn't remain in Kraków.

Luckily Laura found a job in a German bank, but the pay was too low to improve their condition. Moreover, she now had to somehow provide care for five-year-old Zofia during the day. First, Laura paid a small sum to an old woman to look after her. The obese woman in a babushka put Zofia to work every day collecting cigarette stubs in the streets of their neighborhood. She wore a handwritten cardboard sign on a string around her neck that read, "My name is Zofia Tymejko and I live at . . ." whatever their current address was. Zofia would fill her little play purse with the smattering of discarded butts on the cobblestones, then bring them back. The old woman would dump Zofia's haul onto a newspaper and separate out the ones long enough to smoke. The useless ones she would hold up for inspection between pinched fingers and say, "And how do you expect me to smoke this, *kochanie*? With tweezers? Now go and bring *babunia* some more."

Laura soon found a better alternative, dropping her off at a Catholic orphanage in the morning before she made her rounds. The terse nuns gave Zofia a plate of soup and a crust of bread at midday. She was shy by nature, and under her mother's anxious care and ceaseless religious drilling she had grown even more so. Even when she was hungry, and she was hungry almost all the time, she knew how to keep quiet.

Laura managed to establish contact with her sisters, who were both in Kraków as well. Putzi, now living under the name of Ksenia

Osoba, was a maid in a German home, and Fryda, under the name of Zofia Wolenska, worked for a Polish family. Neither of them had heard anything from or about their brother Manek.

A few weeks later, Laura ran into Julek in the streets of Kraków. He acted as if he had no idea what had happened to their luggage weeks before, and Laura would have been a fool to provoke him with accusations. What could she do in a country where a shifty Pole held their very lives in his calloused hands?

"Julek," she said. "Do you know where my brother Manek is?"

The big Pole looked startled. "Oh, there's bad news there," he said, placing a hand on her shoulder.

"How bad?"

"The Krauts caught him at the Lvov train station and hanged him."

"Hanged him?!" she cried in disbelief. "Dear God!"

He said the SS wanted to see his papers and he ran. Julek shrugged. "So terrible," he said without emotion. "I thought you knew."

She would have predicted that Manek, the toughest of the five Litwak siblings, the one who once came home with a broken jaw after a fight with some anti-Semites, would have been the one to survive. She was brotherless now, having already lost the eldest of her siblings, Edek, who had suddenly died in the Holy Land of typhus, or maybe from water poisoned by the Arabs—the family would never know. What was the God she didn't believe in anymore—maybe even the same God she had been drilling Zofia to believe in—doing to her family?

Or perhaps God had nothing to do with it. When Laura learned later from friends that it was Julek himself who had escorted Manek to the Lvov station, as he had escorted Zofia and herself, she couldn't rid herself of the thought that he had betrayed her brother to the Germans.

All that Zofia would remember was moving from one damp, shabby room in someone's home to another. Surely if her father hadn't been taken away, there would be money and her poor mother would not have to be pleading with strangers for a bed. They had so few clothes that her mother seemed to be washing them in the sink every night. She would watch her mother, dark-haired and beautiful, coaxing a pair of stockings up her legs and applying lipstick in a chipped mirror before leaving to look for work.

The drilling didn't stop. Maybe it had to do with Zofia's father's disappearance from their lives, and her praying for his return, but Laura tested Zofia continuously on her catechism from a prayer book. Was it Zofia's imagination, or had her mother actually woken her up in the middle of the night to make sure she knew it?

"Zosia, what are the six principal truths of the faith?"

"'There is one God,'" Zofia would recite sleepily. "'He is a righteous judge who rewards good and punishes evil.' I want to sleep, Mama."

"Who are the three divine Persons?"

"The Father, the Son, and the Holy Ghost. Can I go to sleep, Mama?"

"In a minute, Zosia. 'The Son of God became man . . .'"

"' . . . died on the cross and rose for our salvation.'"

"Good girl," her mother said, kissing her hair. "I love you."

They moved into a better home—a room they rented from a Polish officer and his family.

For Laura, the nightmare simply continued. The officer suspected she was not the Catholic she claimed to be, and tested and baited her mercilessly. When she went off to work at the bank, she feared that he would trick Zofia into a confession that they were Jewish. The officer could report his suspicions to the Nazis anytime he wanted. There were even times when, returning from work, she wondered if she would find Zofia alive. When she went off to work at the bank, her mother reminded her to stay in their room as much as possible and answer as few questions as possible. If the officer or his wife asks where your father is, she told Zofia, say that the Russian soldiers took him away. If they ask why we came to Kraków, say that I came to find a good job. If they ask where we lived in Lvov, tell them in the Christian district.

What else could she do? There was no other world to live in right now but this one. She couldn't bear to move yet again. She had to work, for without her measly income they would starve.

A few weeks after they moved in, there was loud knocking on the apartment door one evening. Three German SS men burst into the apartment, barking in a mixture of German and Polish, and ordered all of them up against the wall of the living room. Zofia was terrified. She stared at the death head medallions on their SS caps and remained very still. Waving his luger at the officer and his wife, one of the SS men demanded to know where the Polish couple's son was. Zofia could make out that the son had escaped from a Nazi prison and was hiding with his brother. The Polish officer stammered that he had no idea. Yelling something in German, his spittle flying, the Nazi brought the muzzle of his luger closer to the Polish officer's face. Then he holstered his pistol and slapped the officer across both sides of his face, using the palm and the back of his gloved hand.

The officer, his eyes watering from the blows, tried to hold back his tears, and the SS man turned to look at Laura.

"Where are they?" he screamed at her. Zofia saw the Polish officer's eyes on her mother, and somehow she knew that her mother knew the answer. Zofia had never thought of her mother as someone who knew things that the frightening Germans didn't, and wanted to. What if they realized her mother was lying? They'd hurt her or take her away like the Russians took away her father, and then what would Zofia do? She would have to find the orphanage by herself and she didn't even remember the name of it. Zofia grew dizzy at the thought that something might happen to her only remaining parent.

Very calmly, considering the terrified officer, his weeping wife, and the general feeling that something quite horrible was about to happen, Zofia's mother began to explain to them—in perfect German—that none of them had seen any sign of the boys, and that she was very sorry that they were not able to help them.

The effect on the Germans of hearing their own language, especially from a woman as pretty as this one, was immediate; they accepted in German what they had doubted in Polish and departed, but not before sternly warning everyone that they would be back to interrogate them again.

The very next morning, the grateful Polish officer's wife left a glass of fresh milk outside their room. It would be the only kindness they showed them during their stay. Zofia—who had not tasted fresh milk in months—would never forget how delicious it was.

The next day Laura placed in one of the Kraków newspapers an ad for a job. It said she sought a position outside the city, preferably with room and board, stressing her fluency in German. She figured that, no matter where they landed, it couldn't be any worse. Of the 15,000 Jews who had been forced into the Kraków ghetto by the Germans a year and a half earlier, only about 6,000 Jews remained. The ghetto contained two forced-labor camps and some businesses where Jews toiled until most of them dropped dead of starvation and fatigue.

Laura passed the ghetto on her way home from work, and she couldn't help but look into the ghetto through the barbed-wire fence between some of the buildings. One day she found all the houses along the fence on fire and German soldiers shooting the Jews as they jumped from the windows. On another, she witnessed a soldier swinging two small children by the legs and smashing their heads against a brick wall. She came close to vomiting there on the street. The ghetto was like a stockyard of emaciated two-legged creatures, waiting to be slaughtered. Yet she somehow envied them. At least they were still living life, however barely, as Jews, to the very end, while she sought to escape death by posing as a member of another religion. If not for Zofia, she would gladly give up her desperate charade and melt back into the ghetto again as Laura Schwarzwald to await the end.

She wrote to her sisters, both working as domestics in Kraków, of her plan to leave the city and waited for a reply to her ad while continuing to work at the bank, where every time she met the eyes of a colleague, she feared she had been recognized. Finally, a miracle! A response arrived in the post, from an SS man named Leming, who was looking for a bookkeeper and part-time translator with office duties. He was in charge of the Polish agricultural cooperative in the spa resort town of Busko-Zdrój, northeast of Kraków. It was just what her landlady in Lvov had recommended. The offer came with a small salary and the promise of a little food from the cooperative's canteen.

Laura accepted immediately and Leming set a date, writing that he would pick her up on his return to Kraków from a vacation in Germany and drive her to Busko-Zdrój. Laura gave notice at the bank, told her landlord she was leaving, and gathered her and Zofia's few possessions. But there was no word from Leming on the appointed day. Frantic, she rushed by bus to the airfield to learn that Leming's flight had been delayed. She waited hours for the plane to arrive and then had him paged. She hadn't known what to expect, but still she was startled when a stern-looking and stubbly middle-aged man showed up in a gray SS tunic and an armband bearing a swastika.

The thought that she had been hired by a Nazi was promptly replaced by the fear that he had already decided to fire her. As she introduced herself, he was complaining about the delayed flight and the "wretched Poles." He promptly informed her that he would have nothing to do with her.

Laura was desperate. She couldn't return either to her job or to their rented room at the Polish officer's house.

"Bitte, Herr Leming—" she began.

"Useless people!" he spat at her, saying he should've hired a German fräulein in the first place.

She reminded him in German of his promise, saying she'd given up her job and lodging. Her little girl and she would have nowhere to go. Tears filled her eyes.

Leming said that was her problem.

"But I have your letters to me. You state very clearly—"

He turned on his boot heels to go, saying that he was sure she would have no problem finding other employment.

She played the only card left in her hand. She took a deep breath and said, "Herr Leming! I don't imagine the Gestapo would be very pleased to know that you are not a man of your word." She could hardly believe the words that were coming out of her mouth.

He could have her arrested; it would be nothing to him. But when he turned back to face her, he looked worried, even frightened. Laura barely knew what to make of his expression. What chance did anyone have against secret police so powerful that an empty threat from a single mother could be instantly effective? Leming looked her up and down, stroked his chin, and said, "Well, well, Frau Tymejko, very good. Your German is excellent and you are obviously not a typical Pole."

It was the biggest automobile Zofia had ever seen that came to pick them up the next day. The chauffeur stared straight ahead behind the wheel while Leming himself opened the back door and beckoned to them. Zofia would have been truly frightened by her mother's new employer if her mother didn't seem so pleased about going to work and eager to get into the car.

Leming had a large, lined face, big for his body, with a pointed, pomaded widow's peak that made him look like the Count Dracula puppet Zofia had once seen in a department store window. Under his deeply furrowed forehead, which featured one sinister groove that bisected his forehead vertically, were two heavy-lidded eyes. His chin was so deeply cleft that it almost looked like someone's bottom, but with stubble. Zofia was fascinated by this chin, as she had been by the *Totenkopf* on the SS hats.

But the part of Leming's face that she could barely take her eyes off of—that she had to force herself to ignore—was the short smudge of a mustache between his nose and thin upper lip, just like Adolf Hitler's.

Zofia sat quietly on the soft gray velour seat with her mother. Herr Leming himself hardly said a word during the two-hour journey to Busko-Zdrój. The town was small and no longer full of the well-dressed people who normally flocked to it for its famous natural sulfur springs. No one looked like they even knew a war was going on. The sanatorium was in a large beautiful park with a garden and chestnut trees, but surrounded by a town that looked like a place where nothing much ever happened.

But, in fact, a great deal had just happened. Busko-Zdrój's little ghetto, which had been created in April 1941, had already been liquidated by the time they arrived. Its two thousand Jews had been transferred to Jedrzejow, joining 4,000 others from the ghettos of Lodz, Wloclawek, and Warsaw on their way to the Treblinka death camp.

Leming offered Laura and Zofia a room in his own apartment, but Laura declined, knowing what that meant.

"As you wish," he said. "I can see you are not *eine Mädchen für alles.*" A woman for all to enjoy.

"But I'll be the best bookkeeper you've ever had," she replied.

Laura and Zofia ended up sharing a room attached to a granary that had only a paraffin stove to warm them. It was early November but so cold it might as well have been January. Zofia, who seemed constantly sick, was sniffling and sneezing more than ever. Her mother wouldn't leave her alone anymore, so she took her to the local grammar school and told the headmaster that Zofia's birth certificate had been destroyed in the war, but that she had turned six—not five—in July. The ruse worked. Zofia was both tall and smart for her age, and her reserve made her seem even older. Within a week of their arrival, Zofia joined the first grade class.

By the spring of 1943, mother and daughter moved again, this time to a two-room, first-floor apartment facing a courtyard. It was much nicer than the granary—in fact, the mayor of Busko lived upstairs with his family—but not at all as nice as the homes of some of Zofia's classmates.

In their new place, Laura and Zofia slept on two single beds in a room with pale green walls. The kitchen, which was painted orange, contained a stove, a table, and three chairs. Zofia started eating better than she had in a long time. There was milk, bread, jam, eggs, butter, potatoes, onions, beets, cucumbers, and even a little meat, and in the nearby woods and fields the two of them picked gooseberries and wild strawberries. Zofia was surprised to learn that her mother was something of an expert on mushrooms who collected wild borowik mushrooms for soups and omelets. Zofia hadn't eaten so well in a long time.

Zofia made a couple of friends, but she sensed a gulf. Many of the children in her class had two parents, bigger homes, even relatives with farms, which meant a steady supply of the meat and fruit that Zofia seldom saw. But she fit in as best she could, giggling with the others at news of the Jews' fate. What were the Jews thinking? Her teacher compared the Warsaw ghetto uprising to a mouse trying to stop a locomotive.

One of her friends had quite a lot of toys, which made Zofia so envious that one afternoon she pocketed a small toy horse. That night, after suffering a great deal over her theft, knowing it was wrong, she confessed the crime to her mother, who said she had to return it. Which, being a most obedient girl, she did.

And her mother was different from the other mothers too—prettier, more sophisticated, but also so joyless and demanding. In her anxiety, she occasionally still drilled Zofia.

"Where's your father? Who is your Savior?" Zofia began to hate her.

"If you don't stop," she snapped at her mother one day, "I'm going to report you to the Gestapo!"

Now Laura knew how Leming had felt. It was the only time she ever slapped her daughter.

When Zofia wasn't cursing her mother, she was trying desperately to please her.

One day she decided to clean the wood floor in the kitchen by pouring a bucketful of water over it. This was apparently not the right method, because when her mother came home and saw the results, she had a fit—which to Zofia seemed wildly out of proportion to the misdeed. She had only a single toy named Halinka to amuse her, a large doll, blond and blue-eyed like Zofia herself, that her mother had bought from a fleeing German family, and so Zofia often resorted to playing in puddles, another activity her mother didn't find amusing. She arranged for Zofia to stay after school with a Polish woman and her two young sons, but one day the boys took a hot poker out of the fire and convinced Zofia that she should touch it. Laura didn't find this funny either and stopped the after-school visits.

Zofia returned to being a latchkey child, condemned to spend many more hours than she would have liked with her two favorite books. One was a Scandinavian fable about a bear named Kurol who was king of the forest. The other was called *Mr. Thermometer*, a poem about a sickly child much like herself. Later her mother would buy her a small walleyed bear with a quizzical expression to keep her and Halinka company, but Zofia barely knew how to play. Tea parties were foreign to her. She knew nothing of nonexistent tea and invisible cakes.

"What do you think of Halinka's dress, Bear?" she'd ask, wait a few seconds, then say, "Well, that just shows how much you know about girls' dresses."

"Halinka thinks you're handsome, Bear," she'd say, then pause. "Now you say something nice about her. . . . Yes, go ahead. . . . That's very nice of you, Bear. Yes, I think she has beautiful hair, too."

The neighbors made sure Laura knew that their furnished apartment had been occupied by Jews before they were deported. Laura lived not among Jews, but among their things. The furniture in their apartment. The sidewalks on which she walked were paved with gravestones from the Jewish cemetery; the dresses the town's poor Polish Catholic girls wore were made from Jewish prayer shawls.

Whenever Laura slipped on the icy stone step by the front door, she was convinced that the previous occupants were reprimanding her from their crowded graves.

Occasionally Zofia would walk around town after school, looking in the gift shop window or the ice cream store, wishing she had a few zlotys. Other times, she'd go to the park, sit under a chestnut tree, and read. One day she saw notices posted in the park that a Pole was going to be executed in the town square the next day. She didn't think she'd like watching a Pole being killed, so she stayed home. On the following day, she did venture into the square to pay her mother a visit at work in the two-story stone agricultural cooperative. Right there, near the front door, at the base of the front of the building, she saw streaks of blood. More blood had pooled, and dried, between the stones of the sidewalk.

Zofia stared, trying to summon a mental picture of the event that had left these stains. Next to her, a man shook his head. He wore a brown overcoat that was too big for him and had probably belonged to a bigger, and now dead, man.

It wasn't that Zofia had become inured to the apparent cheapness of human life in Poland—she still shuddered at what could happen to her mother or her—but like all children, even in a time of war, little pleasures loomed large, none larger than the treat her mother brought home from work one evening: a Suchard chocolate bar that Herr Leming had given her. Zofia couldn't recall ever having tasted chocolate, but she must have. Why else would her mouth water at the sight of it? Chocolate, fresh vegetables, and fruit were almost impossible for most ordinary Poles to obtain. When Zofia came down with scurvy from a lack of vitamin C, one of her aunts in Kraków had somehow acquired an orange and sent it to her. But an orange was such a luxury that Laura was able to trade it to a nearby farmer for enough apples to last the entire winter and cure the scurvy. But chocolate? It was in her mother's hand just inches away, and her eyes grew wide.

Then, just as her mother was about to give her the candy, she suddenly pulled it back.

"Mama!" Zofia protested, but not before the candy had already disappeared into an apron pocket.

Her mother said it might be poisoned.

Zofia was perplexed. "Poisoned?"

"You know Herr Leming, the man I work for?" She explained that she didn't trust him. He was a German and might try to poison them.

"But why would he poison us?"

She explained that the Germans hated the Poles almost as much as they hated the Jews.

This was disturbing news to Zofia. The Jews were detestable, dirty, and worthless. Her teacher had made that clear. Besides, the evidence was everywhere. Why else would some of the streets of Busko be paved with Jewish gravestones? But why would the Germans hate Zofia herself, a Polish girl who went to church every Sunday, even when her mother's headaches prevented her from going with her daughter? The figure of God depicted in the fresco on the church's ceiling, a fatherly-looking man with a flowing white beard, was a great comfort to a girl whose own father had been taken away. She was going to take her First Communion in less than a year. She knew that Jesus Christ was going to be there with her.

"The Germans couldn't hate us. Not like they hate the Jews," Zofia protested.

"They hate us too," her mother explained, "and they have killed plenty of innocent Poles to prove it. Zosia, you must take my word for it. To them, we are slaves and they are the masters. But you must never, ever mention it. Do you understand? When you come to visit me at work, you mustn't speak to Herr Leming unless spoken to, and then you must say very little."

It was all beyond a child's understanding.

"But the Jews killed Christ and they kill Christian children for their blood," Zofia said, repeating what she'd heard so often at school.

"Well, I've known some Jews who were quite nice," her mother said. "Anyway, my little Zosia, you must never look sad. You must always look happy, Zosia. Then Herr Leming and the others won't bother us."

Zofia wished her mother would stop telling her not to speak because she was already an expert at not speaking when not spoken to. She was a master at hiding sadness. She was a genius at not making any noise at all.

After midnight, when her mother was asleep, Zofia slipped out of bed and padded to the kitchen, where she found her mother's apron hanging over the back of the chair by the stove. She slipped her hand into one pocket, and then the other, but both were empty. She stood on the chair, inspected the shelf and the crockery. Nothing. Zofia returned to bed empty-handed.

In the endless present moment that is childhood, Zofia could no more understand the disappearance of the chocolate bar than she could comprehend the disappearance of her father, or remember leaving the Lvov ghetto, or even of having lived there.

Laura and Zofia were walking in Spa's Park one day when a hollow-eyed young woman and her little boy passed them, followed by two SS men with German shepherds. It was apparent from the leaves and twigs clinging to the mother's and son's torn clothes that they had just been found in the woods. And it was just as clear to Laura that the two Jews were about to be shot. Under the brims of their peaked hats with the death's head medallions, the SS men wore the smug expressions of men who were doing their job well. The mother had her arm around her son's tiny shoulder, determined to protect him from the horrible fate she must have known awaited them.

Laura closed her eyes in an equally futile attempt to ignore the situation. The woman was a mother too, trying to shield her child from the truth, but the knowledge that she and Zofia might survive their lie, while the other woman and her child had perhaps only minutes to live, tore at her heart. A wave of guilt and despair passed through her as she tugged Zofia onward. And what made it all even more unbearable was Zofia's apparent lack of curiosity about the doomed pair. Or was it obliviousness? Either way, her own daughter seemed like a stranger to her, and the more successful Laura was in protecting her, the stranger Zofia became to her.

Still, she continued to test her on the catechism, on the invented fates of loved ones, on what she should say to strangers if she was ever questioned.

"Where's your father? Who is your Savior? What is the name of your mother's boss?" She pushed and pushed until Zofia began running away at the sight of her anxious mother approaching. Laura herself was sick of rehearsing the lies because the price of keeping her daughter alive was to lose her affection—even their very relationship.

Yet she envied her daughter's ignorance. Better to believe you really are a Catholic schoolgirl than to know you're a Jew hiding behind a mask of deception, without which you cannot survive. Better not to realize that the mother and son emerging from the woods would be shot and killed.

Was there not a point when terror simply took over a psyche like an invading army and annihilated the self? How was it that during the day Laura could function as well as she did, sitting at her desk in the agricultural cooperative, only feet away from Leming, translating Polish documents into German for him?

As the Polish Resistance in the area grew, it increasingly became Laura's job to translate something far more unpleasant. Young Polish partisans were sabotaging trains carrying supplies to the Eastern Front, and those who were caught in the vicinity of Busko-Zdrój were brought before Herr Leming for interrogation. It was her job to translate Leming's screaming accusations and denunciations from German to Polish, and then the partisans' screaming defenses and denunciations from Polish to German. The adversaries kept having to pause and wait for her translations, which would have been funny if it hadn't been another matter of life and death. Later, she would hear the cries of the partisans being tortured in the cooperative's basement—the ones, that is, who hadn't been taken out and shot.

Laura had to believe that one day soon history would regard Leming and his kind as evil, as a once-in-the-history-of-the-world aberration, or else civilization itself surely would have to come to an end. In the meantime, while she appeared to be doing her part voluntarily to facilitate the punishment of the partisans, she took the extraordinary step of tipping them off to the Germans' military movements she learned about in Leming's office. The Polish Resistance was becoming more active and Laura wanted to do something to help. It was a terrible gamble for Laura, all the more so since many Poles around her in the cooperative had begun to suspect her of precisely the opposite sympathies, of collaborating.

News that she spoke excellent German had circulated quickly in Busko-Zdrój, and her Polish neighbors were beginning to talk, wondering whose side she was really on. Her neighbors began questioning her and, worse, six-year-old Zofia. Now not only did she live in constant fear of being exposed to the Germans as a Jew, but she was suspected by the Poles of being a German spy! Once, when Zofia visited her mother at work during lunchtime, two Polish women followed them to the outhouse and stood outside eavesdropping, hoping to hear pro-Nazi conversation—with her daughter? What were they thinking? When Laura provided them with no ammunition, she felt that her Polish colleagues began to trust her. Laura detected a more general shift in the sentiments of the local, mostly peasant Poles toward the Jews. With news of the Warsaw ghetto uprising and other acts of heroism, contempt for the Jews was now grudgingly mixed with admiration.

However, Zofia came home from school to tell her that her teacher was laughing at the futility of the uprising. Poor Zofia, Laura thought: she had no idea how many times her mother had gotten off the bus because she thought a man across the way suspected she was a Jew, or because a woman's stare might mean that she knew her from Lvov or Kraków. Zofia didn't know how often she had altered her route or slipped down an alley when she thought she was being followed. She wished she could share with Zofia her happiness when the Jewish fighting held the Germans off for a month in Warsaw.

Laura began to care more and more about their appearance, buying a secondhand coal-heated iron. If she couldn't be the mother to Zofia she would have liked, she at least wanted her daughter to look her best. When a neighbor borrowed the iron and didn't return it, she marched over to demand it back. When the neighbor told her that a German soldier had swiped it from her, Laura proceeded immediately to SS headquarters and insisted on getting it back, which she did. In a world ruled by atrocities, correcting even the smallest injustice helped keep you sane.

In case of emergency, Laura kept a green velvet bag with wooden handles by the front door. In it were money, clothes, their identification papers, a few family photographs that she'd sewn into the lining, a bit of flour, sausage, some hardboiled eggs, a bottle of vodka to use as barter, and a humble family heirloom, a hand-hammered silver soup spoon. Twice before, at the sound of approaching German planes flying to the Eastern Front, her mother had grabbed the bag and rushed with Zofia to their apartment building's cellar in Busko-Zdrój.

By the fall of 1944, the tide had turned. Zofia's mother had overheard at her job that the Nazis were going to go door to door the next day looking for Poles to conscript as laborers in a last desperate attempt to win the war, which was not going well for the Germans. The Germans would have been looking for Jews, had any been left in Busko-Zdrój. The Russians were pushing back into Poland, and Zofia had even seen a broken line of bandaged and limping German soldiers trudging westward, tunics unbuttoned, soles flapping, looking as bedraggled as Jews.

Before dawn, Laura, already holding the velvet bag, woke up Zofia and led her through the empty streets of Busko-Zdrój. In her pocket, Zofia squeezed Bear, the small Steiff she had not yet bothered to name, and carried Halinka under her arm. She followed her mother out of the dark town and into a field dotted with conical haystacks. They saw no one else in the field. Laura marched them to one in the farthest corner, near the woods. Using their hands and a pitchfork she found nearby, they worked on the side that faced the forest, the least likely side to be seen. Within minutes, they had scooped out a cave in the middle of the haystack, just big enough for them to sit in.

As Zofia watched the sunrise with both Halinka and Bear in her lap, she hoped her friends were safe, especially Wacka—it was pronounced *Vatska*—her good friend from school, whose father was a shoemaker with a shop on the town square, opposite the gift shop, where her mother had recently bought her the bear. It was Wacka's father who made Zofia's shoes, the lace-up boots and sandals that her mother made sure were at least two sizes too big so Zofia had plenty of time to grow into them. It was one of the things Zofia looked forward to, when the war was over, that her mother would buy her shoes that fit her *now* and not at some time far off in the future.

"We'll be safe here," Zofia whispered to her two little companions, stroking the big doll's hair and rubbing her thumb nervously over the bear's little face with its tiny glass eyes that had been sewn on unevenly.

"Are you two warm enough?" she whispered later that morning, pretending to offer Halinka and Bear bits of hardboiled egg. She sat Bear, who had jointed arms and legs, down between her legs. "Make sure you share with Halinka," she warned him.

This was an adventure, a rare outing for her these past few months. The sun was shining and her mother was relaxed for once, since even she felt safe sitting inside a haystack in a field of identical haystacks. Overhead, black bombers rumbled west like a formation of gruesome geese.

"Zosia," her mother said, "someday it will be like before."

"Like before" meant nothing to Zofia. As far back as she could remember, she and her mother were poor Poles on the move. When Zofia tried to remember things, she couldn't quite get past some invisible sentry who guarded the first four or five years of her life. A couple of memory fragments slipped through, like the wonderful smells in her grandmother's kitchen, her father returning from work, and the memory of her great-grandfather lying dead on his bed, dressed in a black suit. She even dimly remembered that they had buried him the next morning, someone pushing a crude coffin through the streets in a wheelbarrow.

It was toward the end of the war, when Laura couldn't have bought a good night's sleep with a million zlotys, that an itinerant Catholic priest walked into Busko-Zdrój from who knows where and drew a crowd of faith-hungry Poles to a field outside of town. For reasons Laura herself barely understood, she stood in the chilly spring wind and listened to him.

She couldn't take her eyes off of him. With his black moth-eaten cassock and sunken dark eyes, he looked as if he had experienced his own share of suffering. He stood in the pasture with his Bible open in one palm and his other hand pointing to the sky. He told the crowd that they would overcome their suffering with hope and prayer, that Jesus had not forgotten them, and that God would punish the evildoers, and so on and so forth. So where's God been since 1939? she thought.

Laura almost never went to church on Sunday with Zofia and her class, and she couldn't even remember a single Jewish prayer, but the man's message struck some forgotten chord in her. When he finally closed the Bible and made some blessing motions and thanked everyone for coming, Laura was overcome with the desire to go right up to him and ask him to hear her confession.

"*Prosze pani*, I will gladly hear your confession," the priest said, "but only in a church, if you would be so kind as to show me the way to your house of God."

She led him back across the field to St. Leonard's Church, which was empty. She sat in a pew and he took a seat in the row behind her.

"I haven't said a word to anyone for so long, and although I know I am putting my life in your hands by telling you, Father, I feel I must. I'm not even sure why, but please have mercy on me."

"Go ahead, my daughter," came the voice right behind her.

She swallowed and said, "I'm Jewish."

There was silence behind her, which she broke by explaining that she and her daughter had been living as Catholics since 1942. What am I doing? she thought. Am I sending the two of us to our deaths after all this? After coming so far? A word from this tattered priest to the Gestapo and that would be it.

Still, there was silence, and Laura's stomach tightened terribly.

She finally heard the priest say in a low voice, "You should not fear anyone or anything except God. Fear God only and you will be helped and he will have mercy on you. Bless you, my daughter."

The priest mumbled something in Latin and fell silent.

She waited, but the priest said no more. When she finally turned to look at him, he was no longer in the pew. She caught a glimpse of his long coat as he exited the church and turned. She stood up, amazed at what she had done and overcome with the unfamiliar feeling that there was a supernatural being looking out for her and Zofia. Before the war, she had been a nonbeliever, bound only by ethical principles. What sense did it make that only now, after God had abandoned the Jews, she should feel imbued with some fresh hope and renewed strength to survive? And yet she felt a presence.

She really didn't know what to think. She had been the beneficiary of more than her share of sheer luck, but she didn't believe she had been *chosen*. She didn't believe she had *earned* it. She and Zofia had escaped deportation several times. Why? Because she was pretty? Because she spoke perfect German? Because her daughter was blond?

She had lived undetected among the Nazis. Why? Because she did the Polish officer and his family a favor? Because her landlady had given her a Christian prayer book and a good piece of advice?

During the bitterly cold winter of 1944 to 1945, some happiness arrived for both of them in the form of Laura's much younger sister, Putzi, who had against all the odds managed to make her way to Busko in a horse-drawn cart to live with them. She had spent the past two years in Kraków, posing as a Catholic and working under the name Ksenia Osoba as a housekeeper for a German family. Putzi had left her job when her German employers had fled from the advancing Russians back to Germany. Laura introduced her to Zofia by her Catholic nickname, Nusia.

Putzi was shorter than Laura, with a round face and high forehead. It was hard to overestimate the joy Laura felt at this reunion, with her husband, parents, and brothers gone. And Zofia was delighted to have a companion in her twenties, almost as close in age to Zofia as she was to Laura. Where Zofia's mother was so strict and tense—she was the oldest daughter in her family, after all—Putzi, the youngest, was theatrical and fun-loving. At times Putzi seemed more like a child even than Zofia. Her mere presence lit up their two-room apartment and brought out an expressive side of Zofia that her mother hadn't seen in years.

Best of all, Putzi brought with her the most wonderful possession—a goose feather comforter. For Zofia, it was the epitome of luxury—soft, fluffy, warm, and white in a world of black boots, fear, and no chocolate—and it was to rest permanently on Zofia's single bed, which she was to share with the aunt she knew only as Nusia. After just one night, though, Putzi complained to her sister right in front of Zofia that she kicked her legs in her sleep and kept her up all night.

Putzi said that she'd sleep on the floor.

"You will do no such thing, Nusia," Laura said. To avoid any slips, of course, they addressed each other only by their adopted Christian names.

Listening, Zofia thought that her mother might as well have been Putzi's mother too.

"But, Bronia," Putzi said, using Laura's Catholic nickname, "she kicks like a mule!"

Laura proposed they alternate, one week at a time.

"So instead of getting no sleep," Putzi replied, "I'll get half the sleep I need!"

They both laughed—Zofia couldn't remember hearing her mother's laughter, *ever*—and the two sisters hugged each other tightly.

"Now set the table, Nusia. I saved a chicken for you."

"It's a miracle I got here," Putzi wrote her other older sister, Fryda, who was living in Germany, shortly after arriving. "I hope I will manage. I sang Christmas carols, and I just play with little Zosia and make her little things she loves for dinner. I got lucky I came here during the holidays, since everyone treats you with good food. Bronia cooked half a chicken. The little one received some toys and skates. She is a really sweet and good-natured child and very talkative. You cannot stop her! She engages everyone. It's just that she coughs, the croup, though not to a great degree."

For the first time that she could remember, Zofia felt like she had a family. Maybe not like the other girls in school, but a family nonetheless. Having Putzi around softened her mother and took the sting out of Laura's constant anxiety.

"Why does she make me recite the catechism all the time?" Zofia complained to her aunt one day.

"Because she loves you, Zosia my dear. Because she wants you to be a good Christian. Then, if you pray to God for this horrible war to be over, maybe he'll listen."

But it was Putzi who did most of the listening—to Zofia, who at last had someone to talk to after school when her mother was at work. Life seemed almost normal. Putzi began discreetly tutoring Polish students, which Laura was already doing—they snuck in and out of their apartment at night—and they were all beginning to feel somewhat like human beings again. Between her mother's salary and their modest incomes from tutoring there was more food and even the occasional new dress.

Putzi was a talented seamstress who had once bartered her sewing skills for bread with one of her Catholic neighbors back in Lvov. Now, in addition to mending their clothes, she rendered Zofia speechless when she fashioned out of an old blue-striped blouse a little coat for her bear. Zofia was delighted. Putzi's talents extended to the kitchen as well, where she prepared welcome alternatives to her sister's repertoire. So consistently good was her cooking that it would become legendary when one of the peasants she tutored brought her as payment a goose, a rare delicacy, and Putzi managed to burn it beyond recognition.

Putzi's arrival made Laura long all the more for Fryda. All they had was a letter, postmarked Gelsenkirchen, Germany, where she had volunteered for a women's labor camp after her boss at a pharmacy in Bochnia, near Kraków, threatened to expose her when she wouldn't sleep with him. Fryda, a fragile beauty in the best of times, said she was slowly being starved to death and pleaded for food parcels. In addition, she wrote, the Allies were bombing the camp daily and she was hiding in a shelter, wanting to die. Laura tearfully put together a package of what she could spare and sent it off.

There were times when Laura could barely sleep, her fear of exposure was so great, and she would lie in bed with the thoughts flying around in her head like bullets. When she did doze off, sleep was like another occupied country, in which her husband and all the dead were alive again. It is amazing how much a human being can suffer, she thought to herself more and more. One is made of steel. You spring back and carry on. But her secrets were growing too big to be contained, and it was worse because she had no one to share them with but Putzi.

"I've had no choice, but for months, she's been running and hiding when she sees me coming," Laura confided to Putzi, tilting her head in the direction of Zofia's bed, where only a tiny hand could be seen peeking out from under the eiderdown.

Putzi told her that when the war was over, there would be time to make amends.

"*If* this is over. And by then, I'm afraid it will be too late."

Putzi said she'd speak to Zosia. "I'll make her understand."

"She's so hateful," Laura added. "Do you know what I heard her say to her doll the other day? She told Halinka not to play with Jews. She said, 'They kill Christian babies, you know.' Now I understand how easy it is to raise anti-Semites. There's really nothing to it."

A letter from Fryda arrived, this time from the Fraxel Fabrik company in Hanau am Main, Germany.

My Dears!

I already wrote you once that I was transferred to a different factory, in which I am already two weeks. I was taken quite arbitrarily, straight from work. I suppose additional workers were needed here. Although others traveled with me, they were assigned to agricultural work while I was selected to sit here by myself. The town is quite large, the factory as well, but the conditions as usual. Maybe this war will finally end and we will happily tell stories about our experiences. Chin up, don't pick up anything in the street, because there is war going on and one has to be careful. Don't let anyone take advantage of you.

Kisses, Fryda

Like everyone else, Fryda took the precaution of writing in code, so the truth had to be read between the lines. Phrases like "taken quite arbitrarily," "the conditions as usual," and "we will happily tell stories about our experiences" all hid the reality of forced labor and forced optimism in the face of catastrophe. No, they would never tell stories happily, but at least, Laura hoped, they would be able to tell them.

By the end of 1944, there was something in the air in Busko. Even a seven-year-old girl could sense it. Something like confusion and disarray. In Zofia's school there was much talk that the Germans were really losing the war. Soon, people were saying, the skies would be full of Allied planes and the Polish people would finally be freed from their German occupiers.

Around this time, while Zofia was visiting her mother at the cooperative, there was a commotion in the courtyard behind the building and Zofia joined a group of Polish workers at the window. What she saw was inexplicable.

In the courtyard, six uniformed Nazi officials—Herr Leming among them—circled a long, black Mercedes touring car, festooned with tiny Nazi flags. The men were evenly spaced and moved slowly counterclockwise. As each of them passed one of the tires, he would kick it softly without breaking stride. On a command from one of them, they reversed direction and continued to circle the car clockwise. On another order, each man's right arm shot up in unison to "Heil Hitler!" Then they all piled into the car and drove off through the courtyard gate.

Laura couldn't help relishing the sight of German soldiers throwing their weapons away en masse and fleeing just ahead of the Russians. But the killings continued. The retreating Nazis were emptying the camps and forcing the prisoners on death marches westward to relocate them to labor camps for a last-ditch effort to win the unwinnable. As if not enough Jews had already died, hundreds of thousands more would succumb to starvation, illness, and exposure to the cold. And despite Churchill's promise of their imminent arrival, the Allied forces had not yet come to stop them.

In the spring of 1945, with Germany's defeat assured, Laura and Putzi were both concerned that they hadn't heard from Fryda in many weeks. There had been no acknowledgment of the last two food packages. Fryda's new camp and the factory where she worked were close to a rail line, and when reports of repeated heavy Allied bombing of Germany began circulating, Laura feared the worst. Rail lines were a primary target.

Why, she thought? Why hadn't the Allies managed to bomb any of the rail lines carrying Jews to their deaths in the last few years, yet they could somehow manage to bomb her sister, poor Fryda, the prettiest of them all?

Laura accepted that it was just the three of them now, plus a cousin Toncia in Israel, and her uncle Max Schaerf, who had left Austria for Cuba and had since settled in New York City—where Laura now dreamed of going. She didn't allow herself to feel safe even for a moment. The Germans might be on the run, but the Poles in Busko-Zdrój weren't exactly kind to the Jews. When those who had survived both deportation and the gas chambers came filtering back to reclaim their homes, they found their fellow townspeople ensconced there with no intention of moving, or even letting the Jews reclaim their possessions. Instead the Poles threatened to—and maybe did, as far as Laura knew—shoot their own homeless countrymen. What recourse did the Jews have anyway? Complain to the new Soviet authorities, immersed as they were in setting up a local government, and who despised the Jews even more than they despised the Poles? Every Jew in Poland was doing his or her best to get out of the country.

The Soviets came and were as loud as the Germans. They were peasants. They camped with their horses in courtyards, including Laura's and Zofia's, drinking vodka all the time, paring off chunks of black bread from huge round loaves (and offering pieces to Zofia), and biting into raw onions as if they were apples. They relieved themselves wherever they wanted, even in the courtyard—even in an empty office at the agricultural cooperative, where Laura continued to work. They moved into Poles' apartments. They ate horse meat.

Most of the Soviet soldiers seemed to know nothing of modern life. Laura's daughter stared in amazement one day when a soldier, frightened by a ticking pocket watch, shot it with his service revolver.

But the cloud of fear had lifted for Laura. In the May Day parade, she marched behind her neighbor, the mayor, with a rainbow ribbon across her chest, and with Zofia by her side.

Putzi was a bigger concern for the moment. She was tempting fate with a new boyfriend she'd acquired after starring opposite him in a local play at the cooperative. He was a handsome Polish Catholic named Tadeusz, a member of the Resistance and the brother of one of Laura's coworkers. The two had fallen in love and were seeing each other regularly, much to Laura's distress. It would still be dangerous if anyone, even a Resistance fighter, discovered that Putzi and her family were Jewish. The Poles had already proven themselves to be more than capable of murdering Jews without any help at all.

Laura begged Putzi not to fall in love with the boy.

"It's too late," Putzi said. "I already have."

"It can't end well. Someday we will leave Busko-Zdrój. We can't stay here forever. And then you'll have to forget him."

"Then I'll stay with him here."

"No. We must stick together. He's not right for you."

"How can you say that? You see me with Tadeusz! You see how in love we are! He wants to marry me!"

"You'll see. You'll regret it. How can you put our lives at risk?" Laura said, who was haunted by her own ill-advised confession to the priest. "Haven't we lost enough family? His brother probably already knows we're Jewish. I've worked alongside him for the last two years and he's no dummy. You know the Poles are better at identifying Jews than the Germans."

As it happened, Tadeusz himself soon figured out without much difficulty that Putzi was Jewish. He not only had grown up with a Jewish family—and spoke better Yiddish than Putzi!—but he had been badly treated by the Nazis and sympathized with Jews. The relationship continued—for now.

For Zofia, life was better. The Sunday afternoons she spent with her mother and Putzi in Spa's Park were more relaxed than before, especially when they weren't downwind from the rotten-egg smell of the sulfur baths in the grand building at the far end. From the Danish Red Cross came candy and from the United Nations Relief and Rehabilitation Association came Spam and Crisco, which Zofia greedily spread on bread that had not seen much butter. The Red Cross arranged a trip for the town's children to a convent in Rabka, another spa town in the mountains, where Zofia got to kiss a prelate's relic ring, a moment that transported her.

A few weeks before the first Christmas after the war, Zofia wrote Santa Claus:

> *I am requesting candy or a small doll or cookies or a sled. I am asking for skis, but most of all I would like a small doll, but dressed in that pretty dress in the gift shop window and wearing shoes. Sometimes I was a good girl and sometimes not. I cannot tell exactly how many times, because I did not count. I do not know if I deserve it all. I beg your forgiveness and Mommy and Auntie, but I would like to ask you not to be angry with me, I will be good.*
>
> *Zofia*

What Laura wanted for Christmas was something else: freedom. She had no address for her uncle Max Schaerf, but in desperation wrote him anyway in care of "New York City, America." She sent it off in January 1946, and waited week after week for a reply. In the meantime, the past was impossible to escape—both in her mind and in reality. She heard from friends that Julek, the Pole who had escorted them to Kraków and stole their luggage, had accompanied her brother Manek to the Lvov train station two and a half years before on the day he was, or so Julek had told her, hanged. Suspecting him of betraying her brother, Laura had to fight the urge to report him to the Russians as an anti-Communist.

"They'd know what to do with him," she told Putzi.

"Well, why don't you?"

Laura sighed. "It won't bring Manek back. And, anyway, how can I become what I despise?"

Laura and Putzi played along with the Russians. Although neither she nor Putzi could bring themselves to become members of the Communist Party, as long as they didn't reveal their Judaism they felt safer than before. They didn't feel so alone and different inside, because more and more Polish people around them had also lost family. Yet not to be able to commiserate with the returning Jews made them feel guilty. Putzi, Zofia, and she were neither real Catholics nor real Jews. The war had taken their relatives' lives, but it had also taken the survivors' identities.

Finally, miraculously, on April 12 she heard from her uncle.

My dear niece:

It is the third day since I have received your registered letter of January 14, and still I am shocked about the tragic news contained in it. The Huns have surely done a thorough job, and no one could properly describe or picture their misdeeds because their atrocities were and still are beyond human imagination.

My hands are trembling, and I don't know how to begin this letter. After you have gone through such torture and sufferings, what consolation can a letter—even from your nearest relative— bring to you? . . . All of you need real help. My wife Clara and I are willing to do all what is humanly possible. . . . Write us immediately whether you intend to join us, and to immigrate into the United States. . . .

Meanwhile we will try to send you a few food packages; your

*aunt Rosa, married to Emil Hoenig, is living in London. . . . A
copy of your letter has been airmailed to her; and you may be sure
that she will get in touch with you as soon as possible.*

*With love and affection
Max, Clara, and Howie Schaerf*

It was all very perilous. If the Russians discovered that Laura was
trying to get them to the West, the three of them would be thrown
in jail, if not worse.

Uncle Max advised them to consult an immigration lawyer, since
their birthplace of Lvov was now in the Soviet Union, under whose
quota they would come. He told them to apply for a visa at the nearest American Consulate. *Quick attention is necessary*, he wrote. *The
best alternative for you would be to join us here in America.*

But America's door was not open very wide and would take only a
fraction of Jewish refugees immediately after the war. President Roo-
sevelt seemed far more concerned about not antagonizing the oil-rich
Saudi Arabians than helping the remnants of European Jewry. The
British were blocking immigration to Palestine.

The remnants of Laura's family, Putzi and Zofia, would have to
bide their time in a country now cleansed of Nazis but not of virulent
anti-Semitism. The summer of 1946 suddenly provided ample proof
that the war on Poles had hardly ended. The Nazis had come for
people at all hours, but the Russians made them disappear quietly at
night. One never knew who might be listening to you; Zofia learned
to whisper, even among her friends. Anti-Jewish riots erupted in
Kraków and spread. Every town had its violent incidents. On July
4, 1946, in Kielce, not far from Busko, Polish townspeople accused
Jews of kidnapping a boy who had mysteriously disappeared. A mob
proceeded to murder forty-two Jews, including two children and
a concentration camp survivor. The boy turned up later, safe and
sound; he had been off at a friend's and afraid to tell his parents the

truth. By the end of 1947, more than 2,000 Jews had been murdered after the war in Poland without any help from the Nazis.

The surviving Jews had crossed a great desert against all odds, dragged themselves to what they thought was safety, only to find themselves locked out of their own lives or staring into a newly dug grave.

Zofia remained unaware of the drama around her. The agricultural co-op organized an outing for employees and their families to the Shrine of Our Lady of Czestochowa, a cathedral in the village of that same name. Zofia and the others rode all night in heavy rain in the back of a truck. To make matters worse, the windshield wipers didn't work and the roads, cratered by bombs, provided endless rude shocks. Despite it all, when they arrived in the early morning and Zofia spotted the peacocks strolling the grounds, she was delighted. The shrine contained "the Black Madonna," an ancient icon that would work miracles if people prayed hard enough. According to popular belief, prayers induced the Madonna to halt a Swedish invasion of Poland in 1655, and to drive the Russians out of Warsaw in 1920. Hitler took such beliefs seriously enough that, just to be on the safe side, he prohibited pilgrimages during the Nazi occupation. With the Nazis gone, Poles flocked once again to the cathedral to pray for their nation.

When Zofia's group entered the cathedral to take early morning Mass, the walls were sparkling with silver and gold pieces that they were told represented the parts of pilgrims' bodies that had been cured. It was magical. Zofia knelt before the famous icon of the Black Madonna holding baby Jesus, which was said to have been painted on a tabletop built by Jesus himself. She was transfixed. The photograph of the icon she bought that day was one of the few things she would one day carry out of Poland with her. She had never felt so safe before, although Czestochowa was just sixty miles from the town of Oswiecim, which the Germans had renamed Auschwitz.

I n the fall of 1947, Laura heard there was a small window opening up for emigration—not for Jews, still stymied by strict quotas in America, Canada, and the British occupiers in Palestine—but for non-Jews with job offers abroad. By now Laura had in hand a letter from her mother's sister Rosa and her husband, Emil Hoenig, in London, promising her and Putzi jobs as domestics. Soon after, she sat in a Polish government office with Putzi and Zofia, watching as the official studied their false identity papers.

"So you, Bronislawa, will work for your aunt and uncle, is that it? And they've arranged for you, Ksenia"—he said, reading Putzi's Christian name off her document—"to work for another family?"

The women nodded.

"But you say that you're sisters," he said, tapping the end of his fountain pen against the blotter.

"We are."

"But your last names are different."

Laura stiffened. She had to think of something.

"Your last name is Tymejko," he said, looking at Laura. Then he turned to Putzi. "And yours is Osoba. How can that be?"

"I can explain, sir," Laura said. She paused, thinking about how Putzi looked so much more Slavic than she did.

"I'm waiting," the official said.

"Well, Ksenia was an abandoned child," Laura began. "My mother found her under a tree, in a basket, in Lvov when she was just three months old—and she adopted her. And we grew up as sisters. That's the reason." Laura shot Zofia a look that said, Don't react or change your expression.

Zofia hardly needed the reminder. She sat still while the official quizzed her mother and her aunt, keeping her eyes on her hands, which were folded in her lap. Laura proceeded to tell a story that was impossible to follow.

"I don't understand," the man said. "Why didn't your mother give her your last name?"

"Oh, that. Well, sir, Ksenia went through a rebellious phase when my mother told her she was adopted, she didn't want to be a Tymejko anymore. You know how teenagers are. She decided her last name would be Osoba, the name of her close friend, and later she changed it legally. Our mother was not happy about it, but what can you do?" She turned to her sister.

"Yes," Putzi said, nodding.

The official turned again to Putzi. "Your mother, the one who took you in and raised you, she must have been very upset with you."

"Yes, she was."

"My sister is very stubborn!" Laura said with a laugh.

Zofia looked up only when the man suddenly addressed her.

"Young lady? Did you know that your aunt was abandoned as a baby?"

Zofia nodded.

"Excuse me?" the official said.

"Yes," she said softly, although it was all news to her.

She must have done the right thing, because the man looked at all three of them, stamped the papers on his desk, handed them all to her mother, and said, "I don't like it, but off you go!"

They left the office with precious permission to leave the country. Having jumped that first hurdle, Laura now had to travel to Warsaw to obtain work visas. Uncle Max had told her to see representatives of the Hebrew Immigrant Aid Society there, who were doing their best to help tens of thousands of displaced Jews to emigrate. For once she wouldn't have to pretend she was Bronislawa Tymejko, a Catholic. She would only have to prove that she was Jewish, not so easy for someone holding only false papers, but at least she could speak

Yiddish. Or could she? While preparing for the trip to Warsaw, she realized to her horror that she couldn't remember more than a word or two of it. Nor could she recall the names of her two brothers, or of her parents—and not even the name of her own husband! It was as if she had been in shock since 1939 without even knowing it. The war seemed to have leveled her Jewish identity as surely as the Germans had leveled Warsaw. Now that she was about to become a Jew again, she had forgotten what it meant.

"Putzi," she said, "I can't remember my husband's name!"

Her sister looked at her blankly.

"Oh, come on," Laura said. "You too? What's happened to us? Can you name our siblings?"

Putzi opened her mouth slightly, as if about to say something, then closed it again.

"I can only come up with Manek," Laura said.

"Well," Putzi finally replied, "don't ask me."

Laura didn't think such a thing possible—that the same brain that had dissembled and connived and fought to stay alive could not now produce the most basic information about her own life. While she had used every ounce of energy to endure one horrific hardship after another, she hadn't been aware of the cost, that her previous life was being amputated. Fortunately, only a few days later in Busko-Zdrój, she ran into a Jew she'd known in Lvov, and the strangest thing happened. The man's face was like a window through which she could suddenly see her past. Her husband Daniel Schwarzwald and his parents. Her parents, Josef and Mina. Her grandparents Moses and Sarah, and Mina. Her brothers Edek and Manek and sister Fryda. All gone now. She could see Daniel's parents' Lvov apartment, where they had lived for a year as newlyweds while waiting for their furniture to be made. Putzi, however—maybe because she was much younger and had less to remember—continued to block much of it out, and for months after Laura would patiently remind her of what had been.

The train to Warsaw was crowded and smelly, and when Laura reached the city she couldn't find a place to sleep—an unhappy reminder of her arrival in Kraków with Zofia six years before, robbed of their luggage and having to scrounge a bed for the night. Warsaw had been reduced to a pile of rubble by the retreating Germans in 1944, and only a few sections of the city had since been rebuilt. Laura spotted a fellow Jew from the old days in Lvov, but after locking eyes briefly, they both looked away, still afraid to draw attention to themselves even though the Nazis were long gone.

Laura made her way to the Hebrew Immigration Aid Society, armed with her most valuable possession, a diamond crescent pin, hidden in the heel of her shoe. It was always a good idea to be prepared with a bribe, but nothing could shorten the lines of people outside the Immigration Aid Society, and eventually, she gave up in despair. Her second trip to Warsaw proved equally unsuccessful. But on the third try, in January 1948, her luck changed. This time she was carrying three visas when she returned to Busko. She and Putzi were registered as "maids" and could remain in England only as long as they earned their living as housekeepers—Laura for her aunt and uncle and Putzi for another Jewish family of the Hoenigs' acquaintance.

Not two weeks later, a very anxious Zofia had to leave Wacka and her other friends behind and board a train to Warsaw with her mother and aunt, en route to Gdynia, the Baltic Sea port and the waiting M/S Batory, a luxury liner that, like the three of them, had seen better days. The Batory, named after the sixteenth-century king of Poland, was as lucky to have survived the war as Laura, Putzi, and Zofia. The ocean liner started making the run from Gdynia to New York in 1936, but from 1939 till the end of the war she was a troop transport and a hospital ship for the Allies. In the summer of 1940, she secretly carried most of Britain's gold reserves to Montreal for safekeeping. Two months later, she carried another precious cargo—

700 British children—to Australia. She was involved in the evacuation of Dunkirk, the invasions of Oran, Algeria, and Sicily. She was under attack many times from German planes and submarines but escaped with only minor damage. In fact, her nickname after the war was Lucky Ship.

Zofia boarded with a small suitcase in one hand and her three-inch Steiff bear, named Bear, in the other. Halinka, unfortunately, hadn't made it. She had slowly fallen apart after the war. Much of her hair had fallen out, then one of her eyes refused to open anymore, and soon Halinka was lying awkwardly in the corner. By the time they left for Gdynia, she had disappeared altogether.

On the *Batory*, Zofia shared a third-class cabin with her mother and aunt in the bottom-most part of the ship, which turned out to be a blessing: the Baltic crossing was very rough, and the rolling of the ship was less severe below the waterline. The waves could get so high that they sometimes crashed onto the deck, and seasickness was rampant among the passengers. Most of them stayed in their cabins for the whole voyage, unable to carry on a conversation, let alone indulge in the copious amounts of food served at the daily buffet. Despite their comparatively unrocky accommodations in steerage, Putzi and Laura were as nauseated as everyone else.

Everyone, that is, except for the seasoned crew—and the eleven-year-old Zofia, who was strangely unaffected by the endless rolling of the huge vessel. The girl, who had last tasted an orange at age six, now had hundreds of them to choose from, along with numerous varieties of bread, cheese, and sausages. Oh, and there were five types of herring and a dozen different desserts. Other than the odd passenger who ventured in during a momentary hiatus from vomiting, Zofia had the dining room all to herself.

This cheered the food staff to no end; they were overjoyed that *someone* was eating and kept applauding Zofia's appetite and her hardiness.

It wasn't just the dining room either. The entire ship became her private playground. Zofia had a grand time exploring every public corner of the immense *Batory*, and none was more impressive to her than the bathrooms. All she had known in Poland were outhouses; Zofia and her mother had shared one with the mayor of Busko-Zdrój, no less. Between the bountiful food and the sparkling bathrooms with flush toilets, Zofia felt she had died and gone to heaven. A heaven that kept heaving back and forth, but a heaven nonetheless.

In Southampton, Laura disembarked and stood on the pier overcome by emotions that had been bottled up for years. Only now that she was actually free did she begin to register some new measure of the horror she, Zofia, and Putzi had survived, and also the true miracle that her own courage, strength, and luck had somehow carried them through. Laura felt as if some literal, physical weight had just been lifted from her shoulders, and the tears, which she hid from the others, came.

Then the impossible happened. Even though the three of them had finally made it to freedom, disaster loomed again in the form of an immigration official who didn't seem to want to let all three of them into England together. He scowled at the Christian identification papers that had passed muster with dozens of Nazis. He and dark-eyed, dark-haired Uncle Emil, who had traveled from London to greet his relatives, were shouting at each other in English while Laura and Putzi tried—and failed—to follow the argument. Zofia, frightened by this latest complication, sat very still. Laura suddenly interrupted the men, talking urgently and firmly in German. Uncle Emil tried his best to keep up with her as he translated for the official.

"She says that either all three of them must be admitted to the country, or none of them. Now she's saying that for any of them to be separated is unthinkable after what they have been through. . . . And if they return to Poland, they will be imprisoned for the crime of trying to escape to a non-Communist country. Do you want to send us back to prison or worse, she's saying, after everything we've been through?"

Once again, Laura had prevailed; after all she'd endured, she was not about to let a British functionary defeat her. They had at last left Poland behind; in five years, if all went well, they would become British citizens.

Emil finally led them through customs, and soon all four of them were on a London-bound train, much nicer than any train Zofia had ever been on before. She caught the attention of an older woman in a tweed suit, who noticed on Zofia's face the look of a bewildered immigrant—it was, in fact, sheer anxiety—and offered her some unfamiliar coins, while muttering in an equally unfamiliar language. Zofia, who had been told her entire childhood not to talk to strangers, drew back and Uncle Emil had to intervene, first comforting her in German, and then apologizing to the lady in heavily accented English. Laura studied the landscape out the train window, surprised to see spent shells littered among the rubble of burned-out Southampton buildings. It reminded her of some child's building-block project that had been destroyed by a resentful older brother. It hadn't sunk in that the war had reached so far beyond Busko.

The journey ended for Zofia and Laura at 109 Belsize Road in Hampstead, where Emil and Zofia's great-aunt Rosa lived. Rosa welcomed them by serving real English tea and cakes. Their home, one in a line of tidy three-story row houses, had escaped the London blitz, but just barely. While Rosa and Emil were in a shelter during a bombing raid on the railroad tracks behind the house, a German bomb had pierced the roof of their third-floor apartment but failed to explode. The bomb had been defused and removed, but not before the couple had moved to the second floor, where they lived with their dark and heavy Viennese Biedermeier furniture, which matched the mood in the apartment.

Because Emil and Rosa couldn't get away with claiming to need two domestics, Putzi worked as a domestic for a Jewish family in Hampstead with small children that lived within walking distance from the Hoenigs'. They had barely enough room for Zofia and Laura, anyway; Laura slept on the couch in the living room, while Zofia slept on a foldout armchair in Emil's study.

"Isn't it nice," Rosa said to Zofia that first night as she tucked her in, "that your great-uncle and I can give you such a nice home? I hope you're a neat child. Do you put your things away?"

Since Zofia, as far as she could remember, had never had enough things to put away to make putting them away any kind of issue, she could answer her aunt with a clear conscience.

"*Immer*," Zofia said. Always.

It was not a happy household. Rosa and Emil had left Austria after Kristallnacht in 1938, having lost their only child to tuberculosis, and between that loss and their reduced circumstances—he came from a wealthy Austrian family that owned oil fields in Eastern Poland, and he himself had been the business adviser to the Vienna Boys Choir—the atmosphere at 109 Belsize Road in northwest London was tense and overbearing. Rosa treated Laura more as an employee than as a niece. She was a perfectionist about the housework who demanded that Laura dust, clean, and wash just so, and was never satisfied. Rosa, who had recently broken her leg, kept barking instructions to Laura from an armchair, with her leg up on an ottoman. The thought was grossly small-minded, Laura knew, but she hadn't endured enslavement by the Nazis only to be enslaved by her dead mother's sister. For Laura, there were miserable moments when being back in Poland, just the three of them, almost seemed preferable to her new role as Aunt Rosa's Cinderella.

Rosa repeatedly demanded gratitude for opening her home to them, and no amount of Laura's and Zofia's sincere thanks seemed to placate her. It was ironic that the two of them, who had managed to squeeze whatever small happiness they could out of their anxious situation in Busko-Zdrój, had somehow landed with dyspeptic relatives who seemed more joyless than they were.

Of course, the memories of their suffering—it was too weak a word—followed her to England. The sound of SS boots stomping in her dreams ruined her sleep. Her ambiguous religious identity had followed her as well. She had asked Rosa and Emil not to let on to Zofia that they were Jewish—at least not yet. Rosa and Emil, who were not observant Jews and did not attend synagogue, complied. Laura felt no pressure to reclaim her Judaism, but Zofia's ignorance of her origins weighed on her more and more. Several months after arriving in London, when she wrote her cousin Toncia, who had left for Israel before the war, she was still struggling with the ordeal of survival.

My Dearest Toncia,

I got your letter two weeks ago, but I was so shaken that I didn't have the strength to answer. I saw before my eyes all I lost. If Danek and Manek had crossed the border in 1939, they would have survived. It was not in the cards. I have changed a great deal since I became dependent only on myself. I am not as healthy as I used to be and I do not trust people like I used to.

I think you got my letter written in the summer, so you know how my life in hiding in Poland was. If I hadn't had the opportunity to go to England, I would have stayed in Poland and I would have sunk into Christian life. I have to admit that the church can make a charming impression on simpletons like me. I was completely cut off from the life of Jews. For a few years, I even forgot what a Jew looks like.

Zosia, my daughter, looks just like Danek, light blond. Her light skin and light hair rescued me many times from disaster.

I am surprised that after all I have been through that I still look like a human being. I am most depressed by the awareness

that I have lost my independence, and who knows for how long.
My English is quite weak, but I am making progress. I cannot look
for another job because I am registered as a maid. My relatives are
good to me, but we live with them and not on our own. Here, we
have nothing, that's why I am somewhat sorry that I left Poland.

Laura wasted no time getting Zofia started on English lessons with
a teacher who lived on the first floor named Mrs. Dora Camrass. On
Zofia's way up and down the stairs, she often ran into the occupants
of the other apartment on the second floor, an elderly woman named
Levinson and her middle-aged daughter, who were Jewish. She practiced her English salutations on the two of them when they met on
the landing, but Zofia was otherwise afraid to engage them in a conversation. She saw no reason to despise them just because they were
Jews, despite having been taught to do so at school in Busko-Zdrój,
but that didn't mean she had to like them any more than she liked
the Jewish refugees she sometimes saw in the neighborhood, with
their secondhand clothes and used faces.

For Zofia, life in London was at first full of wonder. Treats that
had been impossible to find were now all around her, thanks to her
great-uncle's small candy and tobacco store near Victoria Station.
Her mother, having finished her housekeeping by noon, usually
brought Emil his lunch and stayed to work there, illegally, during
the afternoons. Zofia spent quite a bit of time there as well, where she
could help herself to Cadbury chocolate bars and Wall's ice cream,
which Emil did not seem very good at selling, so that she was welcome to all the ice cream that showed early signs of freezer burn.
Zofia overheard Rosa complain to her mother that, despite his business expertise back in Vienna, her husband was simply not very good
at selling retail.

Just as she had gorged on oranges aboard the *Batory* to the point
where she couldn't eat another one, now she gorged on Neapolitan
ice cream until she couldn't even bear to look at it. How strange,

Zofia thought, that one reality could so quickly be replaced by another.

Given Laura's own weakened sense of her Jewishness, it crossed her mind to try to avoid the question of Zofia's Catholic identity. However, now that they had escaped a country where to be a Jew was still a condition often enough punishable by death, she felt a strong ethical compulsion to reunite Zofia with her original faith. Moreover, if Zofia was her life and her salvation, which she was, how could Laura allow her to continue to be a pretend Catholic anti-Semite? It was pretend, wasn't it? A necessary deception? No, Laura knew that it wasn't pretend to her daughter. But even if it wasn't pretend for Zofia, how could Laura go through life with a daughter who believed that Jews drank the blood of Christian babies and whatever other garbage they had filled her with in school? What mattered more—Laura's own sanity or sparing her daughter the shock of learning, after everything she'd been through, that she was Jewish? To spare Zofia, to sustain the deception on her behalf, was tantamount to handing the Nazis yet another victory. Not that Zofia would understand that now, but she would thank her mother in the long run.

If Zofia didn't know she was a Jew, how could she ever know her own mother? And if Zofia was truly an anti-Semitic Catholic, how could Laura ever truly love her own daughter?

The only question was how and when to tell her. The rapid approach of Passover just two months after they arrived in London supplied the perfect opportunity.

The neighborhood around the new Swiss Cottage tube stop was full of Jewish refugees, most of them alone, having lost their entire families to Hitler. Rosa and Emil, following the seder tradition, invited a few of these strangers who had nowhere else to go, to share the Feast of the Unleavened Bread.

A few days before the seder, Laura decided she could wait no longer and asked Zofia to accompany her on a neighborhood shopping trip.

Zofia, who was very well attuned to her mother's moods after so many years of togetherness under stressful situations, noticed that she was unusually silent as they walked; she could feel her mother's discomfort as they made their way toward the stores.

Was there bad news? Was it something about her father? Zofia and Laura never talked about him—or anyone else from Lvov—but sometimes Zofia was terrified by the thought that her father had been shot and buried alive in a mass grave. At other times, though, she believed that he was alive and had escaped the Russians and would soon track them down.

Had her mother learned his fate? Had she found out what happened to her other aunt, the one also called Zofia, who had visited them once in Busko and taught her the proper way to brush her teeth? Or maybe they were going to have to move again, which wouldn't surprise her. Rosa and Emil may have opened their home to them, but not so much their hearts.

"I need to ask you something," her mother finally said, turning.

"What is it, Mama?"

"Zofia, do you remember what your name was before you were five?"

Zofia tilted her head and looked quizzically at her. "What do you mean?" she asked. "My name has always been Zofia."

"No, darling, it hasn't."

Zofia stared anxiously at her mother.

Suddenly Laura saw a whole cascade of consequences. Something inside whispered to her not to go on, since it had been only with a great effort that she had been able to repair some of the damage to their relationship brought on by her anxiety and obsessive need to create an airtight identity for Zofia in Poland. Her heart was breaking already for her clueless eleven-year-old and the new damage she was about to inflict.

She led her daughter to the small park near the shopping district and sat her down on a bench. "Darling, do you remember when the Germans made us move to a much smaller apartment in Lvov?"

"Not really."

They were sitting close together, but, as always, in different worlds.

"Well, I had to give you a new name when you were about five and Daddy was taken away by the Russians. You remember about Daddy, don't you?"

Zofia looked down. "Yes," she said.

"You were five years old when the Russians took him away," Laura continued, "and after that the Germans wouldn't let anyone leave the ghetto. That's when I gave us new names. You were Zofia and I was Bronislawa. We pretended to be different people so we could escape the Germans and get to Kraków. Remember that train ride?"

"But I didn't know we were pretending. Why did we have to?"

"Because if we didn't, the Nazis would have killed us. They were going to kill everyone in Lvov. Only a few people in our family escaped—you and me and Aunt Nusia, whose real name is Putzi, and Aunt Fryda."

"Why did the Germans want to kill us?" Zofia said, and suddenly her eyes widened at a memory. "Herr Leming, you thought, wanted to poison us with the chocolate bar, but he didn't."

Laura took her daughter's hand and held it. "Look at me, Zofia," she said, drawing her breath. "They wanted to kill us because we were Jewish."

Zofia pulled her hand away. "Because we were Jewish? That's silly. We're Catholic."

Even though she and Putzi had blocked out so much themselves, Laura was taken aback. It simply hadn't occurred to her that Zofia would have no memory at all of ever being Jewish.

"No, Zofia. Until you were five, you were a Jewish girl named Selma Schwarzwald, and your family was Jewish. Your parents and grandparents and aunts and uncles—all Jews. When the Nazis came, there was only one way to stay alive if you were a Jew and that was to pretend you were a Catholic."

"You're making this up," Zofia said.

"No, darling. Daddy and I were Laura and Daniel Schwarzwald, and when you were born, we named you Selma."

Zofia shook her head violently to make it go away, but her mother wouldn't stop.

"And Nusia's real name is Adele, and we call her Putzi. We pretended in order to survive. You were too young then to understand this, to be able to pretend to lie. So I had to make you believe you were Zofia Tymejko. I was Bronislawa and we were Catholic. That was the only way I could keep you—us—alive."

Zofia kept staring and Laura kept talking.

"In a couple of days, Aunt Rosa and Uncle Emil are having a big dinner. You've seen Rosa cooking, yes? They're preparing a Passover seder. Do you know what that is?"

"That's when the Jews use the blood of Christian children to make their special bread."

"No, they don't. That's a lie. Passover is a festival, a Jewish holiday. It celebrates the Jewish people's escape from being slaves in Egypt many thousands of years ago. In Poland, we became slaves again, the victims of Nazis instead of Egyptian kings."

"They killed Christ!"

"Those are lies, Zosia. People spread all kinds of lies about Jews."

"How do you know, Mama?"

"Because I'm Jewish."

"No, you can't be. Because if you were Jewish, I would be too, and I'm not because I'm Catholic."

Laura, despairing, took her daughter's hands in hers and tried again to get through to her. She explained about the papers Zofia's father, Daniel, bought for them, but then the Russians took

Daddy, and Zofia and Laura had to sneak out of the ghetto without him.

But there was only so much truth a person could take in.

"Zofia, do you remember how I drilled you in the catechism? You had to know what any Catholic girl would know or someone might figure out you weren't who you seemed to be, and if the Germans found out you were a Jew, they would take us both away and kill us."

"But I'm not a Jew!" Zofia was yelling now. "I'm *Catholic*."

"Yes." Laura sighed. "Perhaps you are by now."

For a few minutes, no one said anything. To Laura, speaking now seemed futile. Zofia wasn't even trying to process what her mother was telling her.

Zofia spoke first. "And everyone knew except me?"

"You were only five, Zofia. Too young to understand that your life and mine depended on a lie. If you accidentally told the Germans or even the Poles or Ukrainians, or Russians, the truth, they'd kill us. I had to make you *believe* you were Catholic. I know all the drilling made you so angry, but I had no choice if I wanted to keep us alive."

"Well, now I wish I *was* dead!" snapped Zofia.

Laura recoiled. She felt as if she'd been slapped. But she knew her daughter was experiencing something far worse—a frontal assault on everything she knew to be true. On the one hand, did her daughter have *no* idea what her mother had endured to keep them alive?

Laura leaned over and kissed the top of Zofia's head, murmuring, "It's all right, darling, it's all right."

Around them, Londoners were rushing in all directions.

"We are the lucky ones," her mother whispered.

"I am not lucky!" Zofia cried. "I became what you wanted me to become! And now you want me to become a Jew?"

Zofia shifted on the bench to face her mother squarely. "Who," she said, breathing hard, "who would want to be a JEW?"

For several days, Zofia was inconsolable. When she wasn't sobbing beneath the eiderdown quilt on Rosa and Emil's bed, she stormed around the apartment, breathing loudly through her nose, and refusing to talk or to look any of the adults in the eye. She also refused to continue her English lessons with Mrs. Camrass, who she knew was Jewish.

For Laura, accustomed as she was to a daughter who barely raised her voice and had always done everything expected of her, the transformation was frightening. But somehow Zofia managed to calm down in time for the seder, during which she sat in silence at the table, making a bed out of parsley sprigs for her stuffed bear. After calling him just "Bear" for years, she now bestowed a real name on him: "Refugee," a word she heard increasingly, applied to her and most of those around her.

At the seder, she refused to pick up the Haggadah, which was written in a language she recognized only from the fragmented inscriptions on the Jewish gravestones that paved some of Busko's streets. Emil, who conducted the service in Hebrew in his rich baritone, pretended not to notice Zofia's silence, and twenty-eight-year-old Putzi asked the Four Questions as if she really were the youngest person there. But when the meal was served, Zofia's attitude suddenly shifted. She wasn't about to pass up Rosa's excellent brisket and potato kugel.

A week later, when her friend Wacka's parents wrote from Busko-Zdrój to ask for Zofia's help in obtaining antibiotics, she was too ashamed to answer; in fact, she stopped writing Wacka entirely. Zofia hated having deceived everyone she knew in Poland—however unintentionally. She also stopped speaking Polish with strangers. On the rare occasions when her mother tried to talk to her about Judaism, Zofia wouldn't listen. When Laura made the mistake of asking her daughter whether she now wanted to be called "Selma" again, Zofia yelled, "Go away! My name is Zofia Tymejko and I am a Catholic, not a Jew!" Her habit of curtaining off the past—both the Catholic past she embraced or the Jewish past that was being foisted on her now—prevailed. Zofia was determined to forget everything, to move ahead. She wanted to be English.

Soon after arriving in London, Zofia was placed in primary school. Although still far from fluent in English, she was thrown in the deep end with all the native-born children preparing for the exam that would determine their secondary-school track. Zofia's English rapidly improved, thanks partly to Helen Ardmore, the girl who was assigned to look after her. Helen was an outsider too—a talented, artistic girl from a poor family. She was the only student who invited Zofia over to play, but even her very modest flat made Rosa and Emil's apartment seem depressing by comparison.

Helen, who had done well on the exam, was accepted by the highly regarded Paddington and Maida Vale High School. Zofia was, of course, allowed to skip the exam, but she was already showing signs of promise. After a few months in England, she was no longer at the bottom of the class, which the headmistress considered an achievement, even if the ambitious Zofia did not. The headmistress arranged for Zofia to start with Helen at Paddington and Maida Vale on a trial basis. Zofia immediately liked her new headmistress there, Miss Spong, a very attractive, soft-spoken woman in her forties who came from an upper-class background and wore tweed suits. She administered a quiz to Zofia, whose performance on it convinced Miss Spong to let Zofia join Helen's incoming class for the year, at the end of which they would see if she could continue.

That left one sensitive matter to decide, said Miss Spong: was Zofia Jewish or not? Miss Spong called Zofia and Laura in for a meeting. Paddington and Maida Vale provided its Jewish children with Jewish instruction once a week. For morning prayers Jews went separately to the school library while the Protestants and Roman

Catholics went elsewhere before everyone, even the Jews, convened for an Our Father.

Miss Spong reasoned that since Zofia once had been Jewish and, despite her six years as a Catholic, apparently still was, then she *was* Jewish.

And so a girl who had no idea until recently that she'd *ever* been Jewish, began spending every weekday morning in the library, praying with her Jewish classmates, a tiny minority—fifteen or twenty in all—of the school's population. Zofia, to put it mildly, did not feel at home in this group, and not only because its members were Jewish. They were among the brightest girls at Paddington—as well as the most spoiled. They wore pretty dresses and ballet slippers that were all the fashion. They excelled in class, as Zofia had in Busko-Zdrój, and they stuck together. Every morning in the library, she sat with these girls and listened to them pray in two languages, neither of which was her first tongue, one of which—Hebrew—she had been taught to associate with people so vile that they were not quite human. It wasn't surprising that one of Zofia's very best friends was a Christian girl named Elphis Christopher.

Was it because Miss Spong was aware of Zofia's state of religious limbo that she soon appointed her to the important position of Senior Jewess during morning prayers? To ease her reentry into Judaism? Or did Miss Spong thrust the responsibility on her to bolster the young immigrant's confidence and facilitate her integration into the social life of the school? Whatever the headmistress's motivation, the title meant that Zofia chose those prayers. But she knew only one, and not that well either. So day after day, the girls under her leadership recited the same words, "May the Lord bless you and keep you. May the Lord let His face shine upon you and be gracious to you. May the Lord look kindly upon you and give you peace."

Meanwhile her mother enrolled Zofia in Hebrew school, which was held every Sunday at a nearby synagogue, and it was Zofia who won a scholarship prize over the other children, all of whom had been Jews their whole lives. Her academic achievement wasn't the only way in which she stood out there, and the other children didn't try very hard to make Zofia feel at home. Despite her sudden immersion in Judaism, Zofia avoided making Jewish friends. When a boy in Hebrew school took an interest in her, she rejected him outright.

Zofia still didn't feel the least bit Jewish—and she didn't want to either. The only Jews that intrigued her were Israelis. She'd seen Zionist literature for the first time in Hebrew school, and the Jews in the photographs didn't look Jewish. They were young, tan, and muscular, breaking rocks in the fields, clearing the land. Zofia, who was beginning to realize how much living she had missed in the struggle to have a life at all, and how hard her mother had worked to ensure their survival, felt a bond with these Jews. Zofia knew that many others, including her Uncle Edek, had gone to Israel before and after the war, and now she lamented the fact that she, Laura, and Putzi had ended up in England.

Putzi remained a big part of their lives. She was now working as a domestic for a second Jewish family in Golders Green—still unhappily, as she was constantly underestimated by her more poorly educated employers. Fortunately, the job was only a bus ride away, so all three of them stayed in constant touch, although rarely by the luxury of a telephone. In 1950 Laura, Putzi, and Zofia did manage to take a week's holiday together on the Isle of Wight, where Putzi, ever the clever seamstress and dressmaker, fashioned a ballerina outfit out of tissue paper so Zofia could enter a costume competition. In Zofia's view, it was by far the best costume, and she thought she would have won had she not been a foreigner. She was so heartbroken that her mother and aunt, who knew a few things about standing up for themselves and Zofia, complained to the organizers, and she received a prize after all.

At Laura's insistence, Putzi joined the Polish-Jewish Servicemen's

Club, where she fell in love with a Polish Jew named Kazimierz Rozycki who was working toward an engineering degree. He had served in Anders' Army, led by the Polish general Wladyslaw Anders, which had fought alongside the Allies toward the end of the war. V-E Day had found him in Casablanca, from which he had been flown to Scotland before making his way to London. Laura and Zofia adored Kazimierz and welcomed him into the family when he and Putzi decided to marry. Putzi's second employers, initially upset that she was quitting, quickly came to see her in a more appreciative light and gave the couple a generous wedding gift. For Putzi, Laura, and Zofia, the wedding ceremony seemed a miraculous outcome after Putzi's— and their—long journey to freedom.

However, Laura and Zofia both were devastated when Putzi and Kazik decided to immigrate to Canada in 1951.

Laura hadn't been so fortunate in meeting men. Her life with the Hoenigs was dreary. She resented Rosa's resentment of her, felt guilt for imposing on her, and was ashamed at not being able to afford her own place. She was stuck with her obligations to Rosa in an apartment that itself was hopelessly stuck in the past. Rosa and Emil fought constantly. There was no attempt to brighten their home. They rarely had guests over.

Zofia took refuge in her schoolwork. Laura pushed her to excel in every subject, and Zofia's academic reports reflected both of their ambitions.

"Her conduct is always good," her teacher had written at the end of her very first term at Paddington. A year later, the same teacher reported that "Zofia works well and her progress has been good." In the fall of 1949, her new form mistress wrote that "Zofia is a most enthusiastic and helpful member of the class." At fourteen, in 1951, she "had the makings of a first-class scholar" and had "excellent ability in languages, and works most conscientiously in all subjects."

By 1953, however, she was no longer listed as Zofia Tymejko, the name she had continued to use in England and that the British found virtually impossible to pronounce. After five years of statelessness, Laura and Zofia qualified for British citizenship and so were free to change their names. Laura chose the name of one of her favorite British painters as their own and became Laura Turner. And by the summer of 1953, Zofia was Sophie Turner.

With her new name, Sophie had completed a torturous journey from Selma Schwarzwald, Jew, to Zofia Tymejko, Catholic, to Sophie Turner, who didn't quite know who she was.

By now Sophie's relationship with Laura had largely recovered from the shock of the wartime deception. However, having spent her formative childhood years alone with a mysteriously anxious mother who, among other strict instructions, cautioned Sophie about speaking to strangers, Sophie knew little about boys, even at sixteen. The only friend who ever came to the house was Helen, who now had renounced handstands and somersaults for the opposite sex. Although Helen could easily have gone on to university, she drifted away from Sophie into a world that consisted of roughly equal parts boys, smoking, movie stars, and makeup. Watching Helen's experiments in love and sex, Sophie felt like a clueless child. In a few years, Helen would already be married to a butcher and raising a couple of kids.

Meanwhile the once fiercely independent and audacious Laura was becoming a passive victim of circumstance. Between her household chores and unofficial job helping Emil in his store, she had no time to socialize or hunt for a new job, and few prospects for a good one. Her Polish credentials wouldn't get her far, anyway, in Britain's postwar economy. Some money, however, began to dribble in. First, both Laura and Sophie received monthly pensions from the German government as part of reparations for their losses. In

1951, Sophie and her mother could finally afford to rent their own apartment.

They didn't go far, moving into the dark street-level apartment just below Emil and Rosa's. They were hardly beyond Rosa's reach—she complained constantly that they monopolized the single phone line they shared—but Laura and Sophie bought some modern mid-century furniture and made it as cheery as possible. They each began to invite their few friends over.

University loomed, and Sophie, who by now wanted to choose a career that would allow her to help others, applied to a six-year medical school program. It wasn't that she was a genius at science—she was a much stronger student in history and languages, and had some noticeable difficulty with physics—but a career in medicine would also provide security, which had been not so much in short supply as utterly missing in their lives so far. A career in medicine had the added benefit of providing Laura, who had studied economics and once set her sights on medicine in a country where even Jewish men were not welcome in the profession, with a vicarious victory. Sophie applied to several schools and was accepted as a scholarship student at two, choosing University College Hospital, which had a strong liberal arts program—and the advantage of having accepted one of Sophie's best high school friends, Elphis Christopher.

At university one of the first-year students who wanted to be her friend was a Polish woman, but Sophie pretended that she didn't speak Polish. However little she wanted to be Jewish, she wanted to be Polish even less. She could claim no Jews yet among her friends, and she remained silent in the presence of the occasional anti-Semitic remarks made by friends, on whose casual prejudices the annihilation of the Jews during the war had had little effect. Yet she joined Hillel House, whose members for the most part wore their Judaism very lightly and socially, not like the more observant Jewish students. It bothered her that the Orthodox Jews walked around in yarmulkes.

At least, she thought, they should have the decency to confine their *kipa*-wearing to indoors.

But Hillel soon posed its own difficulties for a girl who had grown up in silent secrecy. There were Israelis at Hillel, argumentative ones who seemed so different from the handsome, hardworking, muscular ones she had envied in the Zionist brochures.

A young English law student named Monty, who was active in Hillel, gradually became Sophie's first bona fide Jewish friend. He was very smart, very funny, and also very devoted to his younger brother, whom he had taken care of during the war years when their parents had sent them to the safety of the countryside. Nothing serious developed between them, but she had broken the ice; seven years after learning she was Jewish, she could finally let another Jew into her life.

While Sophie made friends, however few, and attended to her own evolving ambitions, her mother was largely alone and increasingly dependent on Sophie's companionship. Their roles were gradually reversing. There were times her mother wanted to go for a walk, but Sophie now had better things to do. The conflict was growing between what she felt was her duty to her mother and her need for greater independence. There was no conflict, however, over the issue of the importance of Sophie's achievements. They both felt she had to do well because she had nothing else to fall back on. Her religious conflicts took a backseat to the gospel of success: you had to lead your life constructively and do some good; you had to leave some kind of positive mark, saying that you were here, that you did something and you helped somebody. "My mother pushed me a great deal and was very ambitious for me," she would recall when she reached her midthirties. "I felt this tremendous pressure to achieve, not to waste time, to bring something to some conclusion. But with time I became convinced of this myself, and I've carried it on in a way and I think she was right."

Medical school represented financial *and* emotional security. "I would have a profession," she'd recall, "and in our family it was always considered very important to have a profession in case you had to flee for your life. You'd be able to earn a living somewhere else. Medicine is pretty universal."

Through a medical school student organization, Sophie traveled to Germany with a group that slept in schools and other people's modest homes. What made the most impression on her was how well the Germans seemed to be living. When she would think back later on the trip, she couldn't fathom why on earth she had agreed to go, except that she felt very forgiving at the time. That it might have anything to do with her revulsion at being Jewish seems far-fetched, but she would recall feeling that "whatever had happened during the war had happened." On her next visit, twenty years later, the numbness had worn off; this time, as she walked down German streets, she looked at men of a certain age and wondered where they had been during the war, and whether one of them had been the man who murdered her father.

Sophie still had trouble accepting the fact that, on the day before her fifth birthday, her father, Daniel Schwarzwald, had been killed by the Germans. During the few years she and her mother shared the Hoenigs' grim apartment, sometimes she dreamed of her father returning from Russia to save her and her mother, this time from their little ghetto on Belsize Road. Sometimes she could say to herself that the Nazis had killed him; most of the time, though, her father was neither alive nor dead. He just inhabited a different realm—one that was getting farther and farther away, and in which a little girl she used to know, named Zofia Tymejko, awaited his return.

She had only a few possessions from that other world. There was her Christian prayer book, her rosary, and her little bear, Refugee, still wearing the tiny coat that Aunt Putzi—Nusia—had made for him. And there was one other thing that remained from those years in Poland: silence. Time had erected a wall between her and those years, no more passable than the walls of the ghettoes of Lvov or Warsaw or Kraków. She knew that every Jewish refugee she saw in North London had his or her own story, protected by the barbed wire of forgetting, and that for all of them everything was better left unsaid.

The past was their secret. Not once did Sophie talk about the past with her mother. Not once. And they quickly learned to keep it even from themselves.

In 1963, after completing a rotating internship at a couple of suburban London hospitals and falling in love with several specialties, Sophie settled, at least for the time being, on obstetrics and gynecology. With the encouragement of one of her professors, she decided to work in the United States, where there was a shortage of doctors. Her New York cousin-by-marriage Alice Herb (Emil and Rosa's niece, who had immigrated to America with her family after Kristallnacht) contacted a successful plastic surgeon named Lou Feit, who was able to arrange a permanent visa and get her a job at his hospital, New York Polyclinic Hospital in Manhattan.

Sophie's mother would have to remain in London where, freed of her original work restrictions, she was hired to teach accounting at a secretarial school. It would be the first time she and Sophie had ever been apart for any length of time. Laura, who had watched most of her own family be destroyed twenty years before, and her sister Putzi move to Canada a dozen years before, would now be separated by an ocean from the little girl, now a twenty-six-year-old doctor, she had single-handedly saved from the fires of the Holocaust. It felt every bit as painful as all the other, and more permanent, losses in her life. But what could she do? Laura knew that Sophie had to leave even this nest.

Shortly before she left London, Sophie was preoccupied with the impending marriage of one of her closest medical school friends, Avril Sillitoe, in an Anglican Church in East Anglia. Sophie was asked to be one of the bridesmaids—the only Jewish one. When told that she would have to kneel during the ceremony, Sophie's emerging Jewish consciousness surprised her. She told Avril she couldn't bring herself to do it. She had never discussed her split identity with Avril or even discussed her years in Busko-Zdrój—it was simply not a subject that ever came up with anybody—yet kneeling in a church didn't seem right. Remarkably, Avril didn't argue, and it was decided that if one of the bridesmaids couldn't kneel, then *none* of them would have to kneel.

In May Sophie said her complicated farewell to her mother and flew first to Canada, where she visited Aunt Putzi and her family, who lived comfortably in Montreal. (When Putzi's last English employers visited the Rozyckis in Montreal on a trip to the United States, they were amazed that their "humble" former domestic now lived in such a lovely home.) On the eve of Sophie's departure for New York, visa complications arose that kept her in Canada until August. She spent the summer accompanying Putzi, Kazik, and their seven-year-old son, Henry, on trips to Ottawa and Quebec. When her permanent visa finally came through, Sophie arrived at the newly named John F. Kennedy International Airport in a heavy woolen suit, which had been appropriate apparel in chilly Canada, only to be hit by blasts of ninety-degree temperatures the moment she left the terminal and headed to the taxi stand. Since she was long overdue at her new job, she asked the driver to take her directly to the New York Polyclinic in Manhattan, which she had envisioned as a beautiful modern hospital with gorgeous nurses and especially good-looking male doctors. Her heart sank when the cab pulled up on West Fiftieth Street in front of a dilapidated facility that had seen better days, although it still treated the occasional high-profile celebrity patient. In 1926, while in New York promoting *Son of the Sheik*, Rudolph Valentino had been rushed to Polyclinic for emergency abdominal surgery, only to die soon afterward from peritonitis and pleurisy. And just two summers before Sophie's arrival, Marilyn Monroe had had gallbladder surgery at Polyclinic while husband Joe DiMaggio paced in the waiting room.

Sophie's first months were horribly lonely. She did little but work and sleep, commuting to the hospital on West Fiftieth Street from her room in the Belvedere Hotel on West Forty-Eighth by running across an uninviting parking lot next to the old Madison Square Garden.

Back in London, her mother was busy taking courses at Pitman College in typewriting, bookkeeping, secretarial duties, handwriting, and spelling and diction. Before long, she was offered a job as a part-time student-teacher, and then as a part-time teacher of bookkeeping and general commercial studies at six pounds a week. But in her letters to Sophie, she complained that Sophie didn't write often enough and wasn't paying her enough attention. She wrote that perhaps she and Sophie would live together again one day.

Her neediness triggered a complex of emotions in Sophie. Although she and her mother had barely mentioned their life in Poland, even to each other, it was dawning on Sophie, now that she was older and had moved away, that her mother had been nothing less than heroic. Sophie still saw herself as a survivor of World War II, not a Jewish survivor of the attempted extermination of her race, a race she was still far from embracing. If Sophie was preoccupied with Jews, it was not with those who had died, but with those who had lived. She understood that no Eastern European Jew had survived the war without a fight, and that her own mother had defied the odds. Others might have been crushed by their losses, paralyzed by their fears, immobilized by shock, but Laura had forged ahead in the midst of ruin. She had stood up more than once to the Nazis who came for them, she had threatened Herr Leming when he tried to take her promised job away from her, and she had insisted on getting her iron back from the Gestapo, but most of all, and despite the lapses into suicidal despair, she had insisted on living.

Whatever resentment Sophie still harbored toward her mother for her necessary part in depriving her of a childhood was now overtaken by an unfamiliar emotion: she felt guilty for all her mother had done for her. Sophie owed her life to her. She wished she could make it up to her mother, who had lost ten years of her life—her thirties—to the war, and then lost several more in servitude to her aunt and uncle. (Sophie's feelings toward them had been softened by her aunt and uncle's increasingly affectionate attitude toward her, culminating in their generous, but ghoulish, gift to her on her twenty-first birthday of their dead daughter's ring.)

Yet in England Sophie had felt increasingly like a ghost floating next to her mother—insubstantial, a vestige of a past she barely understood. However lucky she had been, she was still a casualty of the Final Solution. Her childhood had been erased, her adolescence had been postponed, and adulthood still seemed unattainable. She may have owed her mother her life, but that wasn't the same thing as *having* a life. And the painful price of having that, she knew, was to now keep some distance between them.

As lonely as she was, and as much as she knew it would hurt her mother deeply, she sat down one evening in her room at the Belvedere and wrote her to say that things couldn't be as they had been anymore. She needed to make a clean break. She needed to stand on her own two feet.

By definition, virtually all children who were hidden during the war had been utterly cut off from those hidden elsewhere. There was certainly no mechanism or organization, even by the 1960s, by which these formerly hidden children could learn of one another's existence. And so Sophie could not know that only a mile south of her new home at the Belvedere Hotel in Manhattan lived Flora Hogman, a year older than Sophie, who had also survived the Holocaust and had also ended up in New York City.

Sophie and Flora wouldn't meet for another fifteen years, by which time they both would have launched substantial careers that were impressive even for women whose childhoods had not been destroyed by the Nazis. Flora, however, had had to overcome even greater obstacles than Sophie to accomplish anything at all. While Sophie had emerged from the war with at least her mother, Flora had lost everything and everybody.

FLORA

My first conversation with Flora Hogman took place at her apartment in New York City's Chelsea neighborhood. As I stepped out of the elevator onto her floor, I could see a tiny figure standing at the far end of a very long hallway, but even at that distance I could see that she was smiling broadly. This surprised me, for although she had agreed to talk to me about her hidden childhood in wartime France, I had already learned from months of interviewing Sophie how sensitive this ground could be.

Throughout my career, I have been reluctant to delve into other people's suffering. As a young reporter, I shrank from invading the privacy of strangers with tragic stories to tell. Yet here I was, unpacking my laptop and tape recorder at Flora's dining room table while she went to the kitchen to get me a glass of seltzer and a plate of her rich homemade chocolate truffles. Flora, a petite and stylishly dressed woman with a charming French accent, had lost everything, even her self, to the Nazis.

Unlike Sophie, who seemed armored against the past despite admitting to me that our interview sessions had left her depressed, Flora from the beginning was agitated about talking to me. I tried to assure her that her story might actually help bring a relatively neglected aspect of the Holocaust to the attention of a larger public, but her tension remained palpable. And her smile failed to mask her wariness.

She seemed especially concerned that I wouldn't get her story right. Not that I blamed her. The whole enterprise of trying to capture another person's life, regardless of the circumstances, is full of pitfalls, to say nothing of the chasm between any writer's ambition and the subject's felt experience and spotty recall. My endless questions frustrated her. Flora lamented the loss of her memory as if it were another person whose disappearance she mourned. Her story sometimes seemed to come out of her in a chronological jumble, like pieces of a jigsaw puzzle emptied onto a table. After a couple of long interviews, I sent her a first draft of what I had written, and heard nothing for a few weeks. Then this:

> Hi Richard,
>
> I have started to read the manuscript over and over again. I hesitated to answer as I am in many regards somewhat dismayed by the writing. There are parts of it which are fine, but others are quite troubling and make it difficult for me to feel that you really concentrated on understanding the person you are talking about and about what happened to her and within her rather than in details which are often wrong.

It ended:

> Sorry, but I must be honest. It is very important to make come across the power of forgetting and silence, it is not so easy. I hope you feel up to it.
>
> All the best, Flora

The next time we met, I reminded Flora that we were in this together, that without her help I would never get it right, and I asked for patience. Fortunately, since we'd last met, it seemed to me that Flora's memory had stirred and stretched; her recall was sharper, the story more coherent than before. I had experienced this with Sophie too.

But getting one's hands on a vanished reality is no easy matter, especially when there's just one living witness. At times our sessions felt a little like hand-to-hand combat—with memory itself.

The fates of millions of Eastern European Jews were decided by a hand. The one holding the gun aimed at the base of the skull. The one gripping the flashlight that panned the hiding place, looking for the sets of terrified eyes in the dark. The hand that had the power, with the stroke of a fountain pen, to condemn or reprieve. The one that separated death camp arrivals to the left or to the right.

Flora Hillel's fate was decided by her own six-year-old hand, and what she didn't do with it. Seventy years later, she would still not understand what play of unrecognized forces in her young mind had prompted her to keep her hands on her desk.

An only child, she was born in 1935 to opera-loving, Czechoslovakian Jewish parents, the granddaughter of the famous Rabbi Dr. Friedrich Hillel, who served in Leipnik, Czechoslovakia, and was himself descended from the great Jewish sage and scholar Hillel the Elder, who led the Jewish people around the time of Jesus Christ. Flora spent her first two years in San Remo, Italy, where her father, a maker of false teeth, had decided to go because of his tuberculosis. After he died from a recurrence of TB in November 1937, her mother, Stefanie—a pianist and writer—kept Flora in San Remo with her until she decided to join friends who lived across the border in Nice, then part of the Unoccupied Zone administered by the Vichy government.

In June 1942, Stefanie moved the two of them thirty miles west to Nice to a small apartment on Avenue Monplaisir, a mile inland from the Mediterranean, where they started their new life together. Flora did not have to share her mother's love with anyone and grew so accustomed to maternal adoration that she would never forget the few times she provoked disapproval instead. On one such occasion, Flora's mother chastised her for making fun of an amputee on the street, and she reprimanded Flora when she caught her and some friends singing popular ditties mocking Hitler and Mussolini.

Desperate to make ends meet, Stefanie Hillel took in sewing. She expertly embroidered Flora's name on the clothes she wore to her new school, which was a short distance away. Each morning her mother tied a ribbon into a bow near the part in Flora's hair and sent her off to school with her friend Rachel, who lived nearby. There wasn't much food—not in the markets near them, anyway, or at least not much that her mother could afford, and Flora worried about her mother's weight, since she gave most of what she had to Flora.

The taunts of the children who made fun of her for being father-less brought her to tears. She was helpless to defend herself, since she was not exactly sure how he had died, or why, or even, at times, whether he had died at all. Her mother would often tell her that he was "traveling," which fueled her fantasies that he would return.

When the French police began arresting Jews by the thousands in August 1942, mother and daughter boarded a bus to Vence, a walled medieval village west of Nice known for its natural spring water and—more recently—for a children's home and boarding school run by a Protestant relief organization, Maison d'Accueil Chrétienne pour Enfants, that was taking Jewish children.

The bus lumbered up Avenue Colonel Meyere toward Vence's crested cluster of terra-cotta-roofed buildings and stopped in front of a stucco building with shutters. Holding her mother's hand, Flora watched an assortment of girls around her age wandering around a dirt yard, one of them clutching a soiled doll.

Her mother assured her she wouldn't be there long.

Flora turned to her mother in panic. It hadn't really occurred to her that her mother meant to leave her in Vence. She had never been away from her before.

Her mother straightened her hair ribbon and crushed her in a hug, whispered that it would only be for a while, and was gone.

The days without her mother dragged on among strange children, all of them little refugees from some threat beyond their comprehension. Flora was too numb to concentrate on the games or the songs or the prayers. She wet her bed constantly.

My dear little Flory! her mother wrote just before Christmas, *I hope to kiss you soon. Take care of yourself and don't forget to wear your pants! Lots of kisses. . . .*

Chère Maman, she wrote back in January 1943, *I hug you very hard. I'm sending you this little letter to make you happy. . . . When the letter comes to you I want you to come. . . . I'm eating well and I hope you're eating well also. . . . I'm ending this little letter. Your little girl, Florine Hillel.*

At least there was food—milk, days-old baguettes, a little cheese, a spoonful of preserves.

And then, miraculously, there was her mother. She reappeared toward spring, thinner than ever, to take her home. Flora ran to her, happier than she had ever been in her life. Back in Nice, Flora returned to school and to her best friend Rachel. All was well, or so it seemed to Flora, for many months. Then came September 1943. On the way home from the food market one day, Flora and Stefanie found themselves in the midst of an excited, expanding crowd, and were soon trapped on the sidewalk, pressed against a store window. Frightened, Flora clutched her mother's hand and tried to see what the fuss was about, but at first she could only hear the sound of a clacking drumbeat getting louder and louder. She peered between the bodies in front of her to catch a glimpse of the German army's grand entrance into the city. Flora had never seen anything like it. Helmeted soldiers filed past in perfect formation, the rows bristling with rifles. The clacking sound turned out to be the staccato gun-burst sound of thousands of jackboots striking the pavement in unison. The soldiers were followed by rumbling tanks and armored vehicles—metal monsters out of a nightmare—then more dense rows of goose-stepping soldiers. Then open touring cars filled with unsmiling men, followed by more soldiers.

Flora was terrified, clutching her mother's hand in that forest of silent adults. But what was worse was that she could feel that her mother was terrified too. The parade seemed to go on for hours before the people on the sidewalk began to disperse and they could make their way home.

By the following day, Nice sprouted Nazi flags everywhere, and soldiers on every corner, even near her school.

The victims of history are the last to know what hit them. Only as an adult would Flora learn what had brought the massive *Wehrmacht* to Nice. Following the Allied invasion of North Africa and then Italy, the Italian army had capitulated and the Germans had arrived. Had her mother known by then what had happened in Paris the past July? That the French police themselves, under German orders, had rounded up thousands of Jews and sent them to the Vélodrome d'Hiver near the Eiffel Tower, then on to the transit camp at Drancy, and on their way to Auschwitz?

Flora walked to school with Rachel that day, as usual, and they took their adjacent seats in the classroom and waited for their teacher to begin. This time, however, she departed from her usual routine.

"*Qui est juif?*" she asked, quite suddenly. "*Levez vos mains.*"

Would the Jewish children raise their hands? Flora's stomach fluttered. Next to her, Rachel raised her arm, but Flora hesitated. Had her mother told her not to mention to anyone that she was Jewish? Flora didn't really think about being Jewish, anyway. They were not practicing Jews. Even though her father's father had been a famous rabbi back in Czechoslovakia, Flora and her mother never went to synagogue or kept the Sabbath or said prayers or lit candles. What Flora felt was not Jewish, but scared and numb, yet when the teacher asked for hands, Flora thought that she ought to ask her mother first before doing anything, so she kept her hands folded on the desk.

"Good," her mother said when later that day Flora reported what happened. But despite her relief her mother was agitated. Word reached them that Rachel and her family were probably now going to be something called "deported."

Not only did Flora not return to school after that day, but her mother explained that she was going to send Flora to a new school, a Catholic one where she would be safe. She said that it wouldn't be like the other place. It was just up the hill, right there in Nice.

Flora knew that it would be just like the other place because her mother wouldn't be there.

She would believe for a long time that it was her mother who drove her to the convent that sat on a terraced hillside overlooking the Mediterranean, on a road that climbed between oleander bushes on either side. Below the convent's high walls, olive, cypress, and palms trees ran down toward the sea. Then, with a promise to come visit her as soon as possible, she disappeared.

A towering woman in a long robe spoke to Flora from behind an iron grille, welcoming her to "the house of God." That God had a house was confusing to Flora; that Flora had ended up in it made her want to giggle, except that the woman, obscured by the grille, was frightening her. God must have extremely long legs, she decided, to live both in the convent and in heaven as well. She wondered when she might meet him. She had the idea that she might become his favorite of all the girls there.

And who was this Mother Superior? What was so superior about her?

Afterward she was led up the hill, above the main building, to join the dozen other children congregating in front of a house ringed by rose hedges. It would be Flora's home now, except that Flora would no longer be Flora. She had been given a new name to go with her strange new home. She must now forget she had even been Flora Hillel. That much had been made quite clear. She was now Marie Hamon, born in Corsica. She wondered if she would be the same girl as Marie Hamon. Marie Hamon, Marie Hamon, Marie Hamon.

The sisters had taken a vow of silence—and, it appeared to Flora, a vow of not bathing as well. But bathe *Flora* they did, holding her over an old sink to baptize her. It was yet another new terrifying experience. She barely knew what a Jew was, let alone a Catholic whose salvation required being doused with cold water in what looked like a thousand-year-old sink. What were they doing, pouring water over her head, and telling her she was a child of God?

Among the sisters' jobs was embroidering religious garments and making holy wafers, but mainly, Flora observed, they prayed. They seemed to spend most of their time gliding silently through the halls in their mountainous robes and winglike white cornettes on their heads, or pacing the flat roof of the convent in postures of prayer, hands pressed against their breasts, eyes glued to the sky. Tiny Flora stood in the garden and watched as they paraded back and forth like huge birds of prey. In her loneliness, Flora prayed only that they would look at her, even just once, and not at the sky. Look at me, she wished. Look at me. Look at me.

The one game the children had was: racing to see who would be the first to finish their Ave Marias and Our Fathers and Mothers Who Art in Heaven on their rosaries. To see which of them could produce the fastest stream of prayer provided their greatest amusement.

NotrePèrequiestauxcieuxquevotreNomsoitSanctifiéquevotrerègnevienne-
quevotrevolontésoitfaitesurlaterrecommeauciel. . . . JevoussalueMariepleine-
degrâceLeSeigneurestavecvousvousêtesbénieentretouteslesfemmesetJésusle-
fruitdevosentraillesestbéni.

Worse than the discipline was the time when she was told the
Jews had killed Jesus Christ. Who were these women who claimed
to be married to God, yet never had a kind word for their charges,
and called them killers? First they had taught her to identify with
the baby Jesus, who had so many problems like her, then they said
the Jews killed him? She and her mother had already been blamed,
and had to be separated, because they were Jewish, and now this? At
seven, Flora was not too young to feel the terrible injustice, but not
old enough to understand it or defend herself against it.

There were no classes, as in her previous school. Much of the time
was spent learning all the prayers, and the sign of the cross. At the
large house just across the street, Nazis soldiers came and went, yet
the nuns, who were known to supplement the rationing with extra
food for Christian children in the area, seemed on good terms with
them. To quiet the Jewish children's anxiety, the nuns reassured them
that God was listening. They told Flora that her mother, who had not
even written her a letter, would come back, that God granted wishes
in mysterious ways. Flora couldn't understand his mysteriousness;
after all, this was his house, yet she never saw him. There was no one
to explain anything to her. Still, she prayed to see her mother, who
was so nearby and yet seemed to have forgotten her completely, even
if one of the sisters had helped her write her a letter.

Amid the general misery and loneliness of Flora's months there,
no event was more vivid than what happened one night in early
1944, when the tranquility of the monastery was broken by the
sudden scurrying around of the sisters. They burst into the cottage
where the children were sleeping and began packing up their bags by
candlelight.

"*Levez-vous! Levez-vous!*" they whispered urgently. "*Les gens viennent vous chercher! Ramassez vos affaires! Levez-vous!*"

During the ensuing scramble, one of the sisters began folding Flora's clothes to put them into her suitcase. "Mon Dieu!" she cried, seeing that Flora's mother had embroidered her Jewish name on every piece, while for months she'd been answering to Marie Hamon. Wasting no time, the nun took a small pair of sewing scissors and ripped out every dangerous stitch. The nun was destroying, thread by thread, the visual confirmation of Stefanie's presence in Flora's life, the only proof that she ever had a mother.

As Flora screamed for her to stop, the nun clapped her hand over Flora's mouth. "*Tais-toi, Marie!*" the nun said. "*C'est dangereux!*"

The nun kept severing the threads that spelled out FLORA and HILLEL and yanking them out of the inside of her collars and the waistbands of her skirts. When she was through, she gathered up the nest of black threads in her lap and it all disappeared inside her habit.

Sobbing, Flora was sure now that her mother would never be able to find her.

In a hushed storm of activity, under cover of darkness, and barely saying farewell to the nuns who had hidden them for months and at great risk, the children and their bags were quietly loaded onto a truck that sat with its motor humming in the monastery's driveway. Most of the children held hands, shaking, as the truck, its driver unseen beyond the canvas top, rolled out onto L'Avenue Sainte Colette and into the night. None of them had any idea that they had just escaped right under the eyes of the increasingly suspicious Gestapo stationed right across the street.

The children were dropped off at different locations one by one, the driver walking around to the back of the truck to call out a name and offering a hand to help the child down and into his or her new home. For Flora, the destination was the rural home in Châteauneuf of two middle-age ladies, an Englishwoman and a Russian dancer who liked to prance and twirl about the living room, showing off her long legs. Not only were they much nicer than the nuns, although equally eccentric in their own way, but Flora, who loved to dance, would join the Russian in her improvised pirouettes and arabesques. It had been a long time since she had felt free to express herself. To dance was to feel free momentarily from her confusion and grief and thoughts of her absent mother. After the nuns, the women's warmth, and their delight in the scrawny Flora's lack of inhibition, made it easy for Flora to fall in love with them and bury, for the moment, her memories of the convent and the life that had come before.

She could leave the house only to be in the garden, where she fed the women's chickens. One day, a boy appeared in the garden, thirteen or fourteen years old, almost as thin as she was, dressed in dirty shorts and sandals. For a brief time they became friends. She taught him how to feed the chickens, tossing handfuls of corn and cut-up apples. He taught her how to knit, no doubt a skill he had picked up in hiding. Where he came from she never knew.

The friendship distracted her from her worries, but like everything else it was taken from her. After only a few weeks, the two women told Flora they could no longer afford to keep her. She felt betrayed. A man appeared that night and drove her west to the next village, Magagnosc, where a wife and her husband welcomed her with the stilted congeniality she was getting used to. There her life became quite difficult again. Although she had her own room, the wife paid little attention to her while the irritable husband, an engineer, punished the high-spirited Flora for the slightest infraction of their house rules or her failure to complete her chores. Flora looked on sadly when he offered his wife bread before her. They had no children, and therefore no toys. Maybe that's why he decided to teach her the names of all 206 bones of the human skeleton. She didn't get very far before they both gave up in frustration.

He told her repeatedly that he was an atheist and that those who believed in God were fools, weaklings, or worse.

It was cruel, since Flora needed all the help she could get.

"You do know what happens to you after you die, don't you?" he told her.

"I'm going to heaven," said Flora, thinking of the nuns.

"This is what I'm talking about! There is no heaven. No God, no heaven, no angels. If there was a God, you wouldn't have to stay with us because the Germans wouldn't be taking all the Jews away and you'd be with your mother. I will tell you what happens after you die," the husband said. "They put your body in the ground, but that's not the worst of it." He waited in vain for her Flora to ask him what the worst of it was. "You'll be eaten by worms," he said finally. "*That's* what happens."

She had been left by her mother, abandoned by the sisters, betrayed by the two ladies, and now taunted by the engineer. She spent most of her time talking to the couple's goats and hugging them. What she felt was a faraway, distant sorrow.

Fortunately before long the atheist announced that he and his wife wouldn't be able to take care of her any longer. Unlike the other separations in her life, this one barely touched her. Her life with her mother on Avenue Monplaisir had receded so far behind a scrim of rosary games, nearsighted nuns, and free-form dancing around a dining room table that when the man packed up her things and put Flora and her suitcase on the back of his bicycle one morning, it seemed almost—*almost*—like the normal course of things.

He pedaled her several kilometers to the town of Grasse, known as the Perfume Capital of the World. From a distance, Grasse reminded her of Vence. It was a jumble of medieval stucco buildings with painted shutters, built on a hill. He walked Flora, still on his bicycle, into the heart of the old village, past charcuteries and patisseries with little food in their windows. At La Place de la Poissonerie, a square surrounded by tall, five- and six-story buildings painted yellow ocher and rust, they stopped. There the atheist introduced himself and Flora to a group of people who had gathered to find her a new home.

She sat on a bench, feeling spikes of desperation pushing up through her numbness. The atheist sat around a café table with the strangers, who periodically glanced over at her. She could hear one couple, easily the oldest of them, debating in an unfamiliar language. The tall man with a long face and receding hairline was gesturing with a chopping motion of his right hand at a woman, somewhat younger, who wore a strand of wooden beads and a sort of long, flowing turquoise dress that wrapped around her. Finally, it was this couple, old enough to be her grandparents, who told her that she was coming with them.

"I'm Andrée Karpeles," the woman in the long dress said in French, "and this is my husband, Adalrik Hogman." The long-faced man stood a bit behind her, saying nothing. "Our house is out in the country and we'll have to walk there, but I'll carry your suitcase for you."

The man was holding out his hand to her. In it was a single white sugar cube.

"My husband is Swedish and I'm afraid he doesn't speak French that well," the woman said.

Flora took the cube and licked it a few times, finally resting it on her tongue and letting it dissolve in slow, quiet ecstasy.

After a brief word with the engineer, the three of them set off on foot through the narrow streets of Grasse and into the surrounding countryside. With Andrée carrying her suitcase and Adalrik marching silently next to them, they traipsed through woods and past springtime fields of sweet-smelling white jasmine flowers. It was the perfect setting for a girl named Flora, but she didn't notice or care. Flora was thinking, Who are these old people? and wondering what was to become of her now.

After what seemed like several hours on foot, they came to the end of a dirt road in the hills and Flora saw a huge, three-story stone house with a terra-cotta tile roof hidden behind a row of Italian cypress trees. The property was dotted with cacti, some growing out of enormous urns. Low hedge-bordered paths led to a rectangular pond into which a fountain shot a high-arcing jet of water. While Andrée showed Flora around the property, a white mutt with brown markings, the couple's pet, pranced behind them.

She was given her own room upstairs. It seemed like paradise, but the very next morning, as Flora was exploring the downstairs rooms, there were several loud raps on the front door. Andrée told Flora to run upstairs and hide in her room, but instead she stopped and sat at the top of the stairs, from which she could just see the bottom of the front door, which Andrée opened to a pair of glossy black boots.

"Je m'excuse de vous déranger, Madame Hogman," a man's voice said, *"mais j'ai été informé que vous hébergez une jeune fille. Une jeune fille juive."*

Flora froze at the sound of a gendarme who already seemed to know of her presence there. Hours of walking over hill and dale to what seemed like the end of the world, and her existence had been discovered the first day?

Flora listened as Andrée explained that, of course, there was no Jewish girl living with them, she would never allow such a thing. After a brief pause, Flora heard the policeman say, *"Quand même, je vous conseille d'être prudente, si vous me permettez."* All the same, be careful, he said.

Only a few days later, a *Kübelwagen* pulled up to the house and a German soldier jumped out and knocked on the side door. This time Mr. Hogman accompanied his wife to answer the door.

"Sprechen Sie Deutsch?" the soldier asked.

"Français," Andrée replied.

In broken French, the soldier insisted on coming inside to search for metal objects for the Third Reich to turn into much needed ammunition in a war they were now losing.

On hearing this, Adalrik stepped outside and escorted him to the front door to point at a document taped to it. By this point, Flora had run to the kitchen in the back of the house and hidden herself in the pantry, closing the door behind her.

"Comme vous voyez clairement, monsieur," she faintly heard Andrée explain to the solider.

After the German had driven off, Andrée and Adalrik showed Flora the official stamped document taped to the inside of the front door's window.

"This says that our house is protected by the Swedish Consulate," she explained to Flora, "and no one can come in unless we want them to. As long as you stay in the house, you're safe."

The next and most stable phase of Flora's life began a few months later, when the war ended and the Hogmans eventually adopted her, after which she became Flora Hogman and grew to adulthood. Andrée was over sixty and an accomplished painter by the time Flora arrived, and was unlike any adult she had ever met before. As a close friend and devotee of Rabindranath Tagore, the prolific Indian Buddhist poet, musician, and the first non-Westerner to win the Nobel Prize in Literature, Andrée had become a yoga aficionada who occasionally dressed in saris. She knew a lot of people, such as the sister of the Nobel Prize–winning French writer and mystic Romain Rolland, and she had met the famous French writer Colette. After a year and a half of austere nuns and capricious hosts, Flora felt in some ways an immediate affinity for this woman, who treated her like a child to be loved, and took time to tutor Flora, who had already lost two years of schooling, in arithmetic, reading, and, of course, drawing.

Andrée had a fine sense of life's ironies—with which Flora was already too well acquainted—and the two of them laughed a lot together like schoolgirls. Flora found in Andrée a soul mate who encouraged her love of dancing.

"Let's see you dance some more," Andrée would say.

"Again?"

"Rabindranath, you know, was a big proponent of Manipuri dance. He almost single-handedly revived it back in the 1920s." Flora was fascinated, though she had no idea what her foster mother was talking about.

Adalrik, who had retired from the liquor business, was a different story. He didn't speak French and Flora didn't speak English, but he seemed remote in a way not entirely explained by their lack of a common language. When she brought him his tea, he would simply say "*tack*" or "*tack så mycket*."

"You must be grateful to him," Andrée told her. "He took you in because I wanted to."

That was pure Andrée, the streak of childish insensitivity. She was a woman with her own ideas about things, some of which, to say the least, rubbed Flora the wrong way. With a logic that would forever escape Flora, Andrée, a Jew-turned-Buddhist, made her convert to Protestantism, even though all her classmates were Catholics. In Catholic France, being a Protestant was only somewhat better than being a Jew. Flora endured months of Sunday school, learning the Protestant catechism. It made so little sense to her, this latest visit to the smorgasbord of the world's religions, that at the moment of her confirmation Flora decided to become an atheist.

While Flora could secretly resist Andrée's religious control, she was helpless to defend herself against Andrée's fashion dictates. She cut Flora's hair like an Indian girl she had known in Tagore's family and sometimes made her wear saris at home. Andrée disdained modern culture and denied Flora access to popular music and books, though there were plenty of Bach and Brahms recordings, and Flora had the run of Andrée's library of leather-bound volumes by Tolstoy, Hugo,

Balzac, Rousseau, Baudelaire, and editions of Tagore's poetry, short stories, and novels, some of which Andrée herself had illustrated.

After the war, for a while there was no word of Flora's real mother; rather, the French children's welfare agency L'Oeuvre de Secours aux Enfants, which itself had saved thousands of Jewish children during the German occupation, put Flora in contact with two living relatives she didn't know. There was an eccentric aunt on her father's side who lived in Geneva and who, Andrée would tell Flora later, had been intent on kidnapping her. The other relative was her mother's half-brother, who lived in Haifa, Israel, to whom Andrée wrote in 1945:

> *In the beginning she had to hide and that made her nervous and full of fear, but since the liberation she is a very gay, well-balanced little girl, always in good temper though deep enough to understand what a loss it is to have had her mother snatched away from her.*
>
> *I can't help being very interested in her . . . as if I had known her. I have been looking after her little girl as if she was my own with the hope of a happy meeting one day between mother and child. That hope must be given up.*

Flora's half-uncle was not equipped to deal with Flora. Having spent the war years in an English internment camp in Mauritius, having lost most of his family, and now starting a new life in Palestine, he gave the Hogmans permission to officially adopt Flora as their daughter.

Andrée enrolled Flora in the nearest school, which was a three-mile bicycle ride each way, a long climb in the morning and downhill in the afternoon. She had plenty of time, and was now old enough to begin reckoning with the reality of her life. Her mother's survival during the war remained a possibility in the absence of any news of her, but with the war over, it seemed that nothing but death could explain her failure to reappear. Yet Flora was still shocked to learn the truth shortly after the end of the war, when a handsome Czech military officer named Ali showed up at the house, saying he was an old friend of Flora's mother.

He embraced Flora, who had no recollection of him, and sat in a chair in the living room, twisting his military cap while Flora squeezed in between Adalrik and Andrée on the settee.

"Stefanie—your mother," he began, and the rest of it Flora heard only in snatches as she stared at him, trying to take in what he was saying as she felt Andrée's arm tighten around her shoulder. "I know that she was deported to Drancy . . . ," he said. "I'm sorry to say . . . transported to Auschwitz on October 28, 1943 . . . it can only be assumed . . . no word . . . Flora, I am so sorry . . . but I know she would've wanted me to give the two of you"—he was looking at her foster parents now—"her blessings to officially adopt Flora. . . ."

She couldn't help fantasizing that the military man had at one time been more than her mother's friend, and that, had she survived, perhaps she would have married him. For days a vision of the three of them walking hand in hand down Nice's Promenade des Anglais kept playing in her head. Her never-to-be stepfather wrote a few letters to Flora after his visit, but they stopped and she never heard from him again.

Andrée kept telling Flora how brave her mother was and suggested they all go to Nice and see the apartment where Flora had last lived with her mother. Although others no doubt lived in the two rooms on Avenue Monplaisir, Andrée thought that perhaps Flora could reconnect there with her mother's spirit, resurrect more memories of her, find some acceptance of her death.

So the Hogmans set off with her in the car one morning. To their surprise, they found the apartment door in Nice unlocked and the living room bare of furniture. Only a few useless objects were scattered about the desolate apartment. Flora, wandering the dimly remembered rooms in a daze, found her mother's beautiful box of spools of thread. And there was a shoe box lying on the floor, which, when Flora removed the lid, revealed a jumble of black-and-white photographs, many of her, her mother, and her father. The ones with her father had been taken in San Remo or before, in Czechoslovakia; the ones with only her and her mother were from their time in Nice. There were other people in the photos she didn't recognize, men and women posing with her parents.

"How come you're not crying?" Andrée asked her, looking on.

When Flora got up and went to the kitchen, it had been stripped of everything but the sink. The stove and the squat little refrigerator were gone. When Flora looked in the sink, she stopped short, her heart pounding.

In it were two of her mother's dirty dishes that, after three years, were still waiting to be washed.

After the war, Flora tried her best to approximate a normal adolescence. Adalrik's reserve and Andrée's flamboyance made for an odd combination of influences, but they were devoted to each other. At times, their mutual adoration made Flora feel even more like an outsider. The bloom on Flora's relationship with Andrée began to fade; what had been exotic to a nine-year-old— the saris, the Indian hairstyles, her interminable yoga—was annoying to the teenage Flora. In an attempt to get closer to her adoptive father, Flora asked him to teach her Swedish.

Over time, the Hogmans grew elderly and developed health and financial problems, which necessitated a move to a smaller house. At least Adalrik had been an effective enough teacher of Swedish that he could arrange for her to work for a travel agency in Sweden. It was her first taste of real independence, as opposed to abandonment, but in 1956, when Flora had been living with them for almost a dozen years, Andrée suddenly died of a heart attack. Flora had lost her second mother. After she returned to Grasse from Sweden, numb and guilt-ridden, she soon got rid of Andrée's yoga and Buddhism books. But the rest of the library, including several of Tagore's books, inscribed by him to Andrée, she kept forever.

She had to turn her attention to Adalrik, who was in decline. She hired someone to look after him during the day while she took a job as a file clerk for the Swedish airline SAS in its Nice office, to which she commuted fifteen miles every day by motorbike. In the mornings and evenings, though, Flora spent increasing amounts of time caring for her adoptive father, giving him his medicines and injections and conversing in Swedish.

In 1959, Adalrik died. Flora was now twenty-three, a beautiful petite young woman with a warm smile and her dark hair grown out and parted in the middle. In a photo from that year, she leans against a rock in the sun, surrounded by cypresses and cacti, wearing white espadrilles and a pretty sundress. She could be any attractive young French woman from a good home with her life ahead of her. But she was now without family, and with the war years a distant—indeed, mostly repressed—memory, she had no idea what to do. She had been Flora Hillel, granddaughter of a famous Czech rabbi, then Marie Hamon, then Flora Hamon, and finally Flora Hogman. Her faith, what there had ever been of it, had been fractured beyond any denominational recognition. She had been a Czech Jew born in Italy, a Roman Catholic living in a Riviera convent, a reluctant Buddhist, a French Protestant, and finally an atheist—and all by the age of fifteen. She had put together a life out of spare parts and the kindness of fearless strangers, and had emerged from her fragmented childhood with a fighting spirit. She just had no idea what to fight for. She was as trapped in her confusion as she had once been in a convent. Where her life was supposed to be, there was only numbness.

Incredibly, just as she had been rescued so many times before, someone appeared and, with the help of a coincidence too pat even for pulp fiction, pointed the way to the future. Flora had an aunt she didn't know, the sister of her aunt in Geneva, who had managed to escape from Austria to New York City in 1940. The aunt's son, her first cousin, now in his twenties, decided he wanted to see Vienna. Before he left on his trip, his mother gave him one last instruction: "Go find Flora Hogman in southern France." That was the sum of anyone's knowledge of her whereabouts; not even her sister in Geneva knew any more than that.

On his way to Austria, he stopped in Paris, where he happened to walk by a store for tourists called Maison de Nice. He knew that Flora had once lived in the Côte d'Azur, so, for the fun of it, he stopped in to ask the young salesgirl there—what did he have to lose?—if she happened to know a Flora Hogman in southern France. But what were the odds that, just because the store had "Nice" in its name, someone there would ever have heard of his cousin?

The salesgirl, whose name was Thérèse, smiled at him. *"Bien sûr, elle est une de mes meilleures amies."*

One of her *best* friends? *"C'est incroyable!"* the young man said, exhausting in one phrase a good portion of the French he had mastered, then using up a good portion of the rest by saying, *"C'est possible?"*

Therese knew Flora from the tourist industry on the Riviera, where she had previously worked, and they had stayed in touch. She gave him her address in Nice.

And that was how Flora Hogman received a visit out of the blue from some cousin speaking a mélange of bad French and unfamiliar English. Between one thing and another, one of the lucky survivors of history's most efficient genocide was soon walking down Fifth Avenue in a city that, thanks to that genocide, was now home to more than 50 percent as many Jews as remained in all of Europe.

By 1959, New York City was home to more than its fair share of young adults who had survived the Holocaust in hiding as children, including a woman whose path Flora was destined to cross more than three decades later at the most important event in the lives of hidden child survivors everywhere.

CARLA

My first glimpse of Carla Lessing came in the Manhattan office of the Hidden Child Foundation, an organization that wasn't formed until the world's scattered and isolated hidden survivors had already reached middle age. Carla spends every Wednesday in the office as the Foundation's vice president and volunteer social worker. She works behind a frosted glass wall in a room about twenty-five feet square that contains numerous file cabinets and four computer terminals filled with data about the organization's global membership of roughly 6,000 hidden child survivors—still just a fraction of the unknown total. In one corner stand two bookcases bulging with Holocaust memoirs. These volumes—and the new ones that arrive all the time—are a drop in the bucket of Holocaust memoirs and histories, but there are fewer every year.

Carla is a small, dark-haired, energetic woman in her eighties who looks years younger than her age. She speaks in a very precise, thoughtful manner, her English still bearing inflections of her native Dutch. Like Anne Frank and her family, Carla spent most of her war years in Holland, which lost nearly 75 percent of its Jews, hidden with her family by Christians of uncommon generosity and courage.

Carla was already ten when the Germans invaded Holland, and so it is less of a struggle than it is for Sophie and Flora to remember the feelings and details of her years in hiding. Carla's memories also go back much further, to her very earliest intimations of the disaster to come.

Since the early 1930s, Carla Heijmans had been aware of German anti-Semitism and the trouble being stirred up by Hitler's National Socialist Party. As a little girl, she vacationed at her maternal grandparents' home near Cologne, Germany, where she was constantly reminded not to talk or laugh too loudly, not to skip, and not to draw any attention to herself. She could tell that her grandparents were scared of the men in brown shirts and shiny black boots, and their fear frightened her.

In the spring of 1936, six-year-old Carla returned to The Hague from spending the winter with her grandparents to find that her mother, Herta, and brother, Herman, had moved from the family's nice single-family home to a modest apartment—and that, far worse, her father, Julius, had suddenly died. Carla's mother dodged her panicky questions; strangely, no one at all spoke to her about the cause of his death. It seemed like the vague threat she had felt in Germany had now spread to her own family, but in her mind Carla concluded that he had died of a heart attack. It would be decades before Carla learned for sure that her father had committed suicide in February of that year, an act motivated at least in part by Germany's boycott of Jewish businesses—made official in 1935 by the Nuremberg Laws—of which the trading company run by Julius Heijmans, his father, and brother-in-law had been one.

He left behind a wife, an asthmatic son, Herman, and daughter, Carla, a family whose sudden poverty was masked by their expensive silverware and furniture, so that few friends and neighbors were the wiser. Carla's mother Herta tried to make ends meet by selling linen and coal from home, as well as inventing a method for removing the shine from men's well-worn suits. When Herta's parents fled Gelsenkirchen shortly after Kristallnacht in 1938, leaving all their assets behind, they moved in not with her but with their son, who owned a factory in the east of Holland.

A year and a half later, in May 1940, they watched as the Germans invaded Holland and found no resistance. By 1942, the Germans began deporting Dutch Jews to Westerbork, a camp that the Dutch themselves had created in 1939 to house Jews entering Holland illegally. Now it had become a way station for Jews headed to Auschwitz, Sobibor, Theresienstadt, and Bergen-Belsen.

In a country that had nothing in the way of mountains and little in the way of forests, there were very few places a Jew could hide. Dutch Jews were dependent, more than in other European countries, on the kindness of Christian strangers. Outside of Eastern Europe and Greece, no country would lose as high a percentage of its Jewish citizens to Hitler's Final Solution as the Dutch.

The persecution of Dutch Jews started slowly, and for a while life went on. In 1942, Carla's family lived in a mostly Catholic neighborhood, where she attended a public school with her best friend, Fanny, who was one class ahead of her and also Jewish. "Best friends" hardly described how close they were; they shared everything.

Then the Germans began to show their hand more aggressively. It came as a rude shock to Carla when she was suddenly told that she could no longer attend swimming classes because of her religion. The Germans soon confiscated Herta's valuables, the two gold rings she had given Carla for her eleventh birthday, Carla's radio, and her beloved bicycle, which she had ridden every day to school. She was at least still allowed to go to a Jewish school, where everyone wore a yellow cloth Star of David. One of the teachers there, Mr. Engelander, helped Carla and some of her friends to stage their own operetta, which distracted them temporarily from what was going on beyond the school walls, where a sinister attrition of the student population had begun.

One day Carla walked around the corner to Fanny's house and rang the bell, as she often did after school. When there was no answer at first, she looked up at Fanny's second-floor bedroom window. By now Fanny would have appeared at the window or at the door, and they would have begun to share the day's gossip. Carla rang again, absentmindedly touching her yellow star, but no one came. When she pressed her ear against the door, she heard nothing. Her mother had already explained to her at dinner that many Dutch Jews were either leaving everything behind and running off to England or Denmark, or going into hiding. But Fanny? Disappearing just like that? Carla was well aware of the growing list of restrictions affecting The Hague's Jews, but a world in which your best friend could vanish without saying a word? Carla trudged home in despair.

When her brother, Herman, was soon conscripted to a German work camp, he was the first of their family to go into hiding. A Jesuit priest they knew arranged for him to live with a Christian family in The Hague. One night after school, he simply ripped off his star and walked to his new home. The priest would not tell his mother its location. An official letter arrived shortly after, instructing Carla and her family to take the trolley to the train station a few days hence, from which they would be taken to Westerbork for "relocation." Herta immediately contacted the priest, begging him to send her and Carla to the same family Herman had joined.

The next night Carla's mother made her take off her vest with the yellow Star of David sewn on it. Carla was afraid. At first she had been proud of the star, proud to be Jewish. Then she became so accustomed to wearing the proof of her Judaism that she barely noticed it anymore. It was as much a part of her as her dark hair, and, ironically, she felt exposed without it.

"When we get outside," her mother said after they packed their bags, "I want you to just drop it in the gutter. From now on, you're no longer Jewish."

The two of them walked alone, along the trolley tracks, until they came to a house right by the trolley. To Carla it hardly seemed like a place to hide, but, sure enough, Herman was waiting inside for them, along with Mrs. Van Nooyen, the owner of the house, and the foster son who lived with her. Carla's relief at having a safe haven soured soon enough as the three Heijmans crowded into a small, dark, stuffy room in the tiny apartment. They had to avoid all windows and ask permission to go to the bathroom. Carla's asthmatic brother Herman was under strict instructions from Mrs. Van Nooyen to wheeze and cough only while muffled by blankets, for fear that the neighbors would turn her, and them, in.

At times Carla felt there was nothing to do but watch the minutes pass. At least Mrs. Van Nooyen could cook. Her kidney bean soup almost made life bearable. The most priceless diversion in their tight quarters was a dictionary that helped relieve the mixture of boredom and fear that now ruled their lives. The only good thing that could be said so far about the Third Reich was that it led to a rapid expansion of the two children's vocabulary.

After just three months—though it already felt like a dark and idle eternity to Carla—Mrs. Van Nooyen's foster son knocked on their door one morning to tell them that their presence had been discovered by neighbors and that they would have to leave immediately. As plausible as this was, they all suspected that having two quietly bickering teenagers hiding in her little apartment, one of them asthmatic, had simply proven to be too much. The real mystery was why Mrs. Van Nooyen had agreed to shelter them in the first place. How badly did she need the small amounts of money they could pay her? Only later would they learn from a priest that she felt she had sinned quite a lot in her life and that she believed that hiding a Jewish family would be just the thing to restore God's confidence in her. However, her anxiety over past transgressions was no match for the reality of risking her life for total strangers.

The Jesuit priest made new arrangements, and one night, after being engulfed by Mrs. Van Nooyen's farewell embraces, Carla, Herman, and their mother were on the street again in the dark, this time headed to the Haag train station. They had not been outside the apartment for three months and the life of the city was a jolt to their systems. The trolleys startled her. The streetlights alarmed her. Carla felt unseen neighbors scrutinizing them from darkened windows. Even without their yellow stars, she wondered if it was obvious they were Jews. At last they were on a train for the short ride to the city of Delft, with directions to their new home, an apartment over a barbershop.

The apartment was bigger, but so was the family. The Van Geenens—it was Walter's barbershop; his wife, Corrie, was the beautician—already had seven children, most of them hungry teenagers. Mr. and Mrs. van Geenen slept in the dining room while Carla, her brother, mother, and the van Geenens' eldest daughter stayed in the front room on the third floor. The other six children were scattered in the third floor's other bedroom and in the hallway just outside. Why had this good couple, who didn't have enough space for their own brood, taken in three Jews? It was not something anyone talked about, yet it didn't take long for the Heijmans family to discover that the bespectacled, chain-smoking Walter van Geenan was a very unusual man.

"What's three more?" he'd say at the dinner table, where he didn't expect them to say grace with the rest of the family. He actually seemed to relish the challenge of defying Nazi orders. Referring to the German soldiers among his barbershop clientele, he said, brandishing a phantom straight razor, "When they come in for a shave, *I'm* the one with the upper hand!"

Although Carla, her mother, and her brother were largely confined to their room on the third floor, from time to time they might be helping Corrie van Geenan in the kitchen on the second floor when Walter would come up the stairs from the shop, whispering that one of his German customers needed to use the toilet. This was the Heijmans family's cue to retreat soundlessly to the third floor and remain there until well after they heard the toilet flush.

While Walter seemed to take their intrusion in stride, Corrie van Geenen was quietly oppressed by their presence, and unhappy about stretching food meant for nine to feed twelve. She never said anything, but her lower lip quivered when she thought no one was looking.

There couldn't have been less privacy in their situation; not only was everybody on top of one another, but the house sat on a square that became a sheep and pig market once a week, so the opportunities for being discovered were never ending. The Heijmans family was hiding in a busy house in one of the busiest parts of town above a barbershop where Nazis came and went daily.

After only a month with the van Geenens, the Heijmans family found out just how close they had come to being discovered at their previous sanctuary, with Mrs. Van Nooyen. Word filtered from The Hague that a neighbor in the same stairwell as the Van Nooyens' apartment had recently been betrayed—not for hiding people, but for hiding Jewish property—and taken away. It seemed to confirm that the Heijmanses hadn't actually been "discovered" while they were there, but rather that Mrs. Van Nooyen just couldn't take the stress of hiding them any longer. But what a stroke of good fortune that seemed now; another two or three weeks and the Germans surely would have found them.

Herman soon discovered that the neighbors' radio, tuned to the BBC, could be heard through the wall of the van Geenens' toilet. He began to spend more time there than was necessary and would emerge armed with news of the latest German atrocity or Nazi propaganda. To put this new information to use, and to relieve his boredom, Herman would occasionally pick political arguments with the van Geenen teenagers, which frightened Carla. Would the van Geenens throw them all out? Why couldn't Herman keep his mouth shut when even the youngest van Geenen children knew better than to say anything about there being Jews in the house? How much longer would it be before someone tipped off the Germans? What were the odds that all three of them would survive this mess? The growling sound of every truck coming down the street could mean disaster. In any case, Herman's pugnacity just made Carla even more committed to remaining a good girl who said as little as possible.

German soldiers came to the apartment once searching for blankets, and twice to look for boys over sixteen to work in German munitions factories. On one of those occasions, Herman escaped with one of the van Geenen sons to a neighbor's apartment, whose owner, a carpenter, had built a false wall. Walter van Geenen often knew about these searches in advance from contacts in the Dutch Resistance. Another time he arranged for the Heijmanses to walk alone at night to a Catholic church, where the priest concealed them for two or three days in the sacristy, except during Mass, when he instructed them to participate as if they were congregants. The three of them rejoiced not only in the interruption of their tense routine, but also in the entertainment that the church services provided after months of sensory deprivation. The "Kyrie," "Gloria," and "Credo" were joys transcending all religion. And yet, being in church reminded them that, through the accident of being born Jews, they lived on the edge of deportation and death while for the rest of Delft it was business, and religion, as usual.

For the most part, though, their lives at the van Geenens' were so tedious that sleep itself was cherished, since it reduced the number of hours that had to be filled and gave them a break from the fear and boredom that saturated their days. During daylight hours, they couldn't look out a window, walk around the third floor, or even use the toilet, for fear they would be heard and reported by the nosy

Dutch collaborators who surrounded them. In the stifling vacuum of their existence, Carla and her mother savored every chore. They peeled potatoes, chopped cabbage, and helped with the cooking, careful always to stay away from the windows. They helped Mrs. van Geenen darn the endless parade of worn-out socks produced by nine children. Carla learned to knit. The van Geenens were not big readers—the house was devoid of books—so Carla, her mother, and even Herman had no choice but to read and reread the romance novels that the eldest daughter, also named Corrie, took out of the library for them.

Most of the Heijmans family's conversations consisted of reminiscing about the past. They talked so endlessly of what had been, about who had once said what to whom, and when and why, that their hosts could barely stand to hear it. They even bored themselves. New experiences, though usually the product of some fresh threat to their existence, at least gave them something new to talk about. Once, when Walter was warned of an impending house search, he hustled the three Heijmanses into the attic of a neighbor's house. The three of them silently followed the owner up a narrow staircase and entered the dimly lit gabled attic. There in the gloom, blinking like some surprised nocturnal animal, was a poor, unshaven soul in a soiled shirt and suit pants cinched around his diminishing waist by a length of rope.

The man introduced himself. "I was a banker in Amsterdam before all this. Besides the visits from my hosts, I have been here alone for almost a year. Anyway, welcome. I wish I had something to offer you," he added with a dry cackle. "I'm afraid I can't even offer you enough chairs."

Carla was shocked to see another Jew in hiding, and so nearby; she had come to think of her mother, brother, and herself as sole survivors of a catastrophe. She could barely remember life before hiding, and she couldn't imagine there would be life after it. She no longer thought much about Fanny or her other friends who had simply disappeared what seemed ages ago. But now it occurred to her that a big X-ray of Delft would reveal dozens of Jews secreted everywhere. There were dramas just like theirs going on in Amsterdam, Rotterdam, and Utrecht. And surely elsewhere. Carla tried to imagine the staggering complexities of history, the manipulations of the masses, the forces invisible to little girls and even barbers and bankers, that had produced this disaster.

. The banker asked them for news, and Herman was only too glad to tell him of the Russians' production of over a thousand tanks a month, but also of huge losses and famine. Their soldiers weren't very well trained, but there were lots of them, and the Germans were suffering horrendous defeats.

The banker nodded, playing with the knot of the rope that held his trousers up. Here, at last, was someone Carla could feel sorry for besides herself, her brother, and her mother. Gratefulness for having her family welled up inside her. No one asked the banker about his own. No one wanted to ask the question, and no one wanted to hear the answer.

After they were able to return to the van Geenens', Corrie would silently serve up soup and boiled potatoes. Carla watched as she tremblingly passed a serving dish at dinner. She felt too guilty to meet Mrs. van Geenen's eyes, although she seldom looked at Carla anyway. Carla retreated further and further inside herself, becoming in her own mind a mouse: timid, silent, invisible, yet always scared, always listening for trucks, for the sound of boot heels, imagining the Nazis getting their sideburns squared away in Mr. van Geenen's barber chair. His Nazi customers, if they knew of their presence, would think nothing of imprisoning or deporting every last person in the van Geenen household. Death was like the thirteenth person in the household, crowding out all other thoughts, making it hard to breathe.

They had meant to stay with the van Geenens only a few months, while the underground came up with another hiding place for them, but a year and a half passed before Carla was able to get out of the house. When Mrs. van Geenen's sister in Delft had a baby girl, Mr. van Geenen put a scarf on Carla's head and walked her there to help out for six weeks, during which the new mother looked frightened every minute. Other times, especially during the merciless "Hongerwinter" of 1944 to 1945, Carla would venture out in the cold to pry precious bits of coal out of the asphalt with a kitchen knife.

Throughout, Mr. van Geenen remained as friendly as always, but Mrs. van Geenen continued to suffer visibly under the stress, particularly when her oldest son, Walter, received a letter demanding that he leave for a work camp in Germany. They all knew that, had the family not been hiding Jews, Walter might have hid or run away, but defying the order would bring the Germans around to investigate. Walter Jr. had no choice but to go. Apart from the parents' agreement to risk their lives for strangers in the first place, it was by far the biggest sacrifice any of them had made. So Walter went to Germany, and not long after, the eldest girl, Corrie, decided abruptly to marry and left the house as well.

When the parents and their remaining children said grace before dinner, Carla almost couldn't bear it. She too wanted to pray to the God of people as good as the van Geenens, people who asked nothing of them, but who had given them, for more than a year, the daily gift of possible survival.

Delft was among the last cities in Western Europe to be liberated. After the Allies' debacle in September 1944 at Arnhem, just seventy-five miles east of Delft, it was almost eight months before Mr. van Geenan announced that the war was over, and that the Heijmanses were free.

"I don't believe it," Carla said. "It's not true. I'm not going outside. I don't believe it." She was in tears. And, in a way, she was right not to believe it. She couldn't have known yet how unbelievable it was that the three of them had survived. While two-thirds of Europe's Jews were being exterminated with systematic ruthlessness, Carla, Herman, and Herta Heijmans had escaped detection in a country whose Jews had suffered enormously. Of the 140,000 Dutch Jews at the beginning of the war, only 35,000 remained, a loss of 75 percent. By comparison, France had lost 26 percent of its Jews during the war, Italy 20 percent, Denmark less than one percent.

Liberation was enlivened by the appearance in The Hague of a brigade of Palestinian soldiers, robust Jews who threw memorable all-night dancing parties for the gaunt survivors. The soldiers were irresistible to many Dutch girls, particularly the orphans, some of whom ended up in Palestine with husbands. Carla, who lived with her mother (her brother Herman had made it to Palestine illegally), was now going to school full-time in home economics during the day, and to high school at night to catch up on her studies. She was also increasingly involved in a Zionist group of which she was the youngest member.

In the spring of 1946, she met an older Zionist from Delft, a man all of twenty named Ed Lessing, but who, like the rest of them, seemed older. He too had hidden from the Nazis, but his experience made Carla's—which her brother Herman would later call "luxury hiding" compared to others'—seem positively uneventful. If Carla Heijmans's years in hiding amid the Germans were marked by a steady drumbeat of daily jeopardy, Ed Lessing's were filled with high drama and cliffhangers of which any A-list screenwriter would be proud.

But after meeting Carla, Ed had more pressing matters on his mind than regaling her with his wartime escapades. In fact, it would be decades before he spoke of his experiences to her or to anybody at all.

Ed was born in the Netherlands in 1926 into a nonpracticing Jewish family of modest means. They were living in Delft when, on May 10, 1940, Ed woke up at five in the morning to gunfire. Out the window, he could see German paratroopers floating down in the distance like white silk flowers. For a while, the occupation barely disturbed the very law-abiding Dutch, even as a succession of German decrees kept Jews out of public parks, schools, and eventually out of jobs. When the Jews were required to wear Stars of David, some of Ed's clueless Gentile friends said, "You should be proud of that star! We think you Jews are wonderful people." Even after a German SS officer punched the teenage Ed for daring to walk with a cousin of his who didn't wear a star, Ed did not feel in mortal danger.

The Germans then promised Jews "work relief" in Germany. The trains were waiting. Ed's parents had already packed their bags when his grandfather reported rumors circulating in Amsterdam that there was no such thing as "work relief" and begged them not to go.

Engeline Lessing walked into the room where her two younger sons, Fred and Arthur, were playing and told them they would have to take off their yellow stars, and that they were going into hiding. When the clueless boys asked why, she said, "I have to tell you boys something. You are Jewish boys and if you tell anyone, they will kill you."

Early on the morning of October 23, 1942, Ed and his younger brothers, aged six and eight, removed their stars and walked with their parents to a friend's house outside of Delft. That night Ed's parents left to go into hiding at the home of an older, childless couple, and his brothers were picked up and taken somewhere else. Ed remained in the house until his mother found a place for him with two elderly unmarried women in Utrecht. From there, he traveled to a small farm outside of Utrecht, where he could stay in exchange for work. He would have to pass as a Gentile, so he dyed his hair blond and spent the next six months in an increasingly depressed state, awaking at four in the morning to milk the cows, his feet bleeding from the wooden shoes. He seriously considered turning himself in to the Germans.

Meanwhile, in the nearby hamlet of De Lage Vuursche, his parents were confronted by the village's chief of police, a taciturn man named Margrethus Oskam. Oskam revealed that, though he was cooperating with the Germans as head of the village's law enforcement under the Nazis, he was actually the head of the local Dutch Resistance. He helped Mr. and Mrs. Lessing find sanctuary in a hostel for nature lovers.

Later it was Oskam who would rescue Ed from the dreary farm, arranging for him to join a Resistance camp hidden deep in the woods of the Dutch countryside. A zigzagging route led Ed to a crude wooden hut that had been camouflaged by small pine trees and branches someone had nailed to it.

The Resistance fighters didn't want to take Ed. "Too young to die," said the men, who were only a few years older than Ed. "Too Jewish." But Oskam prevailed over the ragtag group. Ed was not entrusted with a pistol and was left behind when the group of assorted Catholics and one Communist made their nightly raids on town halls to steal weapons, uniforms, and German rubber stamps to make fake identity cards. Ed's job was to guard the two Canadian flyers hiding with them. They were from the No. 617 Squadron of the British Royal Air Force—the "Dambusters"—who had been downed during one of their missions to destroy three dams with special heavy-duty bombs in order to flood the industrial Ruhr Valley. The group lived off provisions and intelligence brought to them by couriers. In his spare moments, Ed sketched the inside and outside of the hut with enough artistry to surprise even him—they were his first works of art—and that would eventually lead to a career.

On December 28, 1943, an anonymous caller warned an employee of a nearby convent that the Germans were on their way to raid the group. He sounded the alarm and the Resistance fighters fled the hut to regroup near a hotel in the area. After dark, Oskam appeared to say it had been a false alarm and that no Germans had been spotted in the De Lage Vuursche area. The men returned to the hut and set up watch posts, beginning before dawn. Ed and one other man drew the 4:00 to 8:00 A.M. shift and settled in behind the last row of trees before the gravel road a short distance from the hut.

Shortly before dawn on December 29 the dark forest was suddenly raked by the headlights of five trucks full of soldiers and their barking German shepherds. Ed and his watch partner raced back to the hut and tore the blankets off the others, shouting, "Wake up! Save yourselves! The SS is here!" before escaping on foot through the dense undergrowth until they reached a dirt road. When they paused there, they saw the Germans in the distance preparing to surround the area of the hut. As Ed and his partner slipped across the road and disappeared into the forest, Ed couldn't see how the others would have a chance to make it out alive.

The men had agreed earlier that, in the case of a raid, the survivors would meet at a designated place about eight miles away, which Ed and his partner reached later that day. The two spent the pitch-black night hiding behind some trees, pistols in hand, conjecturing that the Germans would torture their comrades to reveal the location of the meeting place and come to either arrest them or kill them. They had no intention of being arrested and tortured in the basement of Gestapo headquarters in Amsterdam, but at least they hoped to kill a German or two before being mowed down by machine guns.

They soon heard a rattling sound, coming closer in the dark along a dirt road. A small light bobbed in the distance. Would this be the last few minutes of their lives? Eventually they made out the form of a bicycle, but neither of them could make out the rider. Ed figured it was a trap—that the minute they stepped out from behind the trees to investigate, they would be surrounded. The two of them slid the safeties off their guns and waited. The bicycle finally came to a stop several yards in front of them and didn't move. Ed and his comrade raised their pistols, prepared to come out of hiding and start shooting.

But it wasn't a German. Nor was it one of the other Resistance members from the hut.

Incredibly, it was Ed's mother, Engeline, who was in hiding not far away.

"Moeder!" Ed exclaimed as loudly as he dared.

She had found out about the raid that morning, and the meeting place, and on a bicycle with wooden tires—the Germans had taken every shred of rubber in the Netherlands—she had fearlessly pedaled to find her oldest son.

The first thing out of her mouth was, "Bury those guns."

"Are you crazy?" he said.

"They're looking for you," Engeline told the two of them. "We're totally surrounded by Germans—hundreds of *Wehrmacht* and SS. If you have weapons, they will probably execute you right here in the woods. Without weapons, maybe we have a tiny chance."

Ed's comrade said he knew a place where maybe he could hide, but he needed the bicycle to get there.

"Take it," she said, pushing the bicycle toward him, along with its hand-operated flashlight, whose battery was charged with a few squeezes of a lever. The flashlight was invaluable. The Dutch company Phillips had developed it during the war, after the Germans had expropriated all the batteries, electricity, and candles in the country.

"Ed, I have just one idea that we can try," she said after his comrade had pedaled off. "It's probably not going to work. But we have to try."

They started down the path in the forest and saw a German sentry with a shouldered rifle a hundred yards ahead of them, at which point they put their plan into action. Ed and his mother put their arms around each other, their faces close together, and began talking and giggling like lovers. They even made kissing sounds as they approached the German in the dark.

They greeted him affably, but the sentry stopped them at rifle point. After inspecting their faces for what felt to them like an eternity, he finally let them pass, and the two ersatz lovers thanked him profusely as they continued on, safe for the time being.

Ed was now a wreck. He had barely escaped when all of his fellow Resistance fighters had undoubtedly perished. His watch partner on the noisy bicycle could not possibly have escaped the German dragnet. After Ed's mother returned to hiding with his father, Oskam came to his rescue again by finding him a new shelter with a well-to-do elderly man who lived with his sister and a maid. They not only took him in but also gave him his own room. The maid would bring his breakfast to him upstairs, where he had to stay during daylight hours, but he would join the man and his sister downstairs at night for dinner. He lived in this ironic luxury for a few weeks, passing the time reading a copy of the Old Testament he found in his room. It was his first exposure to the Five Books of Moses, which were a revelation to him. He read some of it every night before falling asleep, feeling closer and closer to his Jewish identity. He made a deal with God, that he would follow his laws to the best of his ability if God would only save his family.

Oskam soon moved him again, this time to a farm owned by a prosperous family whom Ed came to love in the few weeks he stayed there. Sadly, in the wake of rumors that there was a Jew in the neighborhood, he was forced to stay at still another farm, then another, each time presenting himself, in his well-worn clothes and manure-stained wooden clogs, as a Christian who needed work. His peroxide bleaching had not succeeded in turning his dark hair blond, but coppery red instead. By now, he was actually adept at plowing and putting up barbed wire and could fit right in. However, because he was flush with his newly discovered Judaism, he ate the bacon that came with most farm meals, and worked Saturdays, under silent protest.

At his fourth or fifth farm, he was once again given room and board in exchange for work. The farmer willingly accepted him, but his wife, a stout woman with a blond braid wound tightly round her head, kept eyeing him suspiciously at the midday meal. He slept uneasily near the animals on a straw-filled bag, listening for the distant whine of shifting truck gears.

The gravest threat to his safety, however, had nothing to do with the Germans. The farm bordered beautiful, wild woods, where a gamekeeper lived in a cottage with a stunning daughter with waist-length hair. The farmer mentioned at a meal that the daughter had noticed Ed and asked his name because she wanted to see him on Sunday after church. Worried that it was a trap, Ed said little, but a couple of days later he looked up from mucking out the cows' stalls to see her waving at him from the cottage. Seventeen and horribly lonely, Ed agreed to a walk with her on Sunday, during which he experienced, and resisted, alternating currents of lust and fear—and even the desire to blurt out that he was a Jew.

Not long after, Ed made one of his secret visits to his parents and mentioned the object of his affections to his mother. Her reaction was immediate and stern. She said that to proceed with her further could get him killed, especially if the girl's father had any Nazi sympathies. Ed had no choice but to make his excuses and regretfully leave the farm.

His mother, whose ingenuity and daring had saved their lives in the forest, now ran out of luck herself. Tensions had arisen between Ed's parents and their rescuers, so Engeline decided to rent a summer cottage in the village of Voorthuizen. First, however, she needed to secure a new hiding place for Ed's seven-year-old brother, Fred. While traveling by train to find one, she was confronted by a Gestapo document specialist who recognized her ID card as fake.

She was arrested and put on another train for Amsterdam, escorted by a Dutch policeman. To her horror, she suddenly remembered that in her handbag she had a scrap of paper on which she had written the addresses of all her family members' hiding places. That her purse hadn't been searched yet was a stroke of unbelievable luck, but with the policeman sitting next to her she had to come up with something. And so, over the course of the next two hours, she periodically slipped her hand in her bag to surreptitiously tear off tiny pieces of the list, then just as furtively, concealing her actions with a cough or a turn of her head, she slipped each shred of paper into her mouth, chewed it slowly to a pulp, and consumed the evidence that might have led to the murder of her entire family.

From Amsterdam she was sent to Westerbork, the transit camp from which more than 100,000 Dutch Jews would ultimately be sent to their deaths.

When Ed managed to visit his grieving father and motherless younger brothers in the little house she'd rented, he saw how helpless they were and decided to join them. The owner of the cottage, a refined gentleman named Van Hamburg who lived with his family next door, kept inquiring after Mr. Lessing's wife. Not yet knowing the truth about her absence, but fearing the worst, Ed's father improvised that she'd broken her leg and was detained in Amsterdam. A month later, after they had received word that she'd been transported to Bergen-Belsen—almost certainly a death sentence—the landlord asked after her again. Ed's father explained that she had become so depressed over her leg that she had been committed to an insane asylum. The landlord never caught on; in fact, he became quite fond of Ed's father, once remarking to him that the war was a terrible thing. Ed's father readily agreed. "Yes," Van Hamburg said, "the Germans are *terrible*. Almost as bad as the Jews."

The last winter of the war, 1944 to 1945, was the harshest, and the hardest on the Lessings, who had to beg, borrow, and even steal to stay alive. Spring brought some relief, but no end to the war was in sight. German V-1 flying bombs whistled overhead, and heavy gunfire in the area kept snapping off small tree branches that fell on the cottage roof. A farmer appeared at their door one day with a dead duck full of German shrapnel, and offered it to the Lessings. After some deft surgery to remove the metal fragments, they began to roast the bird. Unfortunately, while the duck cooked, the fighting came closer and closer, the ground trembling with exploding munitions. After making sure Ed's two little brothers were safely in Van Hamburg's bomb shelter, Ed and his father crawled to the cottage to wait for the duck to finish cooking, then crawled back on their bellies to the shelter with their best meal in months.

After three days in the shelter with the Van Hamburg family, the noise outside stopped. When the Lessings finally emerged, they glimpsed the most incredible sight: the Canadian Army coming toward them through the fields.

But the biggest miracle of all awaited them back in Delft later that spring, when a woman jumped out of an English army truck and asked Ed, "Do you know where the Lessings live?"

Ed stared wide-eyed at the frail woman. Was it possible that Ed had changed so much in the past year that his own mother didn't recognize him? "Mother," he cried. "It's me, Eddie!"

The story she told was almost unbelievable. She had been fading away slowly in Bergen-Belsen, her inevitable death forestalled only by her good fortune in securing a night job in the camp's kitchen. On December 5, 1944, pressed in between two other women in her barracks, she'd had a vivid dream. In it, she'd seen a copy of the *Haagsche Courant*, clearly dated "January 31, 1945." She understood its significance: on that date, she would either be dead, or she would be free. There was no reason for optimism, but maybe the Americans or British would come. With the stub of a pencil, she inscribed the date on the wooden frame of her bunk.

Not long after the dream, her close friend and bunk mate told her one morning that she should walk over to the next barracks, where an SS man was set up at a desk to take information from inmates with foreign papers. Her friend knew that, upon Engeline Lessing's arrest in Amsterdam, she had tried to convince the SS that she was American, providing the address in Jamaica Plain, Massachusetts, where she and her husband and firstborn Ed actually had lived for a few years in the early 1930s. Her husband, Nathan, an accomplished cellist who had worked several cruises for the Holland-America Line, had hoped to catch on with the Boston Symphony Orchestra. When Nathan contracted tuberculosis all seemed lost, but he eventually recovered and found work in 1931 with other BSO musicians at a hotel in New Hampshire before the Depression closed off all further prospects and the family returned to the Netherlands.

"I was lying about being an American citizen and they knew it," Engeline whispered to her fellow inmate.

"But you have nothing to lose," her friend said. "Go."

Engeline made her way to the next barracks, where, sure enough, an SS officer sat at a small table, over a list of names. When she approached, he asked for her name while barely looking up at her.

"Here you are," he said, his finger pausing on the page. "Get yourself ready. You'll be out of here in two days."

Although Bergen-Belsen had begun as a camp for prisoners needed to exchange for German prisoners, Engeline didn't believe the SS officer for a minute. They had lied many times before. She was there to die slowly from starvation or typhus, whichever won the race. But two days later, she found herself walking with 300 other prisoners to the train depot, where Red Cross nurses—they were visions in white, no more real to her than a dream—circulated among them with real coffee, real milk, and real sugar. When they boarded the train, all the window shades were drawn and they were told that looking out the window was punishable by death. Nonetheless, as the train traveled south through Germany, Engeline peeked from time to time, and what she saw filled her with joy: every city lay in ruins. Germany looked like a defeated nation.

Finally, in St. Gallen, Switzerland, her train met another train filled with German citizens who had been interned in Palestine as POWs. The exchange was officially completed, and the former inmates of Bergen-Belsen were led to a school building, where they were fed bread and sardines, and slept on straw spread out on the floor. Engeline dumped tins of sardine, oil and all, on her bread and savored her first real meal—if you could call it that—in months. Her debilitated system couldn't handle the onslaught of calories, and she vomited it all up, as did many of the others.

In the morning, she awoke and stared out the window at the snow-covered Appenzell Alps, amazed that such natural beauty still existed in the same world as Bergen-Belsen, where she had left behind thousands dying of typhus. She and the three hundred other feeble, emaciated prisoners waited throughout the day for further instructions. When evening came, a man arrived to distribute copies of the *St. Galler Tagblatt*.

And there it was, as prophesied in her December dream: *31 Januar 1945*.

The following day Engeline's train moved on to Marseille, where she was given a choice between Palestine, emigration to America, or assignment to a United Nations rehabilitation camp in Europe. Since returning to Holland was not an option—it was still under Nazi control—she chose America and had already boarded the ship bound for New York when she changed her mind, reasoning that if she stayed in Europe, she'd have a chance to be reunited with her husband and children, *if* they had survived. She ended up in a rehabilitation camp in Algeria, from which, five months later, she made her way back to Delft, hitching a ride on a British army truck for the last leg of it.

The night after jumping off the army truck and being reunited with her family, she told them that they were going to America and that she, who was one of five children of poor Orthodox Jews, didn't want to have anything to do with Jews, Germans, or Hollanders for the rest of her life. A year later, Ed and his father obtained visas to immigrate to the United States and establish themselves before sending for Ed's mother and two younger brothers. The only snag for Ed was that he had just fallen in love two months earlier with the teenage Carla Heijmans, to whom a mutual friend had recently introduced him. Ed and Carla had gotten to know each other on Zionist outings, but their blossoming love affair—well, Ed was smitten while Carla was mostly confused—was cut short in June 1946, with promises by both parties to stay in touch and, they hoped, reunite before long.

Ed settled in Schenectady, New York, where he began working at the General Electric plant. For a year and a half, he deluged Carla with love letters—as a stranger in a strange land, he had plenty of time on his hands. Finally, in 1949, Carla's mother obtained a visa to immigrate to America under the German quota (she had been born there), and Carla, as a minor, joined her on the journey. By then Ed had earned a New York State High School Equivalency Diploma and was working on electrocardiographs and gas analysis instrumentation for the Cambridge Instrument Company in Ossining, a town on the Hudson River north of New York City. By 1949, he and Carla were married.

By 1958, they had two children and a house in the New York City suburb of Dobbs Ferry. It looked just like the American dream, but it had been built on a foundation of disaster.

PART TWO

THE GATHERING

Still Hiding

In 1989, Carla Lessing, the mother of two grown children and a social worker in Hastings-on-Hudson, New York, heard about a lecture on child Holocaust survivors that was going to be delivered in Manhattan by a well-known Long Island psychoanalyst and author named Dr. Judith Kestenberg. A prominent researcher in the field of childhood trauma, Dr. Kestenberg's family had been annihilated in Poland during the war. She now headed up Holocaust Survivor Studies, as well as the International Study of the Organized Persecution of Children, which she had started with her husband. She traveled the world with her associates, taping interviews with more than 1,500 child survivors of the Holocaust and *their* children. She had been born in Tarnov, Poland, in 1910, but like her Polish-born husband, she had immigrated to the United States in the late 1930s.

If anyone could speak to Carla Lessing's experience as a hidden child during the war, she figured it was Dr. Kestenberg. Lessing had spent her adult life surrounded by Holocaust survivors. As often happened with children of survivors, Lessing's children had gravitated, almost unconsciously, toward other children of survivors as friends. Lessing's daughter became close with the daughter of a neighbor who was a Holocaust survivor, and her son's closest friend was the son of a refugee of Nazi-occupied France.

The experience of hiding was with Carla always in one form or another. She had done, as she put it, "all the normal things"—school, college, graduate school—but she didn't experience the world as a safe place. She lived on a steady diet of worst-case scenarios—especially involving her children. She awoke, startled, with heart palpitations, in the middle of the night. She saw that others enjoyed life so much more than she did; how could she allow herself joy when so many had suffered, had disappeared? She wasn't sure she knew even *how* to express joy. She was in some ways still the girl obeying her grandparents' warnings not to draw attention to herself, still the adolescent whose very life depended on suppressing emotions. She felt uncomfortable in any group. The years in hiding seemed to have killed in her the capacity to belong.

As a member of the "helping professions" whose job was to assist others, Carla knew she had yet to defeat, or maybe even confront, some of her own fears and anxieties. She had not lost any immediate family members during the war, and she had not even witnessed any Jews being beaten, tortured, shot, or hanged, but an aunt, uncle, three cousins, great-aunts, and many close friends had been murdered.

It was clear that the hidden children had come out of the war burdened by the very silence they had needed in order to survive. They had been the victims of one of history's most malevolent hunts, but survival had left them in psychological pain, quietly excluded from the world around them. Worse, the vast majority had endured their misery alone, not able to broach it, even with loved ones, and had been made to feel unworthy of their own suffering.

In the decades that followed the war, Carla and Ed never talked about their experiences in hiding. They never discussed it with their children either. A detail might pop up in conversation here and there, but not whole narratives or chronologies. Not during the five years they spent in Israel in the early 1950s, when Carla cooked on a kibbutz and worked with infants and toddlers in their communal homes.

Sophie's parents, Daniel and Laura Schwarzwald, on a beach in Zaleszczyki, Poland.
(United States Holocaust Museum, courtesy of Sophie Turner Zaretsky)

Nazi reprisal execution of members of the Lvov ghetto Judenrat in September 1942, on the day that Daniel Schwarzwald disappeared. *(United States Holocaust Museum)*

Document identifying Bronislawa Tymejko (the Christian alias of Laura Schwarzwald) as an employee of the Regional Agricultural Mercantile Cooperative in Busko-Zdrój. *(United States Holocaust Museum, courtesy of Sophie Turner Zaretsky)*

Herr Leming, the Nazi who hired Laura as his bookkeeper at the cooperative. *(Courtesy of Sophie Turner Zaretsky)*

Sophie and her mother hiding in plain sight in Busko-Zdrój. *(United States Holocaust Museum)*

Sophie and her mother at her first communion in Busko-Zdrój, 1944. *(United States Holocaust Museum, courtesy of Sophie Turner Zaretsky)*

The agricultural cooperative where Laura worked. *(Courtesy of Sophie Turner Zaretsky)*

Laura, Sophie, and Aunt Putzi in Busko-Zdrój, 1945. *(United States Holocaust Museum)*

Sophie's bear, Refugee, today, still
wearing the coat made for him by Aunt Putzi.
(United States Holocaust Museum)

Sophie in the tutu Aunt Putzi had
made for her out of tissue paper.
(United States Holocaust Museum)

Zofia Tymejko, the future Dr. Sophie Turner Zaretsky.
(Courtesy of Sophie Turner Zaretsky)

Laura in London with her aunt
Rosa Hoenig. *(Courtesy of
Sophie Turner Zaretsky)*

Sophie with her son, Jeffrey, husband, David,
and mother, Laura, at Jeffrey's bar mitzvah.
(Courtesy of Sophie Turner Zaretsky)

Emil Hoenig in front of his candy
and tobacco store in London.
(Courtesy of Sophie Turner Zaretsky)

Sophie and David with their two sons, Jeffrey and Daniel, at Jeffrey's wedding to Andrea Weinstock. Seated are Sophie's uncle, Kazimierz Rozycki, and aunt, Putzi. *(Courtesy of Sophie Turner Zaretsky)*

Sophie and her husband, David. *(Courtesy of Sophie Turner Zaretsky)*

Flora's parents. *(Courtesy of Flora Hogman)*

Flora and her mother, Stefanie, near Nice, shortly before Stefanie was taken by the Nazis. *(Courtesy of Flora Hogman)*

Dr. Odette Rosenstock and Moussa Abadi, who rescued more than 500 Jewish children in the south of France, Flora among them. *(United States Holocaust Museum, courtesy of Julien Engel)*

Flora with her adoptive parents, Andrée Karpeles and Adalrik Hogman, with whom she lived until she was twenty-three. *(Courtesy of Flora Hogman)*

Flora toasting with shipboard companions en route to New York in 1959.
(Courtesy of Flora Hogman)

Flora in America, age twenty-six. *(Courtesy of Flora Hogman)*

Flora at home in New York City today.
(Courtesy of Flora Hogman)

One of Flora's photographs, using reflections to express
what she calls her "double life." *(Courtesy of Flora Hogman)*

Carla Heijmans as a
schoolgirl in The Hague
(Courtesy of Carla Lessing)

A watercolor of Carla as a teenager
in hiding in Delft, painted
by her husband, Ed Lessing.
(Courtesy of Ed Lessing)

CARLA HEIJMANS-"HIDDEN CHILD"- CA 1943

Ed Lessing (left) as a Resistance fighter in a forest hideaway near De Lage Vuurse, Holland. *(Courtesy of Ed Lessing)*

One of Ed's earliest drawings, of the Resistance fighters' hut. *(Courtesy of Ed Lessing)*

Corrie and Walter van Geenen, who hid Carla, her mother, and brother in their Delft home. In 1979 Israel granted them status of the Righteous Among the Nations. *(Courtesy of Carla Lessing)*

The van Geenens' house, where Carla and her family hid on the third floor.

Ed's mother, Engeline, whose resourcefulness helped her entire family survive the war. *(Courtesy of Ed Lessing)*

Margrethus Oskam, the small-town Dutch police chief who secretly headed the local Dutch Resistance and was instrumental in keeping the Lessing family safe from the Nazis. *(Courtesy of Ed Lessing)*

The Lessing clan. *Left to right:* Son-in-law, Richard Fusco; daughter, Noa Lessing Fusco; son, Dan Lessing; grandsons Peter Fusco, Aaron Fusco, and Jesse Lessing; daughter-in-law, Stephanie Lessing; granddaughter Kim Lessing, *(Courtesy of Ed and Carla Lessing)*

Carla today at the offices of the Hidden Child Foundation in New York City.
(Courtesy of Carla Lessing)

Ed Lessing today. *(Courtesy of Ed Lessing)*

Not during the years after they returned to America, when Ed got his design degree at Pratt Institute and Carla worked as a nursery school teacher in the Bronx and Dobbs Ferry, and earned her college degree and graduate degree in social work from Columbia University. Not when she spent ten years as a supervisor in a day treatment program for chronic mentally ill patients and another ten as a therapist and supervisor in an outpatient mental health clinic.

Carla and Ed treated their wartime experiences as detachable chapters, as easily uncoupled from their life stories as a boxcar. Even when they visited the van Geenens on visits to Holland over the years, the distant past—her mother would refer to it only as "the Hitler time"—was rarely part of the conversation.

The only time it regularly came up was in Ed's psychotherapy, and then he wasn't even aware of it. After twenty-three years of treatment, Ed Lessing said to his therapist in one of their last sessions, "You know something? The most important thing in my life I never talk to you about."

His therapist said, "What was that, Ed?"

Ed said, "The Holocaust."

"Ed," the therapist said, "there hasn't been a single session that you did *not* talk about it."

The audience at Dr. Kestenberg's lecture on Holocaust survivors was filled with mental health professionals, listening attentively as a panel of psychoanalysts talked about Kestenberg's ongoing research into the effects of "genocidal persecution on the child's psychic structure and on development throughout the life cycle."

There was just one problem, as far as Lessing was concerned. Not once during the entire talk did Kestenberg mention Jewish children who had been *hidden*, rather than deported, during World War II. Kestenberg focused only on those children who had escaped extermination in the camps. What about the others? The children whose parents had given them up to Christian strangers, many of them too young to understand the reasons for this abandonment, who lived in terror, often without parental love at all, only to face further trauma at the end of the war, when they were "reunited" with devastated parents they didn't know, and who couldn't properly care for them? What about the children who watched the members of their family deported or murdered one by one? Or learned that their parents were dead, leaving them to be raised by their rescuers, by strangers, or after the war, by relatives who rejected them for not "being Jewish"? What about the hidden children who, as adults, didn't know their given names or more than a scrap or two of information about their biological parents? Didn't "genocidal persecution" also apply to them?

Carla Lessing wasn't in the habit of speaking out, but during the question-and-answer period she summoned the courage to raise her hand and ask Kestenberg, "Have you done any research on children who survived in hiding?"

The answer was a polite no.

After the talk, however, Lessing was approached by another audience member named Nicole David, a Belgian who had been hidden in an orphanage, with a wealthy Catholic family, and finally in a convent during the war. She was now part of a survivors' group that Dr. Kestenberg had started. Some of that group's members, former hidden children, were thinking of organizing a conference devoted to these largely ignored members of the Holocaust survivors population. Would Lessing like to be part of it? After all, there had already been official Holocaust *adult* survivor events and conferences around the world since the 1960s. There had been conferences for children of survivors in New York, Los Angeles, Washington, DC, Philadelphia, and Israel. Just eight years before, in 1981, 10,000 survivors and their descendants had gathered in Jerusalem.

At that gathering in Jerusalem in 1981, another former hidden child survivor and now Canadian psychiatrist Robert Krell had had the same idea as Nicole David and now Carla Lessing and others. Krell listened as Rabbi Israel Meir Lau said, "I am the youngest survivor of Buchenwald. My father, the Rabbi of Piotrowsk, died in Treblinka, my mother in Ravensbrück. I was eight years old at Liberation." At that moment Krell realized that the child survivors "were genocidal war's leftovers." Older survivors were scared of the children of the Shoah; they had their hands full dealing with their own damage. A couple of years later, Krell tried to organize a group of child survivors in Los Angeles, hoping to get something started; similar groups were stirring in Chicago, New York, Philadelphia, and Montreal. In 1988 there was a small gathering of hidden children survivors at a Lancaster, Pennsylvania, motel owned by a survivor, but none of the efforts got much traction. It was as if the children of the Holocaust—especially the former hidden ones—were still waiting for their Moses to lead them out of their silent enslavement.

One other person in the group Nicole David mentioned to Carla had impressive credentials, even though she had been born just after the war. However, Myriam Abramowicz had a personal stake in the matter. Although she was born after the war, her own parents had survived the war in hiding with one family in Brussels, while her older brother had been whisked out of the hospital at birth to hide with another.

Unlike most hidden survivors, her parents didn't protect their children from the Holocaust. Myriam was seven when she learned the truth, which set her on a course to help change the destinies of thousands of hidden child survivors. When the daughter of the local butcher in Brussels called her "a dirty Jew" in 1953, she pushed the girl against a wall and ran home. She showed her father her well-washed hands and said, "See, I'm not dirty." Soon after, her father called his two children into his study and told them of his own brother and sister, and her two children, who had been gassed.

In 1955, Myriam and her family traveled to America on the *Queen Mary* and settled first in Brooklyn. In a closet, her mother kept bags of photos, pictures taken before and after the war, nourishing Myriam's curiosity about her family and the historical gap for which no photos existed. Later, when Myriam read Anne Frank's diary and learned that they shared a birthday, June 12, the thought entered Myriam's head that maybe she had been put on earth to finish the work Anne had begun. She came by her interest in storytelling honestly; she was the great-grandniece of S. Y. Abramowicz—aka Mendele Mocher Seforim, considered by many the grandfather of Yiddish literature.

As an adult, Myriam began attending Holocaust survivor conferences, noticing that the hidden children there were actually told to keep quiet by their elders. The children were on no one's radar screen, not even the other survivors'. In 1977, when Myriam was thirty-one, she visited Belgium and met her mother and father's savior, without whom Myriam would not have existed. On her return to New York City, she took a leave from her publishing job as assistant to André Schiffrin, editor in chief at Pantheon Books, and, inspired by Studs Terkel, whose books Schiffrin edited, she returned to Belgium to interview other non-Jewish hiding parents for a book she wanted to write.

However a book seemed inadequate for capturing her subjects' emotions, and she decided in 1978 to make a documentary instead with a French potter-turned-filmmaker named Esther Hoffenberg, whose father had hidden in Poland. Released in 1980, *As If It Were Yesterday* documented the extraordinary Belgians who had hidden and placed over four thousand Jewish children during the Nazi occupation of Belgium. The title came from several interviewees' response to her asking how well they remembered the day long ago when they brought a Jewish child into their home. The term "hidden child" was used for the first time in the documentary, lending a name at last to a forgotten population and an overlooked problem.

As If It Were Yesterday won awards and played around the world to audiences that included many hidden children, some of whom left their names and addresses in Myriam's journal after the screenings. When she had collected a couple hundred names, her mother suggested that Myriam should invite them all into her apartment on 108th Street and Broadway in New York City. When Myriam proposed this at a survivors meeting in 1989, Dr. Judith Kestenberg and Dr. Eva Fogelman countered with a bigger idea. Fogelman, a New York psychologist specializing in Holocaust survivors and the writer/producer herself of an award-winning documentary about the children of survivors, had been instrumental ten years earlier in organizing the First International Conference on Children of Holocaust Survivors at Hebrew Union College in New York City. She was also a founding member of the International Network of Children of Jewish Holocaust Survivors that followed.

"Wait," Fogelman said. "Wait a year, and let's do it right."

Kestenberg's husband, who was in real estate, loaned the group an office, and what Myriam's mother had conceived as an informal coffee klatch in her apartment was on its way to becoming the three-day First International Gathering of Children Hidden During World War II.

The informal group didn't need to look beyond its members to see the damage that had been done to hidden children since the war. No one embodied as many traumas and tragic ironies of the hidden child survivor as another woman in the group, named Marie-Claire Rakowski. When Marie-Claire was born in Belgium in 1943, her mother placed her with a childless Catholic couple named Hicket, whom she would learn to love dearly. In 1945, unknown to Marie-Claire, her mother, who had survived Auschwitz in terrible health, tried unsuccessfully to reclaim her from her devoted hiding parents. Two years later, her mother authorized a Jewish organization to kidnap her daughter and transport her to Switzerland, where she was reunited with her older sister, who had spent the war years in a convent.

"The first thing she did when she met me," Marie-Claire said in an interview years later, "was to grab the doll I'd brought and rip it apart. From then on she took every possible opportunity to make me miserable." The two sisters were sent to a succession of foster homes—a small tragedy, given the love Marie-Claire felt for the Hickets. There, Marie-Claire's "mentally disturbed" sister continued to torment her, even physically beating her. When their mother finally showed up to visit, Marie-Claire said, "I refused to believe that this flabby, unattractive person who kept pawing me was my real mother. I felt disgusted." After two years of foster homes, the girls were sent to the United States without their mother and placed in a Hasidic family that changed her name to Miriam and subjected her to the completely unfamiliar rigors of Orthodox law. They then landed in the homes of one rabbi, then another, the second of which sexually abused Marie-Claire. "That," she said, "was when I finally felt the full impact of what had happened to me: I had lost my hiding parents (the only people I could ever think of as my real parents)."

While at Jewish summer camp when she was ten, her mother reappeared. The whole camp celebrated her arrival with a party, singing Hebrew songs, while Marie-Claire felt it was too late for her mother to be of any help. Nonetheless, she and her sister moved in with their mother in Brooklyn, who exhibited many of the behaviors common to survivors. "She wouldn't even buy toilet paper or sanitary napkins. If any food spoiled, she ate it and expected us to do the same. There was no such thing as throwing out even a blackened, wet lettuce leaf. We were three sick people, living together." When Marie-Claire was sixteen, her mother raised a frying pan against her, to which she responded by picking up a knife. Her mother called the police, who contacted the Federation of Jewish Philanthropies, which placed

Marie-Claire in a group home, where she was isolated again, this time as a "religious Jewish girl" thrown among juvenile delinquents.

"While I was hanging out with drug addicts and around drugs constantly, I never touched the stuff. What protected me was the solid foundation of love that I'd had up to the age of four. That was something I was able to hold on to in a private place." She managed to finish high school, then worked as a bookkeeper, benefited from psychotherapy, and reconciled with her mother, whom she took care of until her death in 1970. With the sister, there was no further communication.

In her forties, Rakowski summed herself up as "relatively healthy, compared with a lot of other people. . . . But if you look at my history, I should be crazy! I should have killed myself at twenty-one. But I'm beyond that, which says a lot about the human spirit and a person's recuperative powers."

Carla jumped at the chance to be part of the planning for a conference, in charge of forty workshops conducted in three different languages. She realized that it would take time to reach as many members as possible of a group that, by its very nature, had not been in touch since the war—had not, with a few exceptions, even known of each other's existence. With just a handful of names in hand, the planning committee placed announcements in two Jewish publications.

Carla dedicated herself to the conference, devoting virtually all her free time to it for a year. At last, she felt part of a community. She could share the experiences she had always held tightly within herself. She didn't have to worry now; the whole purpose of their project was to create the safest and most meaningful context in which to share the stories and the grief. Calls from a few ambivalent former hidden children trickled in, and each caller needed help in making up his or her mind. It was slow going.

Then, in early 1991, *New York* magazine published an article about the coming conference, and the group started to hear from former hidden children everywhere. Most still needed encouragement and reassurance. Even artist Ann Shore, one of the planners, had her doubts about coming forward. However, the article had featured a large photo of her, and she couldn't back out now. A stranger even came up to her in a parking lot, touched her arm, and said, "I'm glad you're here." Artists she'd known for decades were astonished to learn of her past. Shore considered registering under a false name, as if an alias would protect her from the powerful emotions she suspected would be released by the event.

Hidden children had, in effect, continued to hide, and be hidden, since the war. They didn't even have a name for themselves. Although Myriam Abramowicz had used the term "hidden child" years before, it had hardly caught on; instead, it was "the Jewish children and babies who had been hidden during the war." For most of these survivors, the sources of family stories and intergenerational conversations—a cornerstone of the foundation of an individual's identity—had been exterminated. Even if relatives survived, the family narrative had been badly broken. What often remained were unspeakable memories, shame, and helplessness, which constituted a lingering atrocity. The Nazis had not only stolen their families but their pasts as well.

In a little-known documentary called *Hidden Children*, a Hungarian Jewish writer, therapist, and father of five who hid in Budapest in plain sight during the war would express it most wrenchingly:

"I know I can't be a Jew the way one has to be according to Jewish custom, tradition, law," a tearful André Stein tells the filmmaker, "but on the other hand I can't be whole without embracing who I was meant to be. . . . It's a loneliness with two poles and I just shuttle between the two. . . . I'm passing this on to my children. . . . That's the saddest, is that [the Nazis] got to my kids through me."

As the First International Gathering of Children Hidden During

World War II loomed just a few months away, the influential Anti-Defamation League brought the fledgling group under its wing, spurred by ADL's national director Abraham Foxman. Foxman himself had been a hidden child whose parents left him with his Christian nanny in Lithuania before they fled to escape the Nazis. He was all too familiar with the plight of hidden children even after the war; when Foxman's parents came to claim their son, his nanny refused to give him up, and it took a kidnapping and several painful lawsuits before he was reunited with his biological parents.

With their new ADL affiliation, the organizers forged ahead. But how did you convince people to come out of hiding when hiding was all they had known? Carla and the rest of the group now thought they would be lucky to draw a few hundred former hidden children to the conference at the end of May.

But, incredibly, on the Friday of Memorial Day weekend, more than 1,600 middle-aged men and women from twenty-eight countries filtered into the ballroom on the seventh floor of the Marriott Marquis hotel in Times Square. They were glad to be out of the unseasonable ninety-degree heat, even if almost all of them were anxious about what awaited them inside. With few exceptions, they were strangers to one another, their fellow travelers from an old journey through darkness and terror. But it could also be said that they were strangers to themselves, and had traveled from near and far to learn more about who they were.

Just the day before, 300 last-minute callers had contacted the organization, only to hear a recording encouraging them, please, to come. They arrived from Europe, Israel, Australia, Canada, and all over the United States, and were joined by twenty of their Gentile rescuers—some of the Righteous Among the Nations—many of them poor Catholic Poles who had been flown in courtesy of the Jewish philanthropist and art collector Ronald Lauder.

Carla Lessing, now in her early sixties, watched in amazement as people lined up to get their name tags and packets. She would have felt even more emotionally overwhelmed if she weren't distracted now by whether the attendees would know where to go, whether or not there would be enough chairs for everyone, and whether or not all the workshop leaders would show up.

One of those leaders was Dr. Flora Hogman, who knew more about the collective suffering around her than most people in attendance, since she had been one of the first psychologists to study how these hidden children had managed to surmount their traumas to lead functioning lives. Being a psychologist was not what Flora had in mind when she arrived in New York in 1959—she wanted to be like everyone else. She would have liked to be free to be a dancer or an artist, but eventually her history would leave her no alternative but to professionally explore the very depths in which she had come so close to drowning.

To the casual observer, Flora's life during her first years in New York City looked like a thousand other Bohemian scenarios of the era. Flora had a fifty-dollar-a-month apartment on Horatio Street in Greenwich Village. She had a fireplace. She had a cat. She had friends. She had a beret. She roamed the Village's little streets, dense with brownstones and dotted with cafés, feeling very free and avant-garde. She felt connected again to her mother, who had been a talented artist. She marched—for free speech, against the Vietnam War, for civil rights. She worked as a waitress at a tiny French restaurant, Chez Brigitte, a sliver of a storefront on Greenwich Avenue. The tips were good. Flora learned English there by refusing to speak French.

Of all New York City's wonders, perhaps the most amazing to her was how many Jews there were. Yet they were not Jews like her—she didn't feel *anyone* was like her. Flora was in good company; it was the dawn of the counterculture's rebellion against conformity, and Greenwich Village was one of its epicenters. In 1960, not far from Flora's apartment, an off-Broadway show called *The Fantastiks* opened in a small theater on Sullivan Street. It would run for forty-two years and become famous for one whimsical line that could have been the motto for not only the beatniks and hipster denizens of Greenwich Village, but also for the baby boomers waiting in the wings. Luisa, the show's ingénue, cries, "Please, God, please, don't let me be normal!"

But in reality normal was all Flora wanted to be. She looked at her fellow Greenwich Villagers on the street, longing to know how they managed. For all her ostensible competence, Flora felt she didn't know how to deal with the real world—even the less dangerous one she lived in now—and she had no one to teach her. She didn't feel she belonged anywhere. She didn't know whether to go out with Jews or Christians. She was scared of being intimate with anyone because she felt she had nothing to give. Looking back decades later, she would think, *I had post-traumatic stress syndrome. That's what it was.*

At the time, though, there was no name for the feeling that her sense of self had been overwhelmed and fractured, and that it was her impossible job to fit the pieces together. She had serious memory problems; there were huge gaps, and her childhood was a fog in which she was still trapped. Something in her was always hiding, paralyzed.

However confused in her personal life, she was quite organized in her work life. When she was hired as a file clerk at the Ford Foundation, she was so good at it that, after six months, her boss offered her a promotion to assistant bookkeeper. She turned it down and instead used her small inheritance from the Hogmans to enroll at New York University to finish college. She felt ignorant. In school in France, history class had only covered French history to 1936. Incredibly she had only a vague idea of the very events in Europe that had killed her mother and almost her. There was so much she didn't know. Then Flora soon discovered something very interesting about herself: as uneducated as she felt, and as inarticulate as she was about her own feelings, hesitant and fumbling in her soft French accent, she wrote with clarity. When she was called on in class, she sounded clueless, yet when she sat down to write, she often turned in the best paper.

That she finished college, let alone earned a Ph.D. in psychology, was remarkable. By the early 1970s she was working in clinics and hospitals with children—she was, not surprisingly, very sensitive to children—when she decided it was time to take a good look at her own history. But she realized that her path to understanding and integrating her own trauma would have to pass through the experiences of others like her. She decided to study the psychology of *other* child survivors of the Holocaust.

There was no question in her mind that *someone* had to do it. That had become clear when she attended a meeting of the New York Psychological Association and heard a paper that portrayed Holocaust survivors as a bunch of basket cases. She was furious. What right did some psychologist who had not lived through the Holocaust himself have to label and dismiss a generation of broken but brave child survivors? For all her problems, Flora was hardly a basket case. She had struggled to learn to live in the world. She was in the process of finding a way, and she could help others too.

Flora proceeded to do something that no one had done before: through Jewish organizations and her network of friends and colleagues, she identified eleven adults who had survived the Holocaust as children, interviewed them at length, and wrote the first psychological paper exploring what coping techniques they had used to survive the war and what techniques they used as adults to overcome problems related to their war experiences.

"I had to make my trauma the subject of my work," she would recall years later, "because I *had* to. I couldn't do anything else. I was very upset about it. I wanted to be like everyone else. I didn't want to think about the war. I wanted to go to the beach. I wanted to be a pianist. But the only thing I could do was be a psychologist and understand what the hell had happened to me. My history is so complicated, and I always felt everybody else had done better than I."

No one had thought to do what she had: look at the *positive* aspects of having survived the Holocaust. Flora presented her findings in 1977 at a conference in Israel called the Second International Conference on Psychological Stress and Adjustment in Time of War and Peace. Her paper, titled no more succinctly, was called "Adaptive Mechanisms of Displaced Jewish Children during World War II and Their Later Adult Adjustment." She interviewed eight men and three women who had survived the Holocaust as children. In 1939, their ages had ranged from two weeks to eleven years old. Seven came from Eastern Europe, the other four from Western Europe, and they survived in a variety of circumstances, from roaming Ukrainian forests to being hidden in children's camps to living in Auschwitz. By the war's end, two had lost both parents and other family members, five had lost one parent, and the other three had lost several relatives.

Flora found that the coping strategies used by all of the children fell into three categories, the first of which she termed "maintenance of some emotional link to their families." Children in hiding, separated from both parents, maintained their connection by cultivating fantasies about them. The fantasies may have backfired later when they were reunited with their traumatized real parents, but during the war, the fantasies blurred their sense of loss. One of Flora's subjects, hidden in a French children's camp, reported that kids bragged about their families and made up stories in which the parents became younger and more beautiful. Absence made them heroic. Sometimes children assumed the role of a missing parent, taking care of the others.

The second mechanism she called, simply, "defiance." "The children," she wrote, "may have retained a sense of self by mobilizing their rage constructively," which took the form of taking any initiative to survive, from actual escape to simply buoying up others' optimism. One twelve-year-old boy carried a weapon in hiding; another focused on recalling his father's teachings from the Talmud to support his stoicism in the face of suffering; another, hiding in the forest, practiced long-distance running to prepare for his eventual escape from the Nazis.

Most interesting, however, was the third coping strategy many of her subjects had used: "avoidance of full awareness of traumatic realities." That is to say, their best friends were suppression and repression. In one case, a boy who discovered his dead brother and father proceeded to tell his mother that they had been taken away to work, and the mother chose to believe him, although she knew that he was lying. Older children reframed their fear and terror as adventures, not unlike what Roberto Benigni's character did for his young son in the concentration camp in the movie *Life Is Beautiful*, when he convinces the boy that the camp is actually a game in which the most compliant and inconspicuous contestant will win a tank.

The mechanisms Flora identified—fantasy, defiance, repression— involved strategies essential for surviving a horrifying existence. Flora's most traumatized subject resorted to every strategy he could. At a Czech work camp, he transformed his fear into curiosity about the guards' rifles, pestering them with questions. Later, in Russia, when his father and brother were shot, he simply refused to face the fact that they had died. Living later in the forest, he carried his wounded sister to safety, telling Flora, "I became a Tarzan during the war." Incredibly he then found himself in Auschwitz, subjected to Josef Mengele's medical experiments, which he tolerated through a combination of prayer, partial identification with his aggressors, and volunteering to help the other children.

Of course getting through the war was one thing, but adult life was another. Conclusions reached on the page by a psychologist, even one who had been a hidden child herself, bore little resemblance to the very painful, long, and messy journeys hidden children were taking in real life. In her paper, Flora touched on all the lifelong repercussions for child survivors that would start to become a more familiar litany fourteen years later at the First International Gathering of Children Hidden During World War II: distrust, shame, memory loss, isolation, anxiety, depression, marital and career instability, and an exaggerated need for safety and control. The survivors who found it easier to adjust were those whose parents survived, or who could recall and "describe harmonious family life before the war."

In regard to finding meaning in adult life, Flora wrote, accepting their Jewish identity was "the most powerful way to give meaning . . . to their suffering," even though acceptance involved reclaiming a heritage survivors had no memory of or had been taught to despise and pity. Similarly, in order to liberate themselves from the passivity of victimhood, survivors needed to overcome their resentment for problems that had been unfairly and harshly imposed on them—a process of taking responsibility for one's life that confronts all adults, to some degree.

In none of Flora's cases was there "an account of a loss of interest in living after the war." Her research had found not basket cases but people desperate to live like others. Trauma did not necessarily just create psychopathology; it could also launch new and stronger identities, not through dwelling on the disasters of the past, but by incorporating them into the conscious narrative of one's present life. Courage became part of their identity. One important means of integrating the past concerned the search for work that was in some way related to hidden children's war experiences. Her favorite example was a survivor who had never known his parents and who had spent his adult life in many unhappy jobs until he realized that he had a gift for handling emergency situations. Only when he became the head of a crisis intervention center did he begin to find himself.

So it had been with Flora herself, who turned her own psychological emergency into a study of others like herself, allowing her to clarify her own murky sense of self while helping others do the same. She had found her place in the world.

So when Carla Lessing asked her in the spring of 1991 to lead a workshop at the upcoming gathering called "Who Am I, Christian or Jew?" it hadn't taken her long to say yes.

SOPHIE'S CHOICES

On the periphery that first night of the Gathering stood another woman in her fifties who had decided only recently to attend, even though she lived just a short train ride away in Great Neck, Long Island. Dr. Sophie Turner Zaretsky had managed all these years quite well by refusing to peer too intently into the past. She had never been in psychotherapy because she felt that talking about the past would only make it worse.

Sophie arrived in New York in 1963 for her internship at New York Polyclinic. Inspired by a radiologist there, she began a residency in radiation and radiation oncology at Montefiore Medical Center in the Bronx, a hospital that had been founded in 1884 by leaders of New York's vast Jewish community to treat patients with tuberculosis and other chronic illnesses. Her intelligence and devotion to her work paid off with the position of chief resident. Few people were privy to the original motivation behind the intensity of her drive. Sophie needed to be at the top. As long as she remembered, she had always had to prove herself. She couldn't count on help from her family, because she didn't really have one, or her background, which she really didn't have, either. Colleagues might talk about their old neighborhoods in Brooklyn or the Bronx, or the uncle who had gone into medicine, but what did she have besides her mother? A few forgotten years of being a privileged Jew in Lvov, followed by the murder of her father and almost everyone else in her family, followed by six years as a Jew-hating Catholic schoolgirl, followed by years of confusion and near-poverty.

The chief of the department, most of the staff, and almost all patients were Jews, but Sophie never went out of her way to identify herself as Jewish. Between her ambiguous religious identity and the British formality that had mirrored so well her own diffidence and reserve, Sophie found little in common with the city's America-born Jews. As for the *Hasidic* Jews she saw everywhere in New York, they only reminded her of the racist caricatures promulgated by the Nazis.

At work she was assumed to be one of the minority of non-Jewish doctors. She didn't use any Yiddish words, and, in any case, her British accent would rob them of credibility. She didn't wear a Star of David around her neck, although she'd received several as gifts. More painfully, she lacked the narratives of Jewish life and ancestry that bound her Jewish-American colleagues to the past and to one another. She could hardly join in the small talk about difficult fathers, troubled siblings, or loving grandparents.

In her early thirties, Sophie took a big step out of the shadows of her past. One Yom Kippur, when a colleague at Albert Einstein asked her to cover for him, she heard herself say, "I'd be happy to, but I'm Jewish."

In 1969, she started work as an attending physician in radiation oncology at the Albert Einstein College of Medicine at Yeshiva University. She developed a friendship with a German radiologist for whom she felt sympathy because, as a child, the woman and her family had been starving toward the end of World War II, when all of the country's resources were diverted by the Nazis' lost cause. Sophie could hardly bear a grudge against its innocent German victims. On the other hand, she felt uneasy when the German friend invited her to a party at her home and she arrived to find a gathering of other recent German immigrants—doctors, lawyers, educated people. Who were these Germans drinking cocktails and chomping deviled eggs, whose family secrets weren't known, even by them?

Now that she was publicly a Jew, the head of her radiology department came to her later with a touchy matter. He'd received an application for a residency from a German who had disclosed on his application that his father had been a Nazi. The man was an excellent radiologist, the department head explained, but if Sophie objected, he wouldn't hire the applicant. Sophie studied the application and gave her consent, reassured by the man's candor and reasoning that he had lived with a terrible burden and shouldn't have to pay a price for his parents' crimes. Sophie and he would go on to have a cordial relationship.

In her work, she began extending herself a bit more for her Jewish patients, spending extra time with the older ones. It was not only a sign of her growing comfort level with other Jews, but also a way to connect with the older generation after losing so many of her own family members.

In the 1970s, in an interview that her relative Alice Herb, Uncle Emil's niece, conducted for the YIVO Institute for Jewish Research, Sophie said, "I used to be envious of people who had a family with grandparents, and I've always liked old people for this reason. I get along with them. When I have old patients, really old patients, really leathery old people, I guess this is how I imagine grandparents. I always spend more time with them." Radiation oncology—the use of radiation to kill cancer cells—was more than her occupation. "It's almost like being a missionary," she said as her career took off. "Maybe it's a justification for living. I think that's logically so."

If Sophie pushed herself to "be somebody," it wasn't in any mundane sense. In hard work and achievement she had found an actual identity, some solid ground to stand on from which she could more calmly look back at a remote childhood that didn't quite figure into her calculations of self.

By this time in her career, she had another reason to justify her life. Her serious romantic experience had been limited to one relationship with Monty in London, and another with a Mexican-born resident at Polyclinic during her first year in New York. That relationship had triggered the revelation that what she really wanted was to marry a Jew. A Jewish man, that is, who was neither Hasidic nor uncultured. She wanted—the thought had become conscious—to help rebuild the Jewish race and to deny Hitler his victory.

She had both a colleague and a patient to thank for meeting her husband. Janet Pinner, an Englishwoman and colleague at Montefiore, threw a party at her little Upper East Side apartment in early 1970 and invited Sophie as well as another resident, named Marvin Rotman. However, her mother was visiting from Montreal, where she had moved to be close to Putzi. She insisted that Sophie go— "Don't worry about me"—but Sophie wasn't convinced she should until, the day before the party, she was examining an elderly black woman at Albert Einstein who was dying of cancer. As she often did during her examinations, she asked the woman a bit about her life.

Concentrating to understand her thick southern accent, Sophie made out that the woman told people's fortunes.

"You can actually see into a person's future?"

"That's what they tell me," the woman said. "Now let me see that hand."

As a woman of science used to stories with unhappy endings, whether in her own life or that of her patients, Sophie was extremely skeptical. Not once in her life had she ever visited a psychic or a fortune-teller. But this was one of her beloved patients, who was not going to live much longer.

Sophie gave the woman her hand, which she grasped in the papery palm of her own. "All right, Dr. Turner," she said, "let's see what this hand says."

The woman ran her finger along Sophie's palm and after a moment drawled, "You are very hesitant about something, Dr. Turner. I feel it's an event, a party, you've been invited to. You've been invited somewhere and you're not sure you should go."

Sophie felt a shiver go through her body.

"But you should. You should go, Dr. Turner." Then she added, "Yes, and there will be a lot of travel in your life."

Although that second prediction sounded stock, Sophie was so impressed by the first that the next evening she made her mother comfortable in her Manhattan studio apartment—where Sophie kept only a few relics of their life in Busko-Zdrój on top of her dresser: her catechism, rosary, and little Steiff bear, Refugee—and took a taxi to the Upper East Side.

Janet Pinner's small apartment was filled with men and women in their thirties and forties. Marvin introduced her to his friend, a somewhat older man named David Zaretsky, who was also Jewish. David, in turn, introduced Sophie to his neighbor, a tall, extremely good-looking man dressed casually in a denim shirt unbuttoned to his sternum.

Sophie ended up sitting on the sofa talking to the good-looking guy, who, she soon learned, was one of the rugged models used in the Marlboro Man cigarette advertising campaign. Instead of warning him about the carcinogenic properties of cigarettes, she found herself entranced by this six-foot figment of Madison Avenue's imagination. She even got to hold his hand when he showed Sophie a splinter that she expertly removed. However, her burgeoning interest in him evaporated at his mention of a girlfriend.

"You're very good at that," David said, looking on.

"I'm known for my splinter removals," Sophie replied.

His wound cleaned, the Marlboro Man excused himself, leaving David to Sophie, who soon interrogated him.

David Zaretsky had been born into a large immigrant Jewish family in South Bend, Indiana—it hadn't occurred to Sophie that Indiana *had* Jews—that then moved to Brooklyn when he was three. Now he was a venture capitalist focusing on medical advances. He had served in the Korean War in counterintelligence in Germany, where his job, ironically, had been to visit displaced persons camps and try to identify the Communists among the Jews there. He happily considered himself a failure at this task—he had no interest in making any more trouble for the Jews—and was far more successful at hanging out with his Jewish buddies at a Munich café.

On the basis of this information, Sophie quickly calculated his age as forty or a bit older. When he asked about her, she confined her autobiographical comments to the fact that she was born in Poland. He didn't press her for details then, or ever, really. Maybe, Sophie would eventually conclude, he couldn't face her past himself.

When they parted, David told her, "I'm in the phone book."

Sophie sighed inside; she felt that their comfort around each other warranted something a little more aggressive on his part. She stole another glance at his left hand to make doubly sure there wasn't a wedding ring on it.

She didn't hear from him, and after two weeks her colleague Marvin reassured her that he still thought David Zaretsky was a very good idea and told her to be patient. Actually, she hadn't been able to get him out of her mind. When he finally did call, he proposed they double-date with another friend of his named Frank. Frank had nightclub tickets to see Leslie Uggams, who had recently finished hosting a season of *The Leslie Uggams Show* on CBS—the first black person to host a network variety show since Nat King Cole back in the 1950s.

A limousine came to pick her up. The only other limousine that had ever come for her had contained the Nazi Leming. Her doorman's eyes popped when David emerged in formal wear and helped Sophie into the limo, where his friend Frank was sitting with a beautiful young Norwegian woman. Forewarned that they were going out on the town, Sophie wore a cocktail dress she'd bought in London under a short lynx coat made by a Polish furrier friend of the family in Canada.

The limo turned out to be on loan, but by the end of the evening, they were hooked. Three months later, when she met David's family at Passover, her head reeled from all the siblings and cousins she encountered. She wasn't used to big Jewish family gatherings, yet it seemed to be exactly what she was missing. The sudden death of David's brother-in-law in September brought them still closer together. She took David to Canada to meet her mother, Aunt Putzi, and Putzi's family. Sophie and David were soon inseparable. In December, David's good friend Burke and his wife, Gini, from London, came to New York to stay at the Hotel Elysée on East Fifty-Fourth Street. After observing David and Sophie, Burke and Gini asked the two of them, "Why aren't you getting married? Look, David, you were the best man at my wedding, and if you want me to be the best man at yours, I strongly suggest you get married in the next ten days, before we go back to London."

Why not, indeed? David had what Sophie craved: a great feel for family and friends, and plenty of both. Everyone who seemed to come into David's orbit remained there. He made her laugh, he was loving and could show his love, something Sophie didn't know how to do, but which she suspected he could teach her. And it didn't hurt that he wrote her romantic poems, especially since Sophie hardly thought of herself as romantic.

Suddenly the wedding machinery was in frantic motion. David's newly widowed sister Mollie drowned her grief by organizing the entire event with the help of her three daughters—Ellen, Ilyne, and Debbie. Her brother Bill owned a catering company and wedding facility on

Long Island, with an open date on December 19, the day before David's friends were scheduled to return to London. Mollie supplied her own rabbi, Saks Fifth Avenue supplied the dress, a jeweler named Arthur King supplied the wedding rings. Without a formal proposal, without ever having discussed whether to have children, without even much of a chance to get to know each other's bad habits, David Zaretsky and Sophie Turner, née Selma Schwarzwald/Zofia Tymejko, were married. In the insane rush of it all, they forgot to eat at their own wedding and had to stop for sustenance at a diner in Queens on their way to the honeymoon suite at the Hotel Elysée that David's friend, the owner, had donated for the night.

They were both back at work on Monday (the honeymoon in Mexico came a month later). In 1972 and 1973, they had two sons, Daniel and Jeffrey. In the mid-1970s, Sophie left Albert Einstein for Long Island College Hospital in Brooklyn, and they moved from Manhattan to Neponsit, an exclusive neighborhood on the Rockaway Peninsula in Queens. She stayed at Long Island College Hospital until 1985, when she took a job at North Shore University Hospital in Manhasset, Long Island, and their family moved to nearby Great Neck, one of the most Jewish suburbs in America.

Sophie saw her mother regularly now. Before Sophie met David, they were both single, lonely, and ecstatic to be together again. Laura would come down to New York from Montreal to see the sights and take the Circle Line Sightseeing Cruise around Manhattan. Sophie would fly to meet her in Canada for car trips to Niagara Falls and the Finger Lakes region of upstate New York. Laura had always loved nature and was interested in all forms of culture, but it was the art of enjoying life that she practiced best, and they talked and laughed their way through New York's wine country. Laura started to travel widely and once, in Israel, discovered by chance her only living relative on her husband's side, a niece named Aliza Schwarzwald Bar, who had been hidden by Polish peasants and lost both her parents.

Aliza was almost exactly Sophie's age, but she had always known she was Jewish, and after the war had made it to Palestine, where she became a prominent educator.

"I always had this problem with not knowing where I came from," Sophie had told her cousin Alice several years before. "It was like being a person with a void around her, except for my mother, which was a saving thing because she's a very strong person and I think she somehow managed to direct me in some way. That I was able to function, that I didn't crack up or anything like that, like a lot of people have. So I think it's to her credit, really, that she kept things going the way she did." There was no telling how far Laura Turner would have gone had she not had the misfortune to be a Polish Jew in the fourth and fifth decades of the twentieth century. She spoke five languages fluently—Polish, German, English, French, Yiddish—and she could get by in a sixth, Hebrew.

When Sophie became eligible for citizenship by 1968, she was entitled to bring her mother to the States on a visa, but her mother was ensconced in Montreal and Sophie was single and still not committed to staying in America. By 1971, however, Sophie, married and settled in New York, brought her sixty-two-year-old mother to the city, where David had found her a bookkeeping job at a Wall Street firm. She moved into Sophie's old studio apartment in the same Upper West Side complex where Sophie and David and their two sons lived. She followed the first job with another at Merrill Lynch, where she handled international accounts. She was so efficient that, on retiring, she had to be replaced with two full-time employees. Avid about learning, Laura made full use of Manhattan's educational institutions and also began auditing courses at Hunter College in Manhattan—linguistics, art history, comparative religions, and philosophy.

Sophie and her mother were once again in each other's daily life, but they kept one secret from each other, and it was the same one:

what had happened during the war, and that they each endured their separate realities during those years. Once in a great while, Laura would gently broach the subject of their lives in Poland, but Sophie didn't want to hear about it. Sophie had learned too well from her mother how to put the past behind her and move forward. She avoided movies and books about the Holocaust, limiting her knowledge of World War II to a single volume, Herman Wouk's *Winds of War*. As for psychiatry, that was for others. By 1970, history's greatest genocide was already the subject of numerous books and movies, remembrance days and academic conferences, even caricature and satire. But it was a subject that Sophie knew almost nothing about.

Sophie had met only a few other hidden child survivors by chance in the New York City area. A fellow resident named Ruth Rosenblatt, herself a survivor, introduced her to a former hidden child she thought Sophie would like. Sophie and Flora Hogman hit it off immediately. The two women were joined not just by history, but also by a similarly wry sense of humor. They also shared something else: frustratingly impaired memories of their childhoods. Sophie referred to her brain as "Swiss cheese." Flora just liked to say that she couldn't remember anything.

They met often, including at Flora's ecumenical holiday parties, which featured a mix of Christmas carols, Hanukkah songs, and Japanese New Year songs introduced by Flora's Japanese companion, Naka. Yet their bond was real: two child survivors who had been in their forties before they could grieve at last for the little girls who had almost died and who could do nothing to save the parents and relatives who did.

In the spring of 1991, when Flora told Sophie she had been asked to lead a workshop at the Gathering, Sophie decided to attend after all.

Carla's husband, Ed Lessing, now a sixty-four-year-old graphic designer with a full head of curly brown hair and a short beard tinged with gray, had fought attending the gathering harder than anyone, even though his wife had spent much of the past year help-ing to make it all happen.

"Aren't you coming?" Carla had asked him just ten days before, realizing that he'd yet to make a commitment.

"Naw," he'd told her. "Why should I come? And what would I do there? You're going to be busy and I will just have to hang around until it's over." As far as Ed was concerned, Carla was the Holocaust survivor—or "hidden child," the new magical term that the media had seized upon. The television networks had already been out to the Lessings' carriage house in a suburb of the city to interview them while they sat on the new swing set with their grandchildren—the grandchildren who never would have existed had the two of them not been sheltered and saved by Christian strangers.

"Don't you think it will seem a little strange, Ed, if you're not there?" Carla said. "The husband of one of the organizers? When you're also one of us?"

He was still not convinced.

"My own brother is coming from Israel especially for the confer-ence, Ed," Carla added. "It would be nice if you could be with him."

Ed relented. Had he not suffered too—suffered in many ways more than his wife?

The remarkable thing, Ed thought, watching the hidden child survivors at the hotel, was the power of repression and denial, and the fear of touching old wounds. Ed had behaved for the entire last year as though none of it concerned him. What did he have in common with these miserable survivors? He prided himself on not being one of these people who came from Poland or Russia and could barely speak English. He had his own graphics design business right here in New York City. In any case, he was, perhaps understandably, not much of an optimist; his philosophy was that he'd seen it all, and the rest was going to be "a repetition of the same damn thing."

Ed hung out near the registration desk on the seventh floor of the

Marriott in Times Square, curious to see what kind of people would show up at the First International Gathering of Children Hidden During World War II. They poured out of the elevators, balding men and freshly coiffed women, most of them in their fifties, with a few, like Ed and Carla, in their sixties and a smattering of people in their forties, born during the war. He stood to the side and watched as they registered at a long table, received their packets, their meal tickets, and pinned their name tags to their shirts and blouses. They looked quizzically at their programs and stopped by tables selling Holocaust-related books. One table, soliciting oral histories of the attendees, belonged to the not-yet-opened United States Holocaust Memorial Museum in Washington, DC.

Within minutes, they were turning to one another, forming clusters, shaking hands, peering at name tags, hugging. The conversations bubbled with a variety of accents and languages. Ed clung to his pride, indulging his lifelong tendency to stand apart and observe. He stood in wonder as some men and women began to cry, their defenses needing only the sight of other hidden children to give way. The air was alive with something hard to describe: a mix of sorrow, history, humanity, connection, and release. Ed inched closer and squinted behind his eyeglasses to see what was on some of the name tags: not just their names, but beneath them, "Hidden in Poland," "Hidden in France," "Hidden in Hungary."

Ed realized that he was looking at the greatest rebuke to Hitler's evil. The Nazis had murdered Jewish children with an unconscionable single-mindedness and thoroughness. As Himmler pointed out to senior SS officers in 1943, there was no point in "eradicating the men" yet "allowing the avengers in the shape of the children to grow up for our sons and grandsons." But he had missed a few, and here they were.

Ed blinked and saw not a confusion of middle-aged men and women, but the frightened children they had all once been. In an instant, he crossed over the border from aloofness and began to cry with the rest of them for their losses, and for all the other children who had perished. The dead too had been hidden children; they just hadn't been hidden long enough. As for the living, they had come so close to death in so many cellars and closets and convents and fields all over Europe, and yet somehow they had all ended up together after forty-five years, members of a secret society of silence, a diaspora that had gone unnoticed and unknown for decades.

I never knew there were so many like me, Ed thought. Everyone he saw was so intimately acquainted with death, harboring a story so implausible, so sad, so haunting, that strangers couldn't be trusted with it. He was embarrassed. Had it not been for his wife being one of the organizers, he wouldn't have come. He would have stayed home, safe in his bubble of forgetting.

Bulletin boards had been set up as a central clearinghouse for information of all kinds:

"I am looking for Michel and Paul R. from Antwerp. . . . we were hiding in the same Flemish village: Belsele . . ."

"Pour Sara F. nous étions aussi à Trelon au Sanotorium . . ."

"If you were hiding in Charleroi, 1942–45 . . ."

"I am looking for the name and address of the convent where I was hidden. Can you please help me find it?"

"If you were in the convent of Egletons . . ."

"Looking for Clara S. living in Bucharest during the war. Call me . . ."

"Spent 1941–44 in Transnistria Labor/concentration camp. . . . Looking to meet anyone from Chernowitz or Transnistria . . ."

"Looking for classmates from Constantza Romania 1942–44 Jewish community school . . ."

"I am searching for survivors of the family of Philippe D (Austria) . . ."

"I am looking for my sister Celeste J. . . . She was badly wounded in August 1941, in Zaliesciche, Poland, in the crossfire between the Germans and the Polish forces. I last saw her in the town's hospital—but the next day I was deported and never saw her again. . . . God bless you for your help in finding my long-lost sister. . . ."

"To anyone who was in Theresienstadt . . . did you know at that time a woman named . . . ?"

On another board were copies of an assortment of notes and letters Jews had tossed out of the cattle cars on the way to the camps, in the hope that they would reach loved ones: "We are going to Poland to work," one said. "Do not worry about us."

Ed—and Carla and Flora and Sophie—sat in the hotel ballroom with the others, listening to the Gathering's opening remarks by Abraham Foxman, the national director of the Anti-Defamation League, the Gathering's godparent organization. Foxman talked about hidden children's "struggle to be with other people." He spoke of the "pressures building over the years. . . . As our presence here demonstrates today, we can be silent no more. Our presence proclaims the need to speak, to bear witness, to remember the monstrous past that robbed us of our childhoods, and that has cast a shadow on our lives ever since."

The unbearable randomness of it all hung over the proceedings like a disturbing cloud. The attendees could spend their entire lifetimes trying to ascribe meaning to the events that had marked the difference between their lives and the others' deaths, and get nowhere at all. How was it that, in Holland, a country that lost three-quarters of its Jewish population, Carla and her immediate family had survived? Why had Flora reached middle age while her mother had not and her best friend Rachel would forever remain an eight-year-old girl with her hand raised at a school desk in Nice, France? What explained the fact that, in the midst of state-sponsored mass murder, Sophie and her mother had stayed alive in Poland under the noses of the very men who wanted to kill them?

MY NAME MAY HAVE
BEEN MIRIAM

The most famous child survivor of the Holocaust in the 1950s was not Anne Frank—after all, she didn't survive—but a young woman named Hannah Bloch Kohner.

NBC television's *This Is Your Life* was one of television's first reality shows, in which host Ralph Edwards surprised a guest, often a celebrity, by reuniting him or her with friends and family members the guest hadn't heard from in years. The program didn't shy away from either political controversy *or* questionable sentimentality, as when guest Reverend Kiyoshi Tanimoto, who had survived the atomic bombing of Hirsohima in 1945, was introduced to the copilot of the *Enola Gay*.

On May 27, 1953, *This Is Your Life* ambushed a beautiful young woman in the audience, escorted her to the stage, and proceeded, in a matter of minutes, to package, sanitize, and trivialize the Holocaust for a national television audience. Hannah Bloch Kohner's claim to fame was that she had survived Auschwitz before emigrating, marrying, and settling in Los Angeles. She was the first Holocaust survivor to appear on a national television entertainment program.

"Looking at you, it's hard to believe that during seven short years of a still short life, you lived a lifetime of fear, terror, and tragedy," host Edwards said to Kohner in his singsong baritone. "You look like a young American girl just out of college, not at all like a survivor of Hitler's cruel purge of German Jews." He then reunited a stunned Kohner with Eva, a girl with whom she'd spent eight months in Auschwitz, intoning, "You were each given a cake of soap and a towel, weren't you, Hannah? You were sent to the so-called showers, and even this was a doubtful procedure, because some of the showers had regular water and some had liquid gas, and you never knew which one you were being sent to. You and Eva were fortunate. Others were not so fortunate, including your father and mother, your husband Carl Benjamin. They all lost their lives in Auschwitz."

It was an extraordinary lapse of sympathy, good taste, and historical accuracy—history that, if not common knowledge, had at least been documented on film. It would be hard to explain how Kohner ever made it on *This Is Your Life* to be the Holocaust's beautiful poster girl if you didn't happen to know that her husband—a childhood sweetheart who had emigrated to the United States in 1938—was host Ralph Edwards's agent.

Hannah Bloch's appearance was a small, if crass, oasis of public recognition for Holocaust survivors—and child survivors especially—in a vast desert of indifference. It would be decades before the media showed them this much interest again.

Now, almost thirty-eight years to the day after Kohner's appearance, child survivors—the hidden ones—were in the spotlight at last, but far more important, they were visible to one another.

Myriam Abramowicz, one of the Gathering's godmothers, watched as attendees approached the large rolling bulletin board on which survivors had posted photographs from the war years. A photo of seven-year-old Sophie in her communion dress was among them. Despite a sign warning survivors to post copies, a lot of them were precious originals. Two survivors, one a few years older than the other, stood at the wall, arm in arm, studying a photograph of a group of girls.

"I remember you liked tomatoes," the older one said to the other.

Tears sprang into the younger one's eyes.

Myriam walked over and asked about the photo.

"We were both in the same home," the older one explained. "I was twelve and she was seven. She liked tomatoes so much she would trade anything for them in the dining hall."

"I'm crying," the younger one said, "because until this moment I really couldn't remember anything. I had no one to tell me how I was as a child. I have no idea who I was then. My parents never came back, and the whole time has been a blank. But the tomatoes—I can see myself now."

Unexpected reunions and connections were the norm. A member of the contingent that had come all the way from Poland had, as a baby, been thrown out of a transport train, tightly wrapped in a pillow, and rescued. Now a grandmother, her only clue to the identity of her biological family was her mother's first name. She was approached by a man at the Gathering who had once lived in her family's Polish town, had known her parents and older brothers, and now had spotted her in the crowd because of her resemblance to her mother. And so, by chance, she was reunited with her lost family through a stranger's memories.

For most of those at the Gathering it was the first time they felt safe to share their secrets with anyone. One man even unbuttoned his shirt and showed others the comforting Christian cross he had worn around his neck for years but had never before shown a soul.

Susan Sanders, a social worker in her thirties, had convinced her entire family to come. Susan had grown up in New York, afraid to ask questions about her mother's experiences and the grandparents missing from their lives. Her curiosity had deepened in graduate school at Berkeley after hearing about groups for second-generation survivors and seeing Myriam Abramowicz's documentary *As If It Were Yesterday*.

When she learned about the Gathering a few years later, she convinced her mother—who by then had moved to Delray, Florida—to sign up and confront her past for the whole family's sake. Watching the proceedings, Susan was mesmerized by the sight of so many people who had "the same investment." Almost immediately she was relieved that her mother had found a community. During a break, a journalist from the *Palm Beach Post* collared her mother, who reluctantly shared her story and wound up on the *Post*'s front page the following Monday, becoming a local celebrity whose background surprised even her closest friends.

Flora Hogman took mental notes as she watched others pour out their hearts and their hidden pasts to journalists. Something about it troubled her. Later, in an article she wrote about the conference for the New York State Psychological Association, Flora would speculate about the paradoxical effects of all the media attention: "Such belated recognition and sometimes 'awe,' while it provided a thrust of energy, with strong beneficial effects for the victims . . . is also safe for the outside world. It is a part of history, distant for those who listen. At times it might feel a bit phony. Why did it have to wait fifty years and happen by chance? In addition, the press, while giving due to the hardships of these survivors, also emphasized resilience against impossible odds. It could provide a temporary feeling of grandiosity for the victim. . . . Does it represent a real sense of acceptance of the suffering?"

Away from the media, however, solidarity, solace, and perspective were easier to achieve. The conference converted feelings of shame into a new currency—pride and a sense of community, continuity, and reconnection.

A surprising number of former hidden children had, like Sophie, Flora, and Carla, gone into helping professions; they were physicians, social workers, psychologists, psychiatrists, and psychoanalysts, and many had written about the "hidden child phenomenon." Not that these career choices were indicative of any inclination to open up themselves. Bloeme Evers-Emden, a child psychologist who had been hidden in Holland until August 1944, when she was caught by the SS and sent to Auschwitz, had not been able to talk about her experiences with her husband or any of their six children. She summed up the logic behind the hidden children's silence: "They adapted very quickly to their new surroundings, hardly crying for their parents—an important survival tactic. The reasoning seemed to be, 'I must surely have been a bad child that my parents gave me away; I must be a very good child now lest these people give me away.'" Moreover, their grief and anger had to compete with survivor's guilt: why had they survived when so many children perished in the camps and elsewhere? And there had been guilt about the living as well—guilt over their lost love for parents who survived and rejoined, or tried to rejoin, their children, many of whom had really known only their hiding parents. Evers-Emden found that while two-thirds of surviving parents felt that the bond with their reunited children had been restored, only a third of the children felt that way.

While many hidden children had become high-functioning professionals, they had also grown up with an impaired ability to form lasting bonds and close friendships, or even to seek temporary therapeutic bonds. After the Gathering, these wounds began to surface in written accounts that were filled with cries of loneliness and isolation. In the Hidden Child Foundation newsletter, which began publishing shortly after the conference, "Felicity G.," who was pulled out of a train bound for Auschwitz, hid as a Catholic, and survived the war to marry an Orthodox rabbi, would write: "All my life I have felt

I lived a lie. Always, even to this day, it seemed that I really did not belong anywhere."

"As I got older," wrote Renee Kuker, hidden for five years by Polish Catholic peasants, "I could not shake that feeling of my unimportance in relation to others and in relation to events. . . . I felt like a stranger on earth, an unwelcome intruder." After being hidden in a Czech orphanage, Chava Kolar became "distrustful of the whole world and of every person in it. . . . I have never succeeded in really belonging, in feeling completely at ease with people, even with friends, in forming one single lasting bond."

Often forgotten, even among the forgotten, were the hidden *infant* survivors. The most heartbreaking entries in the pages of the Hidden Child Foundation newsletter would be appeals for information from former infants, hidden by Catholics, who had lost their real families and never learned the first thing about their original Jewish identities, not even their real names:

I was told that someone found me on the steps of a house on Ochota in Warsaw. . . . I had a ribbon with a note attached on my left hand: "Zofia Jadwiga, born February 17, 1942. Do not give any information at any time."

I am looking for information about my background. I have done lots of research for seven years and have gotten nowhere. I have been told that I was born in a camp in Holland in the first half of 1941. . . . I had dark, full hair, dark eyes, no marks. My name may have been Miriam.

THE HIERARCHY OF SUFFERING

I quickly found that no one wanted to hear about my experience," the Jewish scholar and author Yaffa Eliach told the *New York Times* just before the Gathering. She, her mother, and younger sister had hidden from the Nazis in Poland in a cave under a pigsty. Four months after the Russians reoccupied her hometown of Vilna in July 1944, Polish partisans shot her mother and younger brother, after which an uncle took Eliach to Palestine, where she discovered there was no audience at all for a hidden child's grief.

After psychotherapist Maya Freed's parents escaped the Warsaw ghetto when she was an infant, she was left with strangers and at orphanages. Reunited with them after the war, she didn't complain to her parents about her nightmares of "lonely train whistles, claustrophobic rooms, loud noises, and sensations of hunger" because her own parents either dismissed her dreams when she brought them up or construed them as criticism of them, rather than frightening memories to which she couldn't attach remembered experiences. They thought her ungrateful for all they had done to save her. When, as an adult, Freed asked her mother what she had been like, her mother told her that she was "a cute, happy child" whom everyone admired.

"Nobody wanted to hear what I had to say," Freed wrote. "Moreover, I was 'too young to have suffered.' Even older hidden children assumed that I was more fortunate because I did not remember very much." Yet even in 1991, her psychological wounds were as raw as ever. "What most people do not even notice in their daily routines can precipitate hours of anguish for me: sirens, crying babies, stray animals, even leaving the house to go to work. Every separation causes anxiety."

"I never spoke about my experiences around my family," Marie-Claire Rakowski wrote. "I felt they'd suffered more, and that my suffering was unimportant compared to my mother and my sister. . . . I thought there are the Holocaust survivors, and then there's me." Ann Shore, another of the organizers, heard it from her own husband: "Well, you're not a Holocaust survivor. The only survivors are the ones who were in the camp." This was the consensus, although a 2000 study of 170 Holocaust survivors by Rachel Lev-Wiesel and Marianne Amir of Ben-Gurion University concluded that survivors hidden by foster families scored significantly higher on several of the measures of distress than survivors of the camps and those who hid in the woods and/or with partisans.

A dark thread running through hidden children's lives was the prejudice they'd experienced at the hands of older survivors, the ones who lived through the Holocaust as adults. Adult survivors had too often treated hidden child survivors as the second-class citizens of Holocaust suffering. For the vast majority of child survivors at the Gathering, it was the first time most of these child survivors felt *entitled* to their traumas.

Even at the Gathering itself, where everyone was on roughly equal footing, competition reared its head in other forms. At the workshop led by Flora Hogman, Sophie was shocked when Orthodox Jews attacked nonreligious ones for not living as Jews in Poland after discovering their original faith. She even apologized to them later in Polish on behalf of their Orthodox critics.

"What we have tried so hard to make others understand," Carla

Lessing still says twenty years after the Gathering, "is that there is no hierarchy of suffering. And that's difficult because people suffered so terribly."

It is an unfortunate fact of human nature that other people's suffering often interferes with our own, and that we are not above manipulating our distress until we are able to see it in the worst possible light. Or to quote the British historian Max Hastings on World War II: "One of the most important truths about the war, as indeed about all human affairs, is that people can interpret what happens to them only in the context of their own experiences. . . . The fact that the plight of other people was worse than one's own did little to promote personal stoicism."

The final message of the Gathering was that instead of jockeying for moral positions as victims, the survivors had important collective work to do. At the close of the weekend, Marie-Claire Rakowski told the assembled, "As Serge Klarsfeld said, 'You need to transcend your sorrows.' I'd like to give you a thirty-year homework assignment. I want to ask you to tell your story to your children, your families, your friends, your synagogues. Go to schools and tell your story. Tell your story to someone and you will begin the process of healing."

"Please, don't go back into hiding," said Abe Foxman, who followed her. "Out there, not in Warsaw, in Budapest, but in New York, Los Angeles, there are Jews, children, still in hiding. And that's your responsibility, to leave this room and make sure that you're in the open. . . . Let's help that other thousand, two thousand, three thousand, that weren't ready yet to be with us."

Just as NBC's 1978 miniseries *Holocaust* had made Hitler's Final Solution safe for dinner-table conversation—one in every two Americans had tuned in to at least part of it—the First International Gathering of Children Hidden During World War II detoxified a taboo topic for child survivors: their own experience. *Holocaust*, like Steven Spielberg's *Schindler's List* fifteen years later, sparked controversy over the commercialization of the Holocaust and the rights of others to portray (and trivialize) its victims; after the release in 1985 of his nine-hour documentary *Shoah*, French filmmaker Claude Lanzmann actually tried to dictate who should and shouldn't be "allowed" to represent the Holocaust. The Gathering's effect was quite different; it quietly inspired similar conferences where the forgotten victims themselves could try to reclaim the events that were being made into art and commerce all around them. The Gathering was followed a year later by a Hidden Child Congress in Amsterdam, where the opening address was given by Amsterdam's mayor (later Dutch minister of the interior), Ed van Thijn, who himself was a hidden child who had been freed from the Westerbork transit camp in a stolen ambulance and hidden by eighteen different families.

Standing at the podium, van Thijn removed his mayoral "chain of office" and said, "I am one of you, a hidden child." It was a powerful gesture. "As mayor, people tell me, I'm an excellent speaker, with much personal commitment, when we're dealing with the horrors of the war . . . at the annual Auschwitz commemoration, on Yom Hashoah. . . . But to say something personal, as a hidden child, and that at this venue, is a sheer impossibility." This conference was followed by the Second International Gathering in Jerusalem in 1993, then the First European Hidden Child Gathering in Brussels in 1995. In 1997, the World Federation of Jewish Child Survivors of the Holocaust and Their Descendants was formed, which now has fifty-four chapters (twenty-nine in the United States alone) in nineteen countries.

In an essay about Amsterdam's Hidden Child Congress, Frederik van Gelder of the Frankfurt Institute for Social Research quoted a participant on the subject of why so many child survivors now jumped at the new opportunities to meet:

What makes the difference is this: the feeling of being understood, "contained". . . . For our kind that means: crawling
into a hideout, a hole, with another victim, crying ourselves
to sleep in each other's arms. That is why our kind travel long
distances to speak to people we've never met before. We go to
these lengths to find others who share this feeling of desperation because we know that they too are chained for life to the
same endless nightmares of mass graves and burnt corpses.

Could it be any wonder that the least heralded of Holocaust survivors, the hidden children, took forty-five years to find each other
and attract the attention of the press? The Gathering would turn
out to be part of the leading edge of a revival of Holocaust coverage—a rebirth, really, since, according to James Carroll's study, by
1997 the rate of Holocaust stories was suddenly *twice* that of 1945,
and greater than in any year since. The approaching millennium,
or perhaps it was just the passage of a curiously requisite number of
years, had enabled Americans and the press at last to confront the
Holocaust.

Those two days at the Marriott made it easier for hidden child
survivors, the only people to whom their experiences belonged, to
reclaim their pasts. "Child survivors came out of hiding, literally,
symbolically, and internally. They were no longer isolated, secret
abnormal people," Australian psychiatrist Paul Valent would write
about the Gathering eight years later. "Existential meanings and purpose were difficult to extract from the Holocaust. Values, justice,
trust in fellow humans and a moral Jewish God were all shaken. Yet
other views could now emerge. Child survivors could take special
pride in their survivorship, their own brand of courage and heroism.
The little humiliated children came to defeat Hitler and the Nazi war
machine. . . . The survivors could thus be a sacred bridge between the
dead and the world."

And twelve years after *that*, Valent was still describing it as "one of the most unusual, historically unique gatherings I'd experienced. It was like a *family* gathering where I could sit down and talk to anybody there and it was like talking to a family member. We talked the same language, could understand each other's stories. We were very tolerant, resonating with each other in a way that had never happened to me before."

Flora was overwhelmed. "I was somebody finally! I had a specialty. But it was not the specialty I wanted. I wanted to be famous for something other than the Holocaust." At least the Gathering enabled her to feel suddenly that she was no longer a *hidden* hidden child, that she could finally share her knowledge, wisdom, and even her gallows humor with others.

Twenty years later, Carla still got goose pimples just thinking about it. After the Gathering, Ed and Carla got their car out of the Marriott Hotel garage and drove right into the teeth of a tremendous thunderstorm spiked with lightning bolts—a storm of biblical proportions, Ed thought, as if God himself was showing him the significance of what had just happened.

What Sophie remembered twenty years later was "crying for three days as I realized the scope of it all, with all these other professionals crying. It was only at the convention that I realized I belonged. I was overwhelmed, on top of which *Newsday* ran an article with a photo of me in my communion dress at the age of seven." Colleagues of Sophie who had worked with her for years saw the photo—perhaps never has a Jewish child looked more angelically Christian—but they didn't know the full story or what to say. It was hard for her. Like Flora, she felt pursued by the Holocaust. "I'm very empathic, but it's very hard for me to accept kindness and sympathy." Yet when one coworker, an American Jew, came into her office a few weeks after the Gathering to discuss the *Newsday* article and sat down, something happened that had not happened before the Gathering, not even with her own mother: Sophie cried.

PART THREE

THE GHETTO INSIDE

THE MINEFIELD OF MEMORY

It took many hidden children until the Gathering in 1991 to confront their pasts head-on. But memory, like faith itself, can be a mirage. One buries a memory, remembered in great detail, and finds, on digging it up, quite another.

Sophie, of course, had learned something about this at the age of eleven, when she found out that her conscious identity had been largely counterfeit. The discovery in 1948 that she was a Jew became a greater trauma even than the hazily recalled losses of her father and other relatives. In fact it would be another thirty years before she was able, with her mother's help, to unearth the emotional reality of her childhood.

In the late 1970s, when Laura was taking a course on European history at Hunter College, she mentioned her wartime experiences, and her professor asked her to put her memories down on paper and present them to the class. She balked, worried that it would give her nightmares. Why revisit all of it now, when she was in her late sixties and doing fine? She had friends and grandchildren. Sophie and her husband, David, however, thought it might be good for Laura and encouraged her to write the essay. Sophie knew that the experience pressed on her mother's consciousness, that she felt a need to talk about it. Maybe if she wrote it down, she would stop trying to engage Sophie in conversation.

So Laura sat down and handwrote twenty pages. It was a staccato montage of scenes, some only a sentence long. It was eerily free of emotion. The mentions of persecution and atrocities spoke for themselves.

Sophie and David went to hear Laura deliver her paper to her class. Afterward Sophie wondered what she had been thinking.

"First I used to throw my daughter across the ventilating shaft," Laura addressed the class, reading from her manuscript. "I had to save my child, no matter how. . . . The Germans came three times to get me to the gas chambers, but every time I pleaded with them in German and they left. . . . It was much harder the fourth time, they insisted I come with them, then they changed their mind and asked for the child only, they said the Führer loved children, he would take good care of her."

Sophie thought, How had she made the Germans change their minds, not once, but *four times*? The mother and daughter she was speaking about were *them*. Sophie had always regarded herself as a fatherless war orphan, not a survivor of the Holocaust. Without really being aware of it, she had put the memories away on a shelf, along with her only surviving toy from childhood, Refugee the bear.

"On my way home from work I had to walk outside the Jewish ghetto wall but there was a space through which you could see the ghetto inmates," Laura went on. "I could never pass by without fear, though sometimes I envied them, my life was so miserable, if not for my child I would have gone in there to be done with."

For a moment, Sophie felt as if she no longer knew her mother, just as she hadn't really known her then, or known herself, or understood the unfathomable forces of history that had murdered 90 percent of the Jews in Poland and left them with only the smallest amount of space in which to breathe.

"I never knew what to expect, coming home from work," her mother continued, clutching the pages in her hands. "My child started hating me, running away whenever she saw me coming. I realized one day I was on the way to becoming insane, I was driving both of us to a lunatic asylum. On that day I changed completely, I tried to regain the confidence of my child, gradually she started trusting me again."

And all this, Sophie thought, while her mother was coping with the loss of almost everyone she had loved, and working for the Nazis.

Her mother had been the difference between having memories, however painful, and being other people's memories, although she wondered if there would have been anyone left to remember them.

Finally, after seventeen pages, it came to an end: "I am not sure I did the right thing digging in my past," her mother said. "There are still nights when I wake up screaming. I cannot forget the sound of German boots, it still makes me shudder. This account should be called the 'story of a miracle.'"

In the early 1950s, after five years in Israel, Carla and Ed Lessing lived in Holland for a year and saw the van Geenens often, either at their house in Delft or at the Lessings' near The Hague. Now that they were no longer forced together in close quarters, they became genuinely close. Mrs. van Geenen, once moody and frightened, was very loving, and Walter van Geenen was especially attentive, as was his married eldest daughter, Corrie, who took after her personable, liberal father. She didn't seem in the least resentful that the overcrowding in the house during the war had pushed her to marry early. When Ed, now thirty, was suddenly called up by the Dutch army, Walter actually offered to hide him—again. Ed and Carla, however, used their U.S. visas to return to the New York City area, where they have lived ever since.

Every five years or so they would visit Holland and see the van Geenen family. When Walter died in the late 1960s, Carla remained close to his daughter Corrie. When Corrie died of a brain tumor,

Carla stayed close to her daughter Mieke and *her* daughter. She now knew four generations of the family that had protected her. It was only after both the elder van Geenens were gone that any of the children expressed regrets about hiding Carla, her mother, and brother. In the late 1990s, one of the van Geenen sons, now in his sixties, spoke up to Carla, saying, *We suffered too. We also had a horrible time.* He was under the mistaken impression that Carla's mother could have paid his parents more money after the war to compensate them. In fact, Carla's mother had little—during the war, she sold off her wedding presents in order to pay the van Geenens anything at all—and was being subsidized herself by her businessman brother.

Walter neither sought nor wanted official recognition for hiding Jews during the war, but he received it posthumously in 1979 when Yad Vashem, the Israeli memorial to the Holocaust, granted him and his wife the status of Righteous Among the Nations. Today the van Geenens are among five thousand Dutch so honored, second in number only to Poland's rescuers of Jews.

For Carla's husband, Ed, the postwar revelations were nothing short of stunning. In 1992, he and Carla, still freshly invigorated by the Gathering in Manhattan, flew to Holland for Amsterdam's Hidden Child Congress. In advance, Ed wrote the Netherlands Institute for War Documentation to obtain the contact information for Margrethus Oskam, the unsmiling Dutch chief of police who had saved his life during the war, and whom he hoped to see again and thank personally. Oskam had defied more than the Nazis; he came from a family of ardent Jew-hating, Nazi-sympathizing Dutch people. That fact may have allowed him to escape German suspicion, but keeping a secret of that magnitude from loved ones couldn't have been an easy task. Moreover, Ed found out that Oskam had personally hidden thirty Jewish men, women, and children.

The Institute for War Documentation wrote back that both Oskam and his wife had died, but they were forwarding his letter to their son, Margrethus Oskam Jr., a retired plumber, who invited him to visit.

After Oskam Jr. received Ed at his home in Holland, Ed recounted the events of December 29, 1943, and his narrow escape from the German raid that claimed the lives of the other Resistance fighters. "Listen," Ed asked him, "do you know if the men had any sisters or brothers with whom I could speak and tell them about these last moments?"

Oskam Jr. smiled. He obviously took after his mother, not his poker-faced father. "My father wasn't a very talkative man," he replied, "but, Mr. Lessing, there is one thing he told me that I'm sure of: none of the men in the hut were arrested that morning."

"It can't be!" Ed said.

"Some people came to warn them. They all escaped."

"That was me and my friend," Ed said, dumbfounded.

Ed's cousin suggested that Ed go on a popular call-in radio show, *Address Unknown*, on the Catholic network, hosted by a Jew, Hans van Willegenburg, to see if he could reconnect with the survivors of his Resistance cell. They rushed him on the air, where he told his story about the miraculously surviving group, thinking to himself, Who the hell's going to care about this?

At the end of the show, he was led out of the sound booth to a room where a dozen phones were ringing off the hook. Among the messages Ed was handed was one that said, "My brother was with you in the hut, but he doesn't live in Holland anymore, but I'll tell him. . . ." Another said: "Ed, I was with you in the hut and I live right around the corner from the radio studio. Come and see me when you're done."

It was almost too much to be believed. When Ed rang the doorbell of the apartment complex around the corner, a large woman he didn't recognize buried him in an embrace.

"You don't remember me, do you?" she said excitedly. "I was one of the couriers. I brought guns and newspapers, all kinds of stuff.

Thank God you survived! I didn't think you'd make it! Come, come see my husband."

In the next room, a silver-haired man he *did* recognize as Louis van Tiggelen, one of the Resistance fighters from the hut, rose from his chair. They hugged and cried and reminisced, amazed again to be alive at all. Lou showed him a couple of photographs he'd taken, one a picture of Ed at seventeen in the hut with one of the others, Herman Munninghoff, and another picture of the entire group at the hut's crude table. Ed teased Lou for taking any photos that could have been used by the Gestapo to identify them. Then Ed asked after his buddy, Jan Karman, the one who had escaped with him that day.

"I'm sorry, Ed, but Jan was arrested with two other Resistance men a couple of months later in another German raid and executed."

"I didn't know," Ed murmured, bowing his head. "Oskam's son told me everyone had escaped and I was hoping . . ."

After the Hidden Child Congress, but before he and Carla left for America, Ed mentioned to Margrethus Oskam Jr. that he'd like a splinter of wood or shard of glass from the hut as a souvenir. Oskam led Ed into the forest near the town of De Lage Vuursche toward the site of the Resistance fighters' hut. What had been a dense undergrowth of brush and Christmas tree–shaped shrubs had become in the last half century a forest of stately, soaring pines that bore little resemblance to what Ed remembered. When Oskam stopped and said, "It was here," Ed saw nothing at first. The hut was long gone. The only clue that this was the location of the hut that had been their home, and where Ed and the others had once risked their lives, was a slight depression in the ground, where they had buried their cache of stolen weapons and uniforms.

That December Ed was flown back to Holland to tape a television show, also hosted by van Willegenburg, to be aired on Christmas Day. With the Oskam family and his own cousins in the audience,

Ed recounted everything for the host: the hiding, the hut, the raid, the escape, his mother finding them on a bicycle, which she then gave to Jan Karman, who didn't make it, and how Ed had just visited his grave the day before.

"Let me tell you something, Mr. Lessing," the host said. "We've got part of a diary from your buddy, in which he describes the whole thing and how it was."

But that's impossible, Ed thought to himself. He was executed seven weeks after the raid. There's no way he could have written a diary. Ed didn't want to be a difficult guest, though, so all he said was, "That's very interesting."

"Mr. Lessing," the host went on, "I want you to know that your friend is here to talk to you."

As chills traveled the length of Ed's spine, a door to the studio opened and out walked a tall man, who took Ed's hand and said, "Thank God you're alive, Ed. I'm Herman Munninghoff." Ed was in shock. "Ed, you convinced Lou van Tiggelen that you were with Karman, but it was me—not Jan. Your mother gave *me* her bike and saved my life."

"Oh, my God!" Ed said, hugging Herman. "It was so long ago," he added, by way of excusing his confusion.

"After I took the bicycle, I wasn't more than a mile away when I was stopped by a German. He made me get off the bike and face a little pump house and spread my arms and legs, and then he frisked me for weapons. Thank God your mother made us bury them! I knew German," Herman continued, "and I went on the offensive a bit because I could tell what the German wanted. So I said, 'What the heck are you doing?! I'm coming from night school and my mom is holding dinner for me. What do you want? Do you want this bicycle? Do you want the flashlight? Here, take it! Just let me keep the bicycle so I can get home to my mother.' And he asked me what I was studying and I told him I was studying to be a notary public, which was true, if you remember, Ed. And then he let me pass and I pedaled away from my third brush with death that day."

After the taping, Ed asked Herman where the hell he had come from to be on the show.

"New Guinea, Indonesia," Herman said. "The producers called me, and when I told them I was headed here for medical reasons, anyway, they arranged this little surprise."

"Wait, Herman. What do you do in New Guinea to make a living?"

"Well, I wouldn't call it a living, Ed."

"What do you do there?"

"I became a Catholic bishop, Ed. I'm a Franciscan bishop and we build hospitals there for the natives."

Ed shook his head at how this man, whom he had long thought dead, who had come so close to death at the hands of the Nazis, had in fact survived and grown up to save lives in Indonesia, and he thought of all the other lives, millions of them, that would have been saved by the blameless Catholics and Jews who had not made it out of the Holocaust alive.

It was only well after the war that Flora began to see her childhood for what it was: a miserable drama played out with millions of others as part of a tragedy whose scope neither she nor the world would ever be able to comprehend. Yet Flora didn't know the entire truth even of her own drama. What of her memories of life at the convent? In the 1960s, she returned there, looking for answers, where she was confronted by a middle-age nun behind the same black iron grille.

"I was hidden here during the war," Flora said. "I wanted to thank you for saving my life."

"I was here, but I wasn't one of those involved with the children," the nun replied. "The ones who looked after you"—she rattled off a list of sisters—"I'm sorry to say that they've all died."

It felt like a rebuke to Flora for not having come sooner, on top of which the nun proceeded to lecture Flora, at that point a confirmed atheist, about the importance of religion.

"You don't have to be a Catholic, you know, but you must be *something*."

Flora returned to New York unsatisfied, but twenty years later, in the 1980s, a French friend, Ann, wrote Flora to say that, no, one of the nuns was still alive, the one who had been in charge of the children's chorus back in 1943. She was retired to a cottage next to the convent. But how, Flora wondered, could the nun she'd seen in the 1960s not have been aware of her? Ann volunteered to visit the surviving nun on Flora's behalf, and her subsequent letter to Flora proved how unreliable her memories had been. The old nun had been kind, Ann wrote, and said that she and others had tried so hard to reassure the children, urging them to play. The nun had, of course, understood the children's need for affection; she herself had lost her mother at a young age. Yes, they had taught the Jewish children how to make the sign of the cross, but she emphasized only because of the Germans living across the street.

Flora could barely reconcile this information with her own scrapbook of grim memories at the convent. Surely they had resented the children. Surely they had resented the interruption of their life of silent devotion. She couldn't possibly have hallucinated the nuns pacing and praying on the roof, their eyes heavenward. Flora couldn't have invented her desperate wish that they look at her just once.

The old nun had passed on the address of a Jewish woman named Lucy, who she said had taken care of the Jewish children because at the time she, just thirteen, was the oldest of them. In 1988 Flora flew to France to meet Lucy, now the owner of a bookstore in Paris. After greetings and hugs, Lucy launched into a jaundiced, detailed account of life at the convent that at times approached a tirade. "Yes," said Lucy, "they were constantly on the roof, praying. *I* had the responsibility of calming the children down! You were always so scared. But I never had anyone to talk to! No one to calm *me* down. I tried to get the nuns to look at me, but, you know, it was a sin for them to look at mere mortals! It was a worldly vanity to look at other humans! When there was a problem with one of you, I had to communicate with them through an intercom in the dining room! They never came over from their side of the wall. God forbid they should look at me when I spoke! I had to do everything—the wash, take care of the sacristy, the chapel, teach you the lives of the saints to keep you occupied. Oh, the nuns, they were too busy praying to help out! The only reason they took us in was because the archbishop ordered them to.

"But you know something?" Lucy said. "Despite it all, I've visited them every year since the end of the war. I suppose it's because they did save our lives. I mean, they *were* the closest things to parents in my life. My own didn't make it out of the camps."

Lucy showed Flora an old black-and-white photo of four girls on the steps of the little house that served as their dormitory.

"Am I one of them?" Flora asked her.

"No idea. So many children came through the convent on their way to other hiding places."

Later in her trip, when Flora drove to the convent in Nice, for the first time in twenty years, in her anxiety she turned into the wrong driveway, the one to the private mansion across the street. She explained her business to the guard, who indicated the convent in plain view across the way, adding that, yes, the Germans had occupied the mansion during the war. So close, Flora thought; how could she blame the nuns for keeping their distance from their Jewish charges?

Once in the courtyard with its terraced hill, Flora recognized nothing at first but the eerie silence of the place. What she remembered as an orderly garden was now running amok, and a middle-aged woman in street clothes was trying to weed the chaotic bed. To

Flora she explained that she liked to help the nuns tend the garden because, as a Christian child, she often came here after rationing during the war because the sisters gave out extra food. That's why, she continued, the Jewish children could come and go without being conspicuous. The Germans across the street were used to seeing the little ones. Still, Flora shuddered at the thought of her daily proximity to death. And the night she and the others were herded into the covered truck and driven to safety? How could the Nazis right across the street not have noticed, not have been suspicious?

As Flora looked up the hill to the house, still surrounded by the hedge of roses, the woman said, "You should go see the Mother Superior. She was here."

"But I've been told they were all dead except for one, who was in retirement."

"You were misinformed," the woman said, pointing across the courtyard. "That's the door."

Flora approached the entrance to the convent, wondering if she was about to meet her past in the flesh. She rang the bell and the door opened, as if expecting her. Before her was a row of vertical iron bars that separated the far third of the room from where she stood. Standing behind the bars was a tall figure in heavy robes.

This nun, the Mother Superior, smiled at her as she opened the gate in the iron grille and came toward her.

"You were here during the war?" she asked.

"*Oui*, Mère Supérieure. My name was Flora Hillel, but here I was Marie Hamon. And now I'm—"

"I know you," the Mother Superior said. Her mouth widened in a bigger smile. "I prayed for you. I prayed for you so much!" She clasped her hands, as if Flora were proof of God's existence, the most perfect vindication of her faith.

Flora's tears flowed down her face as she thought of her mother—it was, she realized, the first time she had been able to cry about her—

and she could barely get out the words, *"Merci. Je vous remercie mille fois pour m'avoir sauvé la vie."*

Flora reached out her hand, but the nun dodged it and swept in to embrace her, murmuring, "I prayed for you, Flora. I prayed for you so much. You had such an original name when you came. Flora," she repeated it. "I never saw you because we were not allowed to look at you, but I heard you. We listened to you from the roof."

It was true, then, that the nuns weren't allowed to look at them. But it was also true that they prayed for them on the roof. Unlike the last nun Flora had met here, the Mother Superior didn't lecture her about religion. Instead, unbidden, she started apologizing for prejudice—not the persecution and murder of the Jews by the Nazis, but the denigration of the Jews by the Catholic church. "We didn't know any better," she said. "We were taught we were better than other religions." She straightened to her full height in front of Flora. "We didn't know it was prejudice. We just thought we were better. It was very destructive. I'm sorry. I hope you'll forgive us."

Of course I'll forgive them, Flora thought. They saved my life. "We were so scared," the Mother Superior blurted out, tears on her cheeks. "We were frightened every day. The Germans were so close, across the street. Their boots stomping all the time, their loud voices interrupting our silence every night. We all lived on the edge of death. We all could so easily have been killed. I wish more of you would come back."

Flora promised to return.

"But don't go yet. There is someone else you must meet." She mentioned a nun whose name Flora didn't recognize. "She was a *soeur courière*," the Mother Superior said. "She hadn't taken a vow of silence and was entrusted with worldly chores, mostly making sure you children had enough to eat."

She led Flora by the arm to the door to the courtyard and gestured toward a frail old woman in a wheelchair in the garden, wearing a hat against the Mediterranean sun and dragging a hose as she propelled her chair along a path from one dry flower bed to the other. She watered each bed with a thin stream. A gray cat, leashed to the wheelchair's arm, had no choice but to follow her.

Flora introduced herself. Emboldened by her reception so far, she leaned down to hug the nun. Flora's touch was like a jolt of energy to the old woman, who suddenly became agitated. She began gesticulating wildly even as she continued to roll on to the next sunflower.

"There was so little to eat!" she exclaimed. "Every day I took my bicycle up and down the hill, looking for food in every store. I had to beg shopkeepers, these *merdouilles*!"

Flora winced at the profanity—"shitheads"—but in old age the nun obviously felt entitled to her obscenities.

"They didn't care! They wouldn't give me any extra milk, any extra bread, and with us having more and more children to feed here every day! Once I found a lousy piece of chocolate, but, oh, did I have to fight for it! I wasn't going to leave without it! And that Jewish couple we hid? They were so rich, but they wouldn't part with their black market food coupons! The *merdouilles*! I threatened to denounce them, but no—they wouldn't hear of it. *Merdouilles!*"

It would have been like a scene from a comedy if it weren't for the tragedy she was still railing about forty-five years later. Flora was freshly appalled by the realities she knew nothing about, but the nun's outburst appealed to her own irreverent nature.

"Let me tell you," the nun went on, "everyone is equal under God! Prejudice is nothing but ignorance, jealousy, pettiness"—she shook the hose with each word, sending undulating arcs of water into the flower beds—"and intolerance is responsible for all the violence! It's drilled into children from the beginning."

Flora walked behind her, smiling. The world had clicked one notch further into place. She was so glad to have reconnected with this chapter of her dark childhood. She had the most extraordinary feeling that her mother was near, closer than she could remember in years.

The memory of parting from her mother turned out to be flawed as well. It wasn't her mother who had taken her to the convent at the beginning of 1943. It *couldn't* have been her mother who took her there, since the parents would not have been allowed to know where their children were going, so that they could not give them up under interrogation or torture. Her rescue had actually been the work of one of the most successful Resistance operations of the war, the brainchild of Moussa Abadi. Abadi was a Syrian-born Jewish actor and political activist who earned a degree from the Sorbonne in child psychology, lost his scholarship due to anti-Semitism in 1936, then joined a French theater company, which toured America. After the company dissolved in 1938, he remained in Paris until the summer of 1940, when he set out for Nice by bicycle, where he was joined by his companion, a doctor named Odette Rosenstock. By 1942 they were working with an organization helping Jewish refugees who, like Flora and her mother, had sought a haven in Nice.

At the beginning of 1943, Abadi encountered a man who would change his life and that of hundreds of Jewish children. An Italian chaplain passing through Nice from the Eastern Front of the war told Abadi of Nazi atrocities there. Although the *Einsatzgruppen* and many of the death camps—Auschwitz-Birkenau, Belzec, Chelmno, Majdanek, and Janowska in Lvov—had been in operation for more than a year, the world had heard little of the Nazis' extermination of the Jews and believed even less. When Abadi refused to accept the stories, including the chaplain's reports of atrocities against children, the chaplain laid his crucifix in his palm and swore by Jesus Christ that it was all true. Based on this, as well as the persecution and deportation of Jews they had already witnessed, Abadi and Rosenstock committed themselves to saving Jewish children in Nice.

At the time, Abadi's cover was working for the bishop of Nice, Monsignor Paul Remond, as an elocution teacher for his seminarians. After Abadi presented his plan to save Jewish children to Remond, the bishop replied that saving children was at the core of his being. Together, they set up a network they called Reseau Marcel. Remond gave Abadi, who dressed as a priest, the improvised title of superintendent of Catholic education, an office, and a signed letter giving him access to Christian institutions in the area. Odette Rosenstock became known as Sylvie Delattre, a social worker in charge of refugee children in the diocese. On the strength of this single document, and the courage of Abadi, Rosenstock, Monsignor Remond, and many others, the lives of 527 Jewish children were about to be saved.

When she learned this, Flora's memory of her mother taking her to the convent was replaced by a vague recollection of her mother leaving her on a train platform with a man in a cape, a man who must have been Abadi himself, a hero who survived the war, married Odette Rosenstock, and became for many years a dramatic arts critic on French radio. He lived well into his eighties, but refused until almost the end of his life to discuss his work during the war.

Yet, even after all this, Flora continued to be surprised by her emotions. In the 1990s, she volunteered for an organization called Facing History and Ourselves, which since 1976 had been devoted to teaching teenage students about racism, anti-Semitism, and prejudice. Facing History and Ourselves often sent genocide survivors into classrooms to teach children how "to combat prejudice with compassion, indifference with participation, and myth and misinformation with knowledge."

Facing History sent Flora one afternoon to talk to junior high school students in Manhattan. On the way there, she figured it would be interesting for them to hear the story of how her friend Rachel had raised her hand when their second grade teacher in Nice had asked which students were Jewish. So Flora started to tell them, getting as far as the part where Rachel raised her hand and she didn't, and suddenly she choked up. The tears began to stream down her cheeks, and she couldn't go on. In that moment, Flora realized that she had never talked about Rachel before. For the first time in her life, that moment became real—certainly more real than when it had actually happened and the consequences of Rachel's and her different actions couldn't be known. It seemed to her that, merely to survive her childhood, Flora's psyche had had to put the terror of her narrow escape from deportation in a box and not open it again. Taken completely off guard, she began to weep right there, standing in front of twenty-five preadolescents, children who sat, silent, while Flora tried vainly to compose herself.

For many minutes, she cried, unable to collect herself enough to say one more thing. And yet in those twenty minutes she felt that some totally anesthetized piece of her childhood, the part that had sent one girl to her death and her to a kind of living purgatory from which she had still not escaped, had now regained its feeling. And she felt grateful that these children had freed her.

At the end of her crying, during which the students had barely moved, she wanted to continue the story, but just the thought of it brought new tears to her eyes. She looked out at the faces of the students who hadn't said a word, and knew that there was no need for her to go on talking. She knew that the students already understood what had happened to Rachel beyond what any of her words could have conveyed. The children could see well enough what had happened to her, little Flora Hillel, a child survivor of the Holocaust who had grown up to be a psychologist studying child survivors of the Holocaust, but who had still not fully come to terms with the catastrophe that, to these children, was now much closer and far more real than just another piece of obligatory middle-school ancient history.

AM I A CHRISTIAN OR A JEW?

By forcing so many Jewish children to hide or abandon their Judaism in order to survive, the Germans demonstrated that, while Jewish genes could not be renounced, a child's religious faith could be irrevocably altered.

This aspect of Sophie's story had been a subliminal attraction for me. The idea that the descendant of two long lines of Jews could so readily believe herself to be an anti-Semitic Catholic was fascinating. My own religious identity at times seemed tenuous; I was the product of an upbringing that was Jewish in name, culture, and history but without being religious. When my Catholic neighbor and friend John called me a "Christ-killer" at seven, I had no idea what he was talking about, so devoid of overt anti-Semitism and religious rivalry was the milieu of my childhood.

I was raised in a friendly fog of religious freedom, born into a community where no one appeared to give Jews a second look, even if anti-Semitism still operated openly in my father's textile industry, prompting him to briefly change his name to Ross. I grew up thinking that Jewishness, far from stigmatizing me, actually conferred an extra measure of appeal. Who wouldn't want to be a Jew in the same 1960s society as Sandy Koufax, Paul Newman, and Sammy Davis Jr.?

My parents were founding members of a Reform temple that looked like an extremely large split-level ranch house. The sedate services, which had been shorn of all alien traces of Hasidism, lacked joy. They were enlivened only by our charismatic, rabble-rousing rabbi, but he no longer believed in bar and bat mitzvahs because "thirteen was too young for any important decisions or for acquiring sufficient knowledge to be an adult Jew in any intelligent sense." To me, Judaism was not a world of specific rites and ceremonies, but a comforting community based on deeply humanistic and democratic values, humor, dissent, existential rumination, and a penchant for salty and smoked fish.

I identified with those who had lost touch with Judaism and had to decide later in life what being Jewish actually meant to them. After all, what it meant to be Jewish was not a question I could easily answer either, nor did I feel particularly compelled to answer, since I had always viewed competing religious beliefs as little more than an issue of which set of narratives you happened to grow up with. Although countless people throughout history have died rather than renounce their religion, the Holocaust's hidden children didn't have the luxury of conscious martyrdom. What did their intrinsic Jewishness consist of now if it could be so easily replaced?

And what did it mean to embrace it again?

I didn't know whom to identify with," Flora said of her years after the war. "I knew I was Jewish, but I didn't know I was Jewish."

Like Sophie and Carla, Flora had been born to assimilated parents with only a modest sense of religious tradition and little consciousness, before Nazism, of being the persecuted "other." Her ambiguous or diluted relationship to Judaism was not caused by her wartime experiences so much as exacerbated by it. Instead of simply professing a vaguely apologetic "cultural Jewishness" as an adult, like so many reform and nonobservant Jews everywhere, Flora has had to contend with a more serious confusion of religious identities—and perhaps more than most hidden children—since she had had multiple religions and spiritual disciplines foisted upon her. "I was lost. I was telling everyone I was Protestant, but I became an atheist." When she finally tried to resolve her religious identity in her thirties, "I figured out it was ridiculous." When she finally had a seder, she held it on Easter Sunday.

Flora became interested in studying other child survivors' struggles with split religious identity. In 1988 she published an article, "The Experience of Catholicism for Jewish Children During World War II." She interviewed four Jewish women who, as girls, were saved by being hidden in convents or Catholic homes. All four women she studied were so enamored of their emergency religion that initially two wanted to become nuns, one wanted to be a Catholic Polish girl, and the fourth wished to be a saint. After Liberation, however, they found themselves in a religious prison. "Feeling abandoned by the church after the war," Flora wrote, "alone and disillusioned, they still yearn to belong to the Christian world which is now seen as unreachable, while feelings linger that the adult Jewish world failed to protect them. . . . All four women struggled to develop an identity that would include their contradictory experiences, mostly by finding a connection with their Jewish roots so that they could 'belong' and also feel 'good' through the adoption of Jewish values and qualities."

Flora blazed her own middle trail. She went to synagogue, but only for Yom Kippur. She celebrated Passover, but in her own way, emphasizing the courage and survival of the Jews. She visited her relatives in Israel but didn't like Judaism's "rules" or its "right wing." She liked Judaism's focus on life here on earth. "Somewhere in the Talmud, it says that men look in envy at heaven, but the angels look in envy at men," she said. "My philosophy is 'I'm lucky I'm alive, I have a responsibility to do my best, to be good to other people.'" But it's a philosophy that's often frustrated by the unimaginable inhumanity that blackened her life. "I manage to do what I can in a small way. My value is to enjoy life and not to be overwhelmed by everything."

Flora summed up her religious experience with a shrug, saying "I've got a whole problem with God—or the idea of God."

"Why didn't I rebel against Judaism?" asked Sophie. After all, she was raised as an anti-Semitic Polish Catholic and kept her Jewishness from coworkers into her thirties. A compliant temperament provides part of the answer. "I always did what people said!" When she was five, her mother told her to be a Catholic and she obeyed. Six years later, when her mother informed her that she was really a Jew, the information was shocking, absurd, and initially useless to her, but at a deeper level, she experienced this too as an inescapable verdict. "I never asked myself, I never had the luxury of 'Do I want it?' So now I'm a Jew!" she recalled, laughing. In time she accepted it and even vowed to marry a Jew and raise Jewish children. "I always gave a hundred percent!" she said with a smile.

Still, when she attended High Holiday services at a conservative synagogue, she was extremely uncomfortable. Although she joined a reform temple in Great Neck, it was the aesthetics of it, the beautiful synagogue itself, that appealed to her as much as wanting to belong and connect with her ancestors.

Was Sophie the same adult that she would have been had she remained a Catholic? Since religion plays little *religious* role in Sophie's life, it's easy to believe that, whatever her faith, Sophie would be the same person—and precisely because her experience ultimately freed her from the man-made constructs and exclusivity of religious beliefs and committed her, like Flora, to a nondenominational gospel of kindness and responsibility. But we'll never know, and who's to say that Sophie, who kept her childhood rosary and her catechism until a museum finally claimed it, wouldn't have become a devout Catholic had her mother not survived the war or had she decided to spare her daughter the trauma of religious confusion so soon after all the other losses?

For Carla, who is six years older than Flora and eight years older than Sophie, Judaism had had more time to take root in her consciousness. Moreover, she had only to keep her Judaism secret, not renounce it for Catholicism. But since Judaism for Carla, as for Flora and Sophie, was a cultural tradition rather than a formal religious commitment, she had that much less of it to conceal. "I remember once, in hiding," Carla recalled seventy years after the fact, "thinking that there is no God. If there *was* one, he wouldn't have put me in this position because I hadn't done anything. The whole idea of a God who is good and everything was gone at the age of thirteen."

Regardless, her ethnic and cultural connection to Judaism never weakened. In her eighties, Carla is "very Jewish, a very proud Jew. Ed and I don't have a problem with our Jewish identity. Not only from the Holocaust, but from the Zionist organization after the war. When we lived in Israel on a nonreligious kibbutz for five years, we weren't religious. We didn't have to be!" Although she celebrates Passover, Rosh Hashanah, and Hanukkah at home, she is otherwise nonobservant and doesn't attend synagogue, not even on High Holidays.

The five years in Israel made her husband Ed "a very patriotic Jew. I'm not religious, but there's something mystical that this people have survived. There are more people living now in Israel than were killed in the Holocaust. To me," Ed said, "being Jewish is the most magical thing. It's a privilege to belong to this *amazing* people, who've given more to mankind than any other people in the world."

What *does* it mean to be a Jew?

The question is a matter of endless debate among *unambivalent* Jews everywhere, but for the hidden children the question is more immediate and even more unanswerable. Almost every Jew at the Gathering had been torn from their Jewish families and traditions by the Holocaust. For those hidden in convents, monasteries, and Christian families, the Catholic church and religion provided them with structure and beauty, positive and omniscient authority figures, a surrogate sense of family and belonging, a feeling of active control over their own and their family members' fates through prayer, and a doctrine that made some sense of their suffering. At a time when Judaism was not simply reviled but punishable by death, Catholicism could be irresistible and its God benevolent, while the Jewish one appeared to be on some sort of sabbatical. If exposed to Catholicism at a very young age, they were faced with a later decision of whether to embrace a religion—Judaism—that they never knew had embraced them. If older, they were later confronted with the challenge of reconciling two historically antagonistic faiths they now experienced as competing for their loyalty and faith.

The religious choices child survivors made were influenced by numerous factors: their age, their temperament, the mysteries of personality, circumstance—and often whether they ever saw one or both of their parents again. For Shlomo Breznitz, this last factor may well have utterly changed the course of his life.

In Vrbove, Czechoslovakia, in 1944, no Christian child seemed as Christian as an eight-year-old Jewish chess prodigy named Shlomo Breznitz. When his grandparents, uncles, aunts, and cousins kept disappearing from Bratislava, his parents attempted to escape the Nazis by moving him and his sister Judith to a shtetl named Vrbove, which Shlomo later described in his memoir, *Memory Fields*, as "something out of a Chagall painting or a story by Sholem Aleichem . . . but by the time we arrived, any fiddlers that might have been on the roofs of Vrbove had been taken to Auschwitz."

As a further precaution, the family converted to Christianity and the two children began taking private lessons in Catholicism. When the parents were tipped off about an impending deportation in September 1944, they tried to hide their children in a local orphanage run by the Benedictine Sisters, but they said they'd already taken as many Jewish children as they wished to. Another local orphanage run by the Sisters of Saint Vincent took in Shlomo and Judith, who said tearful good-byes to their parents, assuming they would be deported to Auschwitz.

Eight-year-old Shlomo was abused, taunted, beaten up, and humiliated by the older Christian orphans while all the while taking great pains to conceal his circumcision, even if it meant wetting his pants. Using his remarkable memory, Shlomo, who had already memorized prayers and passages from the Old Testament, now focused his formidable powers on the long Latin litanies that the nuns themselves couldn't commit to memory, but had to read aloud as they walked the corridors and courtyard. That Shlomo had no knowledge of Latin didn't prevent him from being able to recite the litanies at length. The Mother Superior, alerted to his talent by a Sister C., beckoned both of them to her office.

"I have heard that you have a very good memory," she asked the small, bespectacled boy. "Is it so?" And when he had proved it, she asked him how he did it.

"I don't know, Sister," he replied. "The words just come to me on their own."

She made him promise not to mention his gift to anyone. Inspired by this special attention, Shlomo began volunteering for little jobs, making himself useful. One afternoon, Sister C. asked him to wash, change his shirt, and prepare to visit the house of the prelate, the town's highest religious authority, who lived near the church orphanage. Ironically, the prelate lived across the street from the house Shlomo's family had lived in, and which was now occupied by strangers.

The imposing prelate first asked if he was the son of Joseph Breznitz, the Jew who had lived across the street and who had been taken, along with Shlomo's mother, by the Germans. The prelate then asked him to demonstrate his mastery of the Catholic prayers, which he effortlessly did, after which the prelate retired to an adjacent room with the Mother Superior and Sister C., leaving Shlomo to wonder about the significance of his performance and what destiny awaited him.

He wouldn't learn what the prelate had in mind until months after the war, when he was miraculously reunited with his mother, who had, unlike his father, survived Auschwitz. Shlomo's mother found her son's survival equally miraculous. At Auschwitz she had seen the children from the first orphanage where she had tried to deposit her son, and could only speculate that the Jewish children from Saint Vincent had met with a similar fate. That very morning, Shlomo's mother informed him that she had met with the Mother Superior, who told her what had happened behind those closed doors.

The prelate had seen Shlomo's gift for memorizing prayers as a sign that Shlomo might be the Jewish orphan who would one day become pope, foretold in a fable he knew, and familiar to the Saint Vincent sisters as well. The prelate had urged the sisters to protect Shlomo from the Germans at all costs in the hope that Shlomo indeed might rise to become the leader of the planet's Roman Catholics! After the prelate's brutal murder near the end of the war, the Mother Superior remained so convinced that Shlomo was papal material that it was only his mother's reappearance that convinced her to let him go.

Instead of becoming pope, Shlomo and his mother made aliyah to Israel in 1949, where he grew up to be a renowned psychologist and expert on stress, member briefly of the Knesset, and a leader in the use of technology to improve and maintain brain function.

In the case of Jean-Marie Lustiger, perhaps the most famous of all Jewish-born priests, the crucial factor seems to have been a temperamental affinity for Catholicism so strong that, unlike Breznitz, he likely would not have renounced his adopted Christian faith even if his mother *had* survived the war. Lustiger was born in 1926 in Paris to two Polish Jews, but when the Germans occupied Paris in 1940 Lustiger and his sister were sent to live with a Catholic woman in Orleans. Immediately taken with Catholicism, the teenage Jean-Marie decided to convert that same year, against his parents' wishes. Not even his mother's murder in Auschwitz-Birkenau in 1943 deterred him from entering a Carmelite seminary in 1946 and being ordained in 1954, while his Jewish father, a survivor, watched from a seat in the back of the church. He went on to become the pastor of Paris's Sixteenth Arrondissement.

After a spiritual crisis in the late 1970s, when he considered moving to Israel, the stylish but conservative Lustiger was appointed archbishop of Paris by the pope in 1981, a nomination about which his enigmatic comment was, "For me, this nomination was as if, all of a sudden, the crucifix began to wear a yellow star. . . . I was born Jewish, and so I remain, even if that is unacceptable for many. For me, the vocation of Israel is bringing light to the goyim. That is my hope, and I believe that Christianity is the means for achieving it." Two years later he was named a cardinal and gained a broad reputation for his authoritarian manner. A strong supporter of Israel, he was instrumental in pressing Pope John Paul II to order the removal of the controversial Carmelite convent that had been constructed next to Auschwitz in 1984.

When the Ashkenazic chief rabbi of Israel accused Cardinal Lustiger of betraying his people and his faith during the Jews' darkest period, the Holocaust, he replied, "I am as Jewish as all the other members of my family who were butchered in Auschwitz or in the other camps."

"I believe he saw himself as a Jewish Christian, like the first disciples," one of his close friends said.

After he stepped down as archbishop in 2005, the year that pope John Paul II died, he was mentioned as a possible successor, but he refused to discuss the possibility publicly. To a friend who asked him if he might become pope, he reportedly said in French-accented Yiddish, "From your mouth to God's ear." However, to another who asked him the same thing, he reportedly replied, "Oy vey—you think I'm meshugge?"

Jakob Hirsch Greiner was also able to juggle, or reconcile, his double religious identity. In 1942 Jakob, already eleven years old, ran away moments before the Germans shot the rest of his family. He spent most of the rest of the war wandering alone from Polish village to Polish village under the name Jakob Popofsky. After the war, he found a home at a Catholic orphanage, where he didn't reveal his Jewish name for fear of standing out, but he missed having a faith. The children's agency didn't know what to do with him until a nun from the orphanage said, "Well, if he's so religious, I'll take him with me." Popofsky entered the seminary in 1952 and became a priest in 1958. "But all the time one thought kept bothering me," he said. "I was a Jew and I was still hiding. Why was that? It began to torture me." In 1966 he announced in a magazine article about his life that he was a Jew, after which he was better able to reconcile the religious tension in his life.

Things were not so simple for Father Popofsky's brother, who had survived the war and was now living in Israel as an Orthodox Jew. He discovered his long-lost brother through the magazine article and tracked Jakob down. When the priest decided to visit Israel in 1970, his brother warned him that if he insisted on coming as a priest, "You better stay in Poland."

Disregarding this advice, Father Popofsky arrived in Israel wearing a cassock. His brother, who met him at the airport, was upset. "This is how you greet us?" he said. "I can't take you home like this." So Popofsky changed out of his cassock in the airport men's room and went home with his brother to meet his long-lost relatives, who took him to their synagogue for Rosh Hashanah, where the Lubavitcher rabbi said, "Let God bless him." Back home, his brother exclaimed, "Do you realize what an honor that was!?"

"Big deal," Popofsky replied. "*I* could've blessed *him*!"

Somehow Popofsky survived his "dual personality" with a sense of humor. "I'd go to synagogue with a yarmulke on my head, and the next day I'd go to church with the yarmulke in my pocket," he said. "I had to be careful not to cross myself in the synagogue or put my yarmulke on in church."

In the mirror, Popofsky doesn't see a 2,000-year-old rift between two major religions predicated in some large measure on the allegation that the Jews killed Christ. Instead he sees the essential decency and kindness that followers of all religions profess to aspire to. "When I'm alone," he says, "I can talk to myself in the mirror: 'Oh, there you are—a decent guy I can talk to.'"

It's easy to see the priest's renunciation of his Jewish faith, as Popofsky's own brother does, as a betrayal of Judaism and a kind of posthumous victory for Hitler. Yet the relatively peaceful coexistence of both religions within Popofsky might also be seen as a profound spiritual rebuke to the very anti-Semitism that motivated the Final Solution. If the Jew is no longer the Other, no longer the viciously maligned foil for Christianity, but rather Christianity's long-lost brother, a vital member of the spiritual family, then how can you murder him? He too is in you. As Popofsky says, "If Christ's a Jew and I serve him, that means I'm also a Jew."

For Romuald Jakub Weksler-Waszkinel, however, the question of whether he was Catholic or Jewish became a source of great suffering. Unlike Breznitz, Lustiger, and Popofsky, Weksler-Waszkinel never had a chance in childhood to choose his faith. Born in 1943, he was given up as a newborn to a Catholic couple, the Waszkinels, the only parents he would ever know—or know of, until middle age. Still, he harbored faint doubts about his origins; it was as if others knew something about him that he didn't. When he was a boy, two drunks once yelled "Jewish orphan!" at him. He was the target of other taunts about his appearance, so unlike his parents'. At the age of ten or eleven, the dark-haired Weksler-Waszkinel looked in the mirror and asked his mother if he looked like his fair-haired father. On a trip with his father when he was thirteen, an elderly Polish man pointed to him and said to the father, "Where did you conjure up this little Jew?" At fifteen, he was reading to his illiterate mother about some Jews when he saw tears in her eyes. "Why are you crying?" he asked. "Am I a Jew?" To which she replied, "Don't I love you enough?"

At seventeen he decided to enter a seminary, which angered his father. "Am I doing something wrong?" Weksler-Waszkinel asked him. "No," his father replied, "but your life will be very difficult." Shortly after, his father died of a heart attack. In 1966, Weksler-Waszkinel was ordained a priest at the age of twenty-three.

In 1975, now a Polish Catholic priest and professor of philosophy at the Catholic University of Lublin, Weksler-Waszkinel moved his mother in with him in an apartment in Lublin, where he was again encountering rumors of his possible Jewishness. "The question 'perhaps I really am Jewish' nudged its way into my consciousness more and more intensely," he wrote of that period. "I nurtured this question in my heart and the possibility of it having a positive reply no longer terrified me." In 1978, when he was thirty-five, his beloved, now elderly mother, Emilia, finally brought herself to tell him the truth—that in 1943 his Jewish mother, trapped in the Lublin ghetto, contacted Emilia and begged her to take her week-old baby, saying, "You are a devout Catholic. You believe in Jesus, who was a Jew. So try to save this Jewish baby for the Jew in whom you believe. And one day he will grow up to be a priest." And so it had actually come to pass.

Weksler-Waszkinel now considered himself an emissary between Jews and Christians, who themselves had lost three million to the Holocaust. But the belated proof of his earlier suspicions that he had been born Jewish unsettled him, even as, for the next thirty years, Weksler-Waszkinel attended to his university students at an Ursuline convent in Lublin. When he was in his sixties, the knowledge that he was born Jewish gave birth to a determination to settle in Israel and *become* a Jew. For one thing, he had learned that his biological parents had been Zionists who wanted to immigrate there. For another, with the help of a nun who herself had saved many Jews during the war, he had been put in touch with an uncle and survivors from his Jewish parents' small town who now lived in Israel. He at last learned his father's family name and appended it to his Polish Catholic surname. Maybe most of all, he could no longer abide the anti-Semitism in Poland. The country, he said, reminded him of people smoking under a sign that says NO SMOKING. Anti-Semitism was prohibited, but no one complied. "The sermons are filled with it," he complained. A Christian radio station with millions of listeners peddled anti-Semitism to the masses. "I can't bear it," he said. "It's too intense for me."

On a preliminary visit to Israel, Weksler-Waszkinel wore both his priest's collar and a yarmulke at Jerusalem's Western Wall. His plan was to learn Hebrew and Judaism at a religious kibbutz but practice as a Catholic priest on Sunday. However, no monastery in Israel would accept him, most likely because he was Jewish, and no kibbutz would accept him as a Jew if he insisted on conducting a Mass one day a week. Eventually he accepted a place at a kibbutz on the condition that he give up his once-a-week Mass—"Is he a Jew? A Christian? Who are you, Yaakov?" a member of the kibbutz's Ulpan Admissions Committee had asked during his interview. He insisted on having two faiths, but the kibbutzim wanted him to choose Judaism. "I'm going through something very intense," he confided in a friend, a woman who was also a hidden child, but one who returned to Judaism decades earlier after seven years as a Catholic. Under the strain of reconciling his two faiths, he became very depressed and wanted to leave the kibbutz.

Because of a decades-old Israeli law that prohibits a Jew who practices another religion from having the right to return to Israel as a Jew, the Israeli Population and Immigration Authority granted him temporary residence status, not as a Jew, but as a monk, with a home at Abu Gosh, a Benedictine monastery, once run, ironically, by a monk of Jewish origin.

Perhaps the greatest irony of all is that Israel had already granted Weksler-Waszkinel's Catholic parents the status of Righteous Among the Nations for saving a Jewish boy—himself.

Why has Romuald Jakub agonized so over his religious conflict while Jakob Popofsky embraced both religions, and Shlomo Breznitz and Jean-Marie Lustiger made their choices and stuck with them? Where do you go looking for the answer? In the fact that Weksler-Waszkinel was born *during* the war and traumatized as an infant, so that the roots of his conflict were preverbal and more disturbing on a subconscious level and unresolvable? That he happened to lack Popofsky's sense of humor, as well as his feel for a spirituality that transcends all religions? Or is the answer just hidden in the unknowable thickets of personality and personal preference?

The discovery that hidden child survivors were born Jewish continues to this day, but perhaps nowhere is the revelation more perilous than in Poland, the home of an increasing number of people who have learned only as adults that they were born Jewish. As their Catholic hiding parents enter old age, they, like Weksler-Waszkinel's mother, have finally come clean. The number of Jews in Poland—three million before the war, more than any country in the world—had dropped by the 1990s to roughly 4,000, but has climbed in recent years to 20,000 or more. Since 1988, an annual Jewish Cultural Festival in Kraków provides an opportunity for curious Poles to learn about the country's vanished Jewish culture and cuisine, but almost every newly discovered Jew in Poland who embraces his or her Judaism still does so at some risk—to their social status, family harmony, friendships, careers, even their marriages.

In her book *Broken Chain: Catholics Uncover the Holocaust's Hidden Legacy and Discover Their Jewish Roots*, American psychoanalyst Vera Muller-Paisner, the daughter of Polish Holocaust survivors whose first spouses and families had been murdered by the Nazis, recounts the dilemmas of several newly enlightened Polish Jews. Poles who learn they are Jewish and decide to embrace it have resources to help them in the form of educational programs sponsored by the Ronald S. Lauder Foundation, in particular a Jewish "camp" in the countryside, run by an American-born rabbi, Michael Schudrich, who started working in Poland in 1990 and is now the official rabbi of Poland.

Nothing, however, protects them from ostracism, persecution, and the traumatic effects of being identified as Jewish. The friends of one teenage girl who learned when she was fourteen that her father was Jewish called her a "Jew who should be thrown to the gas." Another teen lost his friends after a yarmulke was spotted on the floor of his family's dining room. After a fifteen-year-old girl who learned her mother was Jewish decided to keep kosher, her father stopped talking to her and eventually became estranged from the whole family. One mother who thought she was dying told her child that they were Jewish, but, once recovered, insisted she was "delusional." In a country still as anti-Semitic as any, and with virtually no separation of church and state, many "new" Jews were fearful that being Jewish meant no longer being Polish. One person wondered, "Because of prevailing anti-Semitism I find myself also anti-Semitic. How do I get rid of it?"

Even for older hidden children survivors who always knew they were Jewish, organized religion can seem like a necessary mirage, a wavering vision of safety in an existential desert. Judaism is simultaneously embraced and rejected, a set of inconsistent rituals that nonetheless give meaning to their devastated childhoods. Many survivors (and victims) of a genocide based on religion were not observant to begin with; the beliefs, rituals, and traits for which they were targeted for extermination were often as alien to them as to the Nazis. For some survivors, Judaism lost much of its remaining religious meaning after the war, leaving its cultural, historical, and sentimental values to cling to.

Poet and writer Judith Sherman was hidden in Czechoslovakia and Hungary before being shipped at fourteen to Auschwitz in a boxcar that gradually filled with the dead during four days without food or water. Because of the recent arrivals of tens of thousands of Hungarian Jews, Auschwitz was unable to accept the living contents of Sherman's train on that particular day and she was sent on to Ravensbrück, where she, unlike her parents and most of her relatives, survived the war. There were days, she writes, "when I was surrounded by more dead people than alive ones." Why did she live to enjoy her grandchildren and write, after a long silence, a beautiful, moving memoir, *Say the Name*? The answer, she knows, can be found in a thousand tiny contingencies, and yet nowhere at all.

On a spring day in 2012, the energetic eighty-two-year-old sat in a coffee shop on Ninth Avenue in Manhattan and tried to explain her difficult relationship with God, whom she treats like a stubborn, irrational, and cautiously loved father. She had just returned from an annual two-day event in Scranton, Pennsylvania, for which the Jewish Federation and Catholic Marymount College bring together 1,800 students and numerous survivors to discuss the Holocaust. While on a panel there, she had been asked by a student about forgiveness. "I don't really know what that word means to me," she replied. "Does it mean I forgive the Nazis for killing my father, mother, etc.? I can't visualize forgiveness. My days are not consumed with rage and hatred and vengeance, but forgiveness is not part of my thinking. I have never heard a Nazi express remorse or regret for his crimes, so what 'forgiveness' is that student asking for?"

God was central to Sherman's childhood in Kurima, Czechoslovakia, and although she never believed she was anything but Jewish, she has retrofitted her surviving faith in God with paradoxes and provisos that fit the emotional realities of her life. She attends Sabbath services, but reads the prayers phonetically in Hebrew—a language she doesn't understand—because "I cannot read words like 'The Lord is good to all. He hears their cry and saves them and upholds all who fall.'" As she writes in *Say the Name*:

> With the images I carry I cannot utter such words of praise. God, such words of praise uttered by this Ravensbrück prisoner— number 83621—should be disdained by you. An insult to you. My unanswered struggle continues. On Yom Kippur I get up early, have a big breakfast, and then spend the day in the synagogue. My act of defiance. I will not go hungry for God. But I will pray. Today I say Kaddish, the memorial prayer, whenever Kaddish is said during Services. Silently I say it. I do not stand up as required—how would I explain the frequency of this reciting to fellow congregants?

"Having God is having someone to rage against," she said over coffee. "Where else will I go with that? God is strong enough to take it, like a strong parent. My railing is not only against God, but also against man. Where was God? Where was man?" When she talks to schools now, the focus is on the Nazis and on their victims—"I order the Nazis to 'say the name' six million times"—and on God— "God, please see to it that every name is accounted for." In one of her poems, Sherman writes,

> *God, would you come down that ladder*
> *that ladder Jacob climbed*
> *I will not deal with angels*
> *I'll wait till you arrive.*
> *when You come down*
> *that ladder—that ladder*
> *Jacob climbed*
> *then I will take Your hand*
> *and I will be Your guide*
> *and I will show You sights*
> *not fit for Godly eyes*

She has maintained a relationship with God because it is in her childhood DNA to do so. She has also turned him, in a sense, into a victim of the Holocaust as well. "God needs us," Sherman said. "We should not abandon him. We must not leave God unattended. Nor us. Nor us."

So what of Father Romuald Jakub Weksler-Waszkinel, who at thirty-five hears the call of Judaism, a faith to which he belongs by birth but by no other lived experience, and sets out to become a Jew in Israel at the age of sixty-seven? What is happening when Jakob Popofsky, *knowing* he is Jewish, decides to become a priest but continues to be tortured by that knowledge and, only at the age of thirty-five, comes out of hiding? What is happening when Sophie, who knew herself only as an anti-Semitic Catholic until she was eleven, is determined as an adult, despite her ambivalence toward Judaism, to marry a Jew and raise Jewish children? What is happening when Flora, whose Judaism was buried under successive waves of Catholicism, Protestantism, Buddhism, and atheism, celebrates Passover and is drawn to her Israeli relatives?

Do these individuals simply want to alleviate their guilt at turning their backs on their religion, even if they did so involuntarily? Do they feel an abstract intellectual commitment to rejoin and propagate their original and historically persecuted minority? Do they want to lay claim to their rightful portion of their legacy of revolutionary Jewish humanism? Or does the discovery of denied Judaism strike some deeper nerve, provide a potential missing piece to the puzzle of their souls, and resonate with some rejected strand of their genetic selves?

Could it be enough just to ask these questions?

THE NEXT CIRCLE OF HELL

However well the hidden children get along in the world, they are reminded of the Holocaust by the things they must do, the things they must avoid, and the thoughts that have lives of their own. To this day, Sophie has to eat before bed so that she won't wake up hungry. She has a furniture-rearranging compulsion, a relic perhaps of the need to alter and control *something* in her terrifying environment. When she used to visit her Aunt Putzi, Uncle Kazik would offer to pay her *not* to move their furniture around. As for Aunt Putzi, she would never throw a piece of bread away, no matter how stale, and left the radio on all night to erase the silence she remembered too well from coming home in 1942 to find her parents gone, never to be heard from again. When Putzi's son Henry was ten, he already knew how to protect her from her past; when *The Pawnbroker* was shown on television, he stood in front of it to block her view during the concentration camp flashbacks.

Today Carla becomes very irritable when people talk about dieting. Not her psychotherapy clients, of course, but when others ramble on about all the things they're not eating, it offends her experience during the war, when for years she often went hungry. How can people obsess about *not* eating when there's so much food available? Carla is often afraid she's going to run out of things. If she finds a pair of shoes she likes, she'll buy a second pair, because you never know. . . .

Flora is preoccupied with her inability to remember enough of the past. "I had so many losses, so many identities," she says. Questions about her childhood are met with frequent disclaimers about her "terrible memory." "I have trouble remembering things," she complains, or "My problem in my life is that I don't remember. I forget everything. It's a pain in the neck in my studies. . . ." However, one thing Flora remembers all too clearly are the first pastries she ate after the war: meringues and baba au rhum. "It was my introduction to plenty," she says. They are still her favorites.

Survivor and poet Judith Sherman can't tolerate hunger. She has lunch at ten-thirty in the morning. In restaurants, the only starch she orders is potatoes, in honor of a food once so precious it made the difference between life and death. Another superstition: until she wrote her own book in 2005, she had never read a book about the Holocaust. Maybe most chilling of all, though, is this: in supermarkets she refuses to select fruits and vegetables, taking only those that happen to be on top. "I cannot engage in 'selections,'" she writes, "because of Auschwitz—because of Mengele."

Such post-traumatic behaviors haunt the adult lives of hidden children, but the therapeutic value of meeting other hidden children was well established by the effects of the First International Gathering of Children Hidden During World War II. Not long after the Gathering, Carla told author Jane Marks for her collection of interviews, *The Hidden Children: Secret Survivors of the Holocaust*, "Part of my personality was almost dead, but now it was coming to life. . . . People say my whole demeanor is different now, that I'm jollier, more outgoing, more relaxed."

The Gathering had also popped the lid off her husband Ed's reluctance to deal with the Holocaust. He started reading the books on Carla's Holocaust shelf, the books he had avoided for decades. He began to speak to hundreds of schoolchildren every year, surrounded by enlarged photos of the chief of police who saved his life, himself as a teenage Dutch Resistance fighter, and the all-Jewish Boy Scout troop in The Hague, of which he was one of only three Dutch boys to survive. In the 1990s, Ed volunteered to conduct fifty videotaped interviews with survivors in the suburbs of New York City and the Bronx for Steven Spielberg's Survivors of the Shoah Visual History Foundation. He started his own local hidden children newsletter.

The Gathering also emboldened Flora to take her private Holocaust public. In addition to her speaking engagements, Flora taught a course at the New School for Social Research that examined how different countries and religions struggled with the Holocaust. It helped her to see how others had suffered outside of herself. The Gathering seemed to substantiate the conclusion she drew from her pioneering study of eleven child survivors back in the 1970s: hidden children could be remarkably resilient, and trauma created not only psychopathology, but also the foundation for a stronger identity once the unthinkable and unspeakable past was consciously incorporated into the narrative of the survivor's life.

Survivors must deal with nonsurvivors in their daily life. Ordinary conversations carry the potential for unwanted sympathy and self-censorship. When Flora met a visiting chorus of college students from Cologne, Germany, she was quite conscious of saying nothing to them about her experiences at the hands of their countrymen sixty-five years ago. "I didn't want to ruin their evening," she says. "On the other hand, I couldn't be myself."

"It's a conversation stopper," Carla says. "When I talk about it, the expressions change dramatically. People get that worried face. It brings them closer to a horrible world."

The reach and enormity of the Holocaust can make the mere mention of having survived it deeply disturbing for others. Its commercialization (in treatments both dramatic and satiric, from *Schindler's List* and *Sarah's Key* to *Life Is Beautiful* and *Inglourious Basterds*) has fixed it in Western consciousness as, one hopes, the outer limit of evil on earth. It will always be caught in history's throat. The mention of the Holocaust by a survivor can suddenly make the listener choke on his or her moral assumptions about the world. It doesn't simply bring the listener disturbingly closer to Carla's "horrible world," a world that exists outside of our familiar ethical categories, but to death itself. As a participant said at the Hidden Child Congress in Amsterdam in 1992:

> The survivor reminds the psychically "healthy" (including the psychoanalyst) of his/her mortality, of the precariousness of all human existence, of the ignominies and barbarity with which untold millions of innocents have met their death. . . . This reminder is intolerable, its suppression is a central function of all that passes for contemporary culture. . . . The very witnesses of the pathology of modern society, whose testimony could shake us out of a once again dangerous complacency about the state of the world in which we find ourselves, are stigmatized as neurotic, are treated as a new field of research for the psychiatric PTSD specialists, rather than as a group of people who have something of great importance to say to us all.

For many people, survivors are emotional lepers; no one wants to catch their misery, however presumed or real. Today the Holocaust is talked about more freely than before—Carla gets a fair amount of casual "Oh, you're a survivor! So where were you?"—but a survivor can never know in advance how well informed or empathetic a listener is.

Sophie loathes being regarded by others as a repository of all things Holocaust. "People are always coming up and saying, 'Have you seen this movie, have you read that book, do you know this other survivor?' You know, we work very hard subconsciously to appear normal"—she laughs—"and it's seriously hard work to keep yourself from imploding. We don't need people to keep giving us this negative energy.

"I regard all survivors and the people who saved them as heroes because they overcame insurmountable obstacles. And those who didn't survive, I object to them being called 'lambs led to slaughter.' They fought bravely against their fate too."

Flora no longer worries so much about the effects of bringing up the fact that she survived the Holocaust. She used to get reactions more often either of the "How come you look so normal?" or else "Who wants to hear about it? Enough about the Holocaust!" variety, but now she can mention it more matter-of-factly and "march on to something else" without being snagged on her listener's distress. But the problem persists: how to talk about it without being defined by it.

"The ideal," says Flora, who's given the issue a lot of thought, "is for someone to listen empathically about what happened to you, without making what happened the whole of you, but seeing it as a part of you that doesn't negate the rest of you. That's what's really therapeutic. The issue is how people seem to define the victimization as something so horrendous that they deny it even to themselves."

It can help, she thinks, if survivors reframe their disclosure. "There's a way that the person who survived can talk about it, by saying, 'Hey, you know, I survived the Holocaust' rather than saying 'I'm a survivor of the Holocaust.' The former says it's part of my life, but it's not my whole life. *Survivor* is a label. When people say they're survivors, the other doesn't want to have anything to do with him or her—you know, we're marked by the devil. And we all have to struggle with this," Flora says quietly, "because we want to be authentic."

When Facing History first sent her to speak to schoolchildren, it was with the organization's usual goal of sensitizing students to discrimination and persecution through Flora's terrible childhood experiences. But what Flora learned from the students that day was also important. When she broke down in tears at the very beginning of her account, the students said nothing, and by not interfering with her obvious pain, they allowed Flora to reach her grief for the first time in decades. The children didn't preempt her feelings with their own pity or discomfort.

On other visits to schools, Flora has returned a favor by consoling students of German extraction who feel uncomfortable before her. She reminds them it's not their fault, there's no reason for *them* to feel bad, and in saying it, everyone feels a little better.

"The responsibility," Flora says, "is to remember history instead of feeling guilty about it."

A listener may feel inferior before a survivor because he believes he wouldn't have had the courage himself to survive. Of course, resilience, adaptability, resourcefulness, and determination played their parts, but what survivors know, of course, is that luck played a major role in their survival. If a child happened to wake up alive for a thousand or more mornings in a row, they became survivors.

Despite it all, and whatever their private battles, the hidden children survivors have been unusually attuned to the suffering of others.

In 1990 Sophie was on a committee for cancer services at North Shore University Hospital in Manhasset, Long Island. Committee meetings were not her thing; treating cancer patients was. Usually she sat far in the back of the room at these meetings.

"Any other business?" the hospital committee chair asked as things wound down.

Sophie, who'd always had a major aversion to public speaking—in a sense, she needed to stay hidden—suddenly raised her hand and asked, "Why don't we do something for cancer survivors?"

The first National Cancer Survivors Day had been held a couple of years before, but North Shore Community didn't have an event, and Sophie realized it should. Sophie's patients were in a life-and-death struggle against a killer as cruel and capricious as the Holocaust. She wanted to celebrate them, celebrate with them, and to supply some hope.

The hospital's CEO happened to be walking by, heard Sophie's question, stopped, and said, "What a great idea!"

Before she knew it, Sophie, who had always hid from group activities, was heading up a planning committee. All the networking, organizing, and decision making was stressful, but along the way she realized that she wanted to include *all* cancer survivors who had been treated at North Shore Community over the years, not just the ones currently under her care. That meant identifying the still living, creating and sending out invitations to what looked more and more like a party to be held outside, with tents and balloons and music.

It was scheduled for June 1991, by which time Sophie had just had the profound experience of attending the First International Gathering of Children Hidden During World War II in Manhattan. She therefore knew firsthand how important it was to meet people in similar circumstances, how powerful it was to be among other survivors with whom you didn't have to say a word in order to know what they had been through.

The event was a big success, involving over 600 cancer survivors and their families. Oncology patients were suddenly transformed into excellent conversationalists and virtuosos on the dance floor. Many of them, patients past and present, made sure Sophie knew they were there. With the hidden children's Christian hiding parents in mind, Sophie took pains to have some of the patients get up and honor their caregivers as well.

The hospital adopted Cancer Survivors Day immediately as an annual event, using a videotape of it as a marketing tool. For Sophie, the Cancer Survivors Day represented a personal milestone, the discovery that she could nurture a question she had asked on the spur of the moment one year into an actual event with far-reaching benefits the next. For the first time in her life, she felt she was going to leave something very important behind (after her two sons, of course, and grandchildren), and it helped quiet the guilt felt by all hidden children—why did I survive the Holocaust and not the others?

In her retirement, as a representative of the International Federation of University Women to the United Nations, Sophie attends, among others, meetings of human rights experts on genocide prevention. When she hears about atrocities in various countries, she is enraged that she still lives in a world where genocide occurs regularly, but feels that part of her personal role is to remind others that genocide didn't begin with Bosnia and Rwanda. There are people in many countries who have never heard of the Final Solution. At one UN meeting of the Commission on the Status of Women, when the chairperson asked everyone to introduce themselves, Sophie did something she never would have done just a couple of years before. She overcame her lingering unease about her own place in history and said that she was a survivor of the European genocide called the Holocaust.

The Hidden Child Foundation was established immediately after the 1991 Gathering, and Carla Lessing became one of its vice presidents. More than twenty years later, she still takes the train into Manhattan every Wednesday to the office of the Hidden Child Foundation. Her tasks range from event planning, to details like tracking down billing code numbers and vetting a package on its way to Yad Vashem, or seeing about getting a member's hiding parents posthumously inducted into the Righteous Among the Nations. There is also the mail. When the *Hidden Child* newsletter is mailed out, a lot of them come back: Address Unknown, Undeliverable Address, Return to Sender. Carla moves files from Active to Moved, more and more often to Deceased.

And there are the phone calls. When elderly hidden children call for financial or emotional assistance during the Jewish holidays, Carla refers them to family service agencies. Many callers live isolated lives far from a community of other hidden children, feeling no less alone than they did seventy years ago, hidden behind a strange family's bookcase. She often fields "second-generation calls"—distress calls from the children of hidden children, saying that their mother's acting strangely, or their father's being aggressive.

The calls she likes least, though, are the occasional ones from a hidden child's child, complaining that his or her aged mother is now saying that she was sexually abused during the war.

It is the next circle of the Holocaust survivor's hell, the trauma so perverse and inconceivable that most of its victims dare speak about it only in old age.

If you Google "sexual abuse of hidden children" you'll find only an article on jspace.com, a brief reference to it on jewishvirtuallibrary .org, another passing mention in the script for a United States Holocaust Memorial Museum exhibit about hidden children in 2003 to 2004, and a link to a 2012 article by Carla Lessing in *Kavod*, an online journal for mental health professionals working with Holocaust survivors. Carla's article, "Aging Child Holocaust Survivors of Sexual Abuse," begins bluntly: "The goal of this presentation is that we, the mental health professionals and caretakers of the now elderly victims, will be alert to the possibility that the aging former hidden children, men, and women were molested in hiding and have never spoken about it."

This is not news within the hidden child community. Back in 1990, a year before the Gathering, a paper by Sarah Moskowitz and Robert Kress in the *Israeli Journal of Psychiatry and Related Sciences* claimed that one in six hidden children had been sexually abused. A subsequent study in the Netherlands estimated that more than 80 percent of hidden children interviewed were treated well, while 15 percent were occasionally mistreated, and some 5 percent were treated badly. But any percent is too many. As British Holocaust historian Zoe Waxman wrote in 2010, "Until relatively recently, rape and sexual abuse has remained an untold chapter in the history of the Holocaust. This stems from both the cultural taboo and also because such experiences are not considered to be a part of the narrative of the Holocaust."

In its mockery of all decency and morality, in its profound betrayal of a child's *desperate* trust, the sexual abuse of hidden children by their benefactors is almost as incomprehensible as the Final Solution itself. Given the standard of inhumanity set by the Third Reich, the sexual abuse of hidden children can surprise us only because it is the one atrocity that hasn't really come to light after all these years.

Incest under any circumstances, as Australian psychiatrist Paul Valent said in a 1995 talk about his challenging treatment of a sexually abused hidden child, "ultimately breaks down the meaning of one's life. To be aware that one is abused and perverted by one's caretakers, to realize that the supposed provider of law and order is immoral and perverse, to be totally powerless and, in spite of everything, to be forced to seek their love even as they are destroying one's life and soul is too hard to do for a child, and if they did they would die or wish to die." For hidden children, "the triple trauma of separation, persecution, and sexual abuse," as Carla puts it, is a double-bind cinched even tighter. "They cannot reconcile the feelings of having been saved from death by their saviors, and concomitantly, abused by them while in their care."

While the extent of the problem will never be known, the largest study conducted to date on the sexual abuse of hidden children contains even more disturbing news. In-depth, voluntary interviews with twenty-two sexually abused former hidden children, fourteen men and eight women, found that 60 percent were abused by their hiding parents or other Christians who knew their identity, 12 percent were abused by their foster siblings, and 28 percent had been abused by their *biological* parents or another male Jew. While a Jewish parent might be disturbed enough under normal circumstances to sexually abuse his or her own child, the extraordinarily stressful, prolonged, and confined conditions imposed by the Holocaust on hidden Jewish families might well account for most, if not all, of these cases. Perhaps not surprisingly, victims' attitudes toward Jewish perpetrators was more clearly negative than abused children's attitudes toward their non-Jewish abusers. Moreover, 27 percent of all perpetrators were females. Finally, the study found that three-quarters of the victims, despite their later success in life and in raising families, did not think life was worth living.

"Yes, I did well in business," one participant told his interviewer. "I also have a loving wife; without her I could not have survived. . . . But is my life worth living? No. Every morning for as long as I can remember, I hoped that I would not be able to open my eyes. . . . I wanted to be dead. . . . Life is not worth living!"

According to Valent, who has treated three hidden children abused by their non-Jewish foster parents, the abuse was "most likely stimulated by the total availability of a helpless dependent child who was not a blood relative. Maybe the abusers justified it by feeling 'We've put ourselves at risk for you, and you owe us.'" Therapists who remain even slightly uncertain about the reports of their hidden child patients run a huge risk, according to Valent. "Even being open-minded," he has said, "saying I don't know what happened, but I do believe that you believe it happened, is experienced as an invalidation, like someone saying, I don't know if the Holocaust happened, but I do believe you think it did."

If sexual abuse hasn't been part of hidden children's public narratives until recently—long after sexual abuse of children had become a well-publicized and much-reported issue—one reason must be that the abuse was often buried beneath other trauma that resisted consciousness. It had to wait its turn. The 1991 Gathering, Carla writes, "gave survivors of hiding the essential support and permission to come out of hiding and talk more freely to each other. But there were those who only told a part of their story and left out the cruel violation they endured in hiding. Another ten years went by before the community of hidden children openly acknowledged that many children in hiding had been sexually and physically abused."

As child survivors get older, Valent writes, "Past means of coping such as looking to the future and cutting off feelings and memories no longer have survival value, and negate developmental drives to make sense and generate wisdom. Paradoxically and often surprisingly to survivors, memories that return into awareness for processing bring the past closer than it had been for many years."

But whether memories of having been sexually abused were simply repressed until now, whether victims withheld the information until they felt their loved ones would not be so burdened by it, or whether children of survivors were simply afraid to ask, for fear their mothers had been raped, the recall of sexual abuse in hiding brings not only great pain, but acknowledging it can also threaten to undo the trust in others so carefully rebuilt over the years.

One of Valent's patients, "Anne," told him about her hiding father's regular invitations to join him in his bed: "I did not know all this was wrong, because a child has to be told something is wrong to know it is wrong. Obviously I did not respond well, because he always became angry, angrier and more violent each time. I had bruises everywhere. I was blue." "Anne" may not have known it was wrong, but she knew it wasn't right. "And when I mentioned to the lady of the house something of what was going on," she told Valent, "she called me a liar, opened the wall oven and said she would throw me in there if I lied again."

She was eight.

KEEPERS OF THE FLAME

Sophie is back in the city now, a very active widow in her seventies, living on Manhattan's Upper West Side, not far from where she first landed in New York City. She has two sons and two grandchildren.

Carla and Ed Lessing are both in their eighties, but they have the air and energy of people twenty years younger. They have a son and a daughter and four grandchildren.

Flora also seems younger than her years. Like Carla, she still sees psychotherapy patients, but she has started a second career as "a perfectly imperfect photographer" who uses reflections in her photos to express her double life. In the spring of 2013, she had her first exhibit at the Cornelia Street Café in Greenwich Village and another one in the Catskills in 2014. For more than thirty years, she has lived with her Japanese companion in a building less than half a mile from Flora's first apartment in 1959. Flora and Sophie continue to be close.

The hidden children survivors are all senior citizens now, many with children and grandchildren. For many of the children of hidden child survivors—"2Gs" they call themselves, for "second generation"—the Holocaust burns brightly. In October 2012, at the annual conference of the World Federation of Holocaust Child Survivors and Their Descendants, fifty children of these hidden child survivors gathered in a meeting room of the Cleveland Renaissance Hotel. More and more come to these conferences, both to honor their parents and to find comfort for the pain that their parents' experiences have inflicted on them. While a few 2Gs in the group were reticent, many had a hard time containing themselves. Bursting with the need to testify about their parents' suffering, they rattled off towns, dates, relatives, and losses until the recitation of atrocities became numbing.

After an hour and a half of "introductions," the leader had to cut off a few of the well-rehearsed accounts. The group had already heard about the mother who was on the first train to Auschwitz and survived four camps while her entire family perished. The mother whose immediate family was all killed before a priest hid her. The mother who thought she'd lost all seven brothers and sisters, only to find one of those brothers many years later. The woman pulled alive from a mass grave by a Russian soldier who later became her uncle. The parent who was the only survivor of the Katyn massacre. The parents who were married before the war, then separated at Auschwitz, and reunited after.

It's in rooms like this, not in books, that the human toll of history is most intimately felt. The present never seemed so tightly and hauntingly bound to the collective past than when it was the turn for the son and daughter of a Dutch survivor to speak. Their mother, they said, had been at the birthday party in Amsterdam for a girl named Anne Frank, where her father gave her a present: a diary with a red-and-white plaid cover.

Through the 2Gs, and increasingly the 3Gs—"the designated candles," some call them—the ugly history simmers. Through the survivors' books, the particulars are recorded for posterity. Elsewhere in the hotel, a long table offers a sampling of melancholy titles: *While Other Children Played, Against All Odds, Denied Entry, How We Sur-*

vived, *Chased by Demons*, *Forgotten Voices of the Holocaust*, *Amidst the Shadows of Trees*, *Bitter Freedom*, *No Time to Mourn*, *I Have My Mother's Eyes*. Open any one of them and you're in a secret passageway that leads to the malevolence that not even a survivor's own words can adequately express.

Over two hundred hidden child survivors came to Cleveland, many with their spouses, children, friends, even grandchildren. A few came from as far away as England, Holland, Poland, Israel, and Peru. The World Federation, which had its origins in the late 1980s as a small gathering of hidden children at a motel in Lancaster, Pennsylvania, has been meeting for twenty-four years in various cities around the world. This time the weather, unfortunately, was as depressing as the stories shared at the conference. Hurricane Sandy was just two days from landfall and on this cold, gray, windswept October weekend, the city had a decidedly forgotten look, its stores mostly dark, its wide avenues virtually devoid of people, its many parking lots only dotted with cars. Inside the huge hotel, the attendees schmoozed, easily identifiable by the red pouches hanging around their necks that contained their meal tickets.

These survivors are members of an exclusive club with a dwindling membership that no one ever wanted to be part of. They shy away from the publicity that attended the 1991 Gathering. Journalists must carefully plead their case. Under no circumstances are outsiders permitted to observe the intimate workshops, such as "Abused as Children," "Intermarriage within Our Families," and "Have We Developed Strengths in the Process of Overcoming Our Pasts?"

The term "family reunion" describes the form, but who can describe the content? Child survivors are like victims of a rare, incurable, ambulatory disease with no visible symptoms. They take their stories for granted, but how can an outsider understand what they themselves cannot convey, except to those few others who walked through the fires of the Holocaust and were not incinerated? As

Sophie told her cousin years ago, "I don't think anybody who doesn't go through it can really understand at all and no amount of words or films or description will ever tell them." In Cleveland, one hidden child survivor—now an older man in an expensive suit and tie—buttonholed an outsider by the hotel's bank of elevators and suddenly said, "How can you describe the hunger? To live with hunger day after day? You can say we were hungry for years, but that"—he tapped his own chest with bunched fingers—"cannot tell you what it was like."

In fact, many of the stories told, and retold, are almost too uncanny to be believed. One old German-born Jew, like Ed Lessing a member of the Dutch Resistance as a teenager, told of being recruited after the war as an interpreter by the victorious British and personally placing Albert Speer under house arrest. He had to restrain himself from shooting the architect then and there. In America, he became an actor. His first role? Playing a Nazi in *Stalag 17* on Broadway.

Then there is the woman who owes her life to circumstances so horribly ironic that not even a demonic O. Henry could have imagined them. While hiding in a bunker with her terrified family, a sympathetic Gentile informed them that the Nazis knew of the bunker and that, to save their lives, they should all escape to another bunker nearby. The Jews who were crowded into the second bunker rejected them, and they had no choice but to return to their own and await their deaths at the hands of the Nazis. There they received a second visit from their Gentile friend, who informed them that he had been mistaken: the Nazis had discovered the *other* bunker, whose eleven inhabitants had by now been slaughtered.

It is not a stretch to say that gatherings like the conference in the Renaissance Hotel have helped saved the lives of the remnants of this generation's doomed cohort. Ed Lessing, attending with Carla as well as one of his brothers, Fred, a Detroit psychotherapist, can hardly believe that, before 1991, he lived without the comfort of his child survivor "family." "It's like oxygen," he said. He and Carla have attended almost every conference in America since 1991. "I so look forward to meeting old friends," Ed said in Cleveland, "the ones who always know what we all went through and can never forget. Life demands so much attention to daily issues, but the Holocaust candle is always there, although it burns at a low, wavering flame."

During an interview for this book, Ed, the primary designated candle in his family, happened to mention that his other younger brother was rather militantly opposed to dwelling on the Holocaust, during which he was hidden by different families. I was astonished when Ed told me that Arthur, or Abba, as he is known, had lived in my hometown of Highland Park, Illinois, for the past twenty-five years.

How improbable that this book had beaten a path back to my childhood neighborhood, that Highland Park should be "hiding" one of my subject's brothers. I arranged to interview Abba on a visit to my hometown in the summer of 2012. My parents had now been gone for two years and the house had been sold, fortunately to a couple who had no desire to raze it to build something bigger. They hadn't moved in yet, and when I pulled my rental car into the empty driveway, where I once spent uncountable hours pitching tennis balls against the garage door, I didn't suffer the anticipated surge of sentiment. I could almost feel my brain fending off the nostalgia.

I wondered if it was because Highland Park, the precious bubble that enclosed my childhood and where my parents remained for more than forty years after my escape from it, will never truly recede into the past for me. I've remained close to several childhood friends who settled in the neighboring suburbs as adults, and every time I visit them, I have the eerie feeling of having time-traveled to the past, especially when our conversations focus on ancient athletic exploits or memories of our favorite teachers, or we resume teasing each other about our teenage foibles. I've always treasured these old relationships, but this time, as I thought of the destroyed childhoods of

Sophie, Flora, Carla, and Ed, these friendships struck me as a sweet privilege.

I met half a dozen of these friends for lunch at a local Jewish deli, where I struggled to see us as diners at the other tables must have—just another group of graying suburban guys stuffing corned beef sandwiches into our mouths, not the main characters in a timeless saga we would always be the center of. When I mentioned my interview appointment later that afternoon with Abba Lessing, and explained its significance, it felt like an intrusion, requiring too abrupt a refocusing of everyone's attention. The others barely registered what I said, or the coincidence it entailed. I pursued the subject only long enough to ask if they, like me, were unaware of the Holocaust as children? Yes, they were, they said—and then the conversation settled back comfortably into our personality assessments of old classmates and the problems with the Chicago Cubs' pitching rotation.

After lunch I drove over to Abba Lessing's house, not even half a mile from my childhood home. Abba, the middle of the three Lessing boys, was waiting for me on the porch of the stucco house to which he moved twenty-five years ago from Lake Forest, where he had been a professor of philosophy at the college for half a century. Like his two brothers, Abba is robust for his age, seventy-eight, and the owner of an enviably lush head of hair, crowned with a knit *kipa*.

"My mother walked into our playroom in 1942 and told my little brother and me that we were going to go into hiding, to take off your yellow stars, and that we were going to walk out of the house in ten minutes," he remembered as we sat on his sun-dappled porch, listening to a pulsating chorus of crickets and the tinkling of wind chimes.

While his two brothers have been active in the world of hidden child survivors, giving talks to schoolchildren and interviewing other survivors, Abba has pointedly avoided any public role as a victim of the Holocaust. For many years, Abba didn't have anything to do with Jews either. He took refuge from his childhood experience in philosophy classes at Wesleyan University, his cello (he is an accomplished symphony musician, as his father was), and marriage to a Christian. At Tulane, where he received his Ph.D. in philosophy, he defended Martin Heidegger's unapologetic Nazi affiliation as "unimportant."

Israel's Six-Day War in 1967 shook him out of his indifference. Abba embraced his Judaism, began reading Martin Buber, and realized that being a Jew was something to be proud of. And, while still acknowledging Heidegger as one of the twentieth-century's most important philosophers, he stopped teaching him at Lake Forest College. He and his second wife, who is Jewish and a psychotherapist, joined one Highland Park synagogue (my own childhood temple), then another.

But at every stage of his evolution as a Jew, Abba rejected the mantle of victimization. He went out of his way not to inflict his traumatic experiences on his four children. Of course, had he not survived in hiding, rarely separated from one or both parents— had the Lessing family, indeed, not been the only one of a hundred Jewish families in Delft to survive the war intact—perhaps Abba would not have enjoyed the same resilience. He knows that, had the family tried to go into hiding twenty minutes later, they might have been caught, and he might not be sitting on a porch on a shady street on Chicago's North Shore, referring to other survivors who cannot leave their pasts alone—or behind. His luck has provided him with the luxury of philosophical perspective.

In the last few years, Abba Lessing has found a kind of home in the Highland Park chapter of Chabad, an Orthodox Hasidic movement and the largest Jewish organization in the world. Chabad allows him to have "a private, almost secretive relationship with God, without the interference of any social pressure to belong. No membership dues, no building fund." Even there, though, he's a bit of a misfit; he protests the Orthodox segregation of men and women on separate sides of the synagogue by praying with one foot on either side of the aisle. As for his private relationship with God, he's not even sure he believes in him, citing Jean-Paul Sartre's observation that not only does God not exist, but he couldn't exist. What Abba believes in is paradox, especially his own; "I can't explain," he says, "how I am an existentialist and a Hasidic Jew." It is, in the end, his own version of the hidden survivor's simultaneous embrace of, and escape from, Judaism.

Abba seems generally at home with not being at home. "I am still in exile," he admits. "Neither Israel nor Holland nor the United States is my country."

As the afternoon dimmed, he told the story of a Sears representative who once came to his house to examine a defective mattress Abba had bought. "As soon as the guy stepped into the house, I knew he was a survivor. Something in the eyes, a certain sadness, a certain dead quality about him. Strong accent. 'Where's the mattress?' he said. Upstairs, he sat on the mattress and said, 'This is definitely defective, we have to replace it.' Then I made the stupid mistake of asking him, 'Were you in the war?'

"So he's sitting on my bed, the most private place in the house, and he's telling me this story that is so horrendously awful, terrifying. His wife was shot in front of him, his children were murdered. His parents he never saw again. . . . I couldn't wait for him to get out of my house. Suffering doesn't always bring people together."

Yet—paradoxically—Abba Lessing mentioned that he's been keeping a book next to his bed that fascinates him. It's a painstakingly assembled 1,900-page book of photographs taken in the 1930s and 1940s, of thousands of French Jewish children who all had one thing in common: they would all perish in the Nazi death camps.

A few months later, a high school classmate of mine—one of the cute, social girls from a housing development on the other side of the highway and the best friend of a girl I had dated briefly as a freshman—revealed that, many years before Abba Lessing's arrival, the Holocaust had been in my hometown all along. I had unknowingly been a single degree of separation from catastrophe, after all. Margie Eis found me on Facebook and, having read a mention of my forthcoming book, told me that her parents were survivors. I hadn't spoken to her in more than forty years, and I'm not sure I had said that many words to her in the first place.

It turned out that we had lived one subway stop from each other for the last year and a half, so we met for lunch. Had she ever told anybody back then? "No, I was embarrassed. My parents had German accents. They never talked about what happened." Didn't anyone ask you about them? "No, my friends knew only that they came from Germany." Margie didn't know much more than that herself, but she could sense, as children often do, that there were family secrets. When she was in kindergarten—1954—she was digging in the yard of their house with a large knife she had found in the kitchen—how was she supposed to know it was sterling silver?—when her mother appeared in tears, crying, "No, no, that was my mother's." Margie had never met her mother's mother, or her grandfather. They had sent Margie's mother to Sweden, her brother to Switzerland, before the war. Margie's grandparents and numerous relatives perished, leaving behind, among other things, the sterling silver and memories faded from disuse.

The subject hadn't come up in high school either. The Holocaust—the term was only coming into common use to describe the Final Solution—wouldn't be in the curriculum for many years. Margie never even talked about it with another girl in our class, Marcia Kramer (who grew up around the corner from me), whose mother had known Margie's mother in Germany before she immigrated to America in April 1939, leaving the rest of her immediate family there to perish. The mothers were best friends now, living three miles apart, and the two families spent many holidays together, but without the women's bond, without their very reason for ending up together on Chicago's North Shore, ever being discussed.

But the unarticulated damage found its way into Margie's sleep. Starting in sixth grade, she had the same nightmare a few times a year: men in black were coming to her house to kill her family. In her dream, she'd hide in her parents' closet, then wake up, panicked. The nightmares lasted for six or seven years, through most of high school. I can see her now in her kilt and oversize kilt pin, cardigan, kneesocks and loafers, books pressed against her chest as she passed in a pack of unapproachably pretty girls. If she, who knew nothing of her parents' past, had such dreams, what were her parents dreaming?

Margie's father's journey—about which she would also know nothing until well into adulthood—had been perilous, especially *after* he arrived in America. In 1936, as a twenty-two-year-old in Frankfurt, Maurice Eis could see which way the wind was blowing for the Jews, and how hard, so he bought a ticket for America but was denied a visa. Two years later, on Kristallnacht, he was rounded up with his father and brother and sent to Dachau, not yet then a death camp, but the daily ration was already thin soup and a piece of bread. After five weeks, he was released, apparently thanks to his mother, who had pleaded his case to the Gestapo—"Sir, my son already has a ticket for America!"—and he was given ten days to get out of Germany. He ended up in Shanghai and sent for his entire family.

By 1941 Maurice Eis was in the United States, but hardly out of harm's way. By declaring his intention on arrival to become a U.S. citizen, he became eligible for the draft and enlisted in the army, where he trained as a medic. When Japan bombed Pearl Harbor, his one-year enlistment became permanent. Five months after leaving Shanghai, he was on a troop ship to Scotland in a vintage World War I uniform to fight against the Germans. In four years in Europe, his luck in life held up, and if anyone ever needed it, he did. He landed at Omaha

Beach on D-day, an unarmed medic, and survived. The Battle of the Bulge left him unscathed. Back home, weighed down with medals, he became a traveling salesman for the Western Hosiery Company, built a three-bedroom house in Highland Park, and mainly kept his mouth shut about the past until he was in his eighties.

My Name Is Refugee

As a young woman, Sophie had been a little jealous of her mother, Laura, who had always been a woman who attracted a lot of attention, while Sophie felt very insecure and tongue-tied. Once Sophie was married and had children, she realized that she had built the kind of life that her mother had been denied.

Laura was in her late sixties before she met the right man. She was introduced to Nathan Olbe through friends from Lvov now living in the Bronx. Nathan had brought most of his Polish family to America before the war and, with his wife, had done well in the evening bag and corset business. He was a widower with a second marriage behind him, already in his seventies, but he had a house in Queens, a large extended family, and a big heart. When Sophie and her family lived in Queens, Nathan would make a *babka*—he was very proud of his baking—drive into Manhattan to pick up Laura on the Upper West Side, where she continued to live, and then out to Neponsit, where he and Laura would take Sophie's sons to the beach and give Sophie and David some time to themselves.

Sophie loved Nathan, and loved him for what he gave her mother. Laura began to relax, and Sophie stopped feeling quite so bad that her mother had missed out on a normal life for so many years. By the 1990s, however, when Laura reached her eighties, she was showing signs of diminished cognitive function. Once a bookkeeper, she was frustrated that she could no longer balance her checkbook and had to rely on Nathan and sometimes her younger sister Putzi and brother-in-law Kazik, who came in regularly from Morristown, New Jersey, where they'd moved from Canada in 1975.

As Laura declined, Sophie, who had shied away for so long from dwelling on the past, realized that she was slowly losing her only link to her childhood and the dark history she and her mother shared. On one of her almost daily visits to the nursing home, Sophie implored her mother to tell her about the past.

But Laura had written down as much as she wanted to remember back in the 1970s for her Hunter College class.

"Enough," she said, waving Sophie away.

Please, Sophie pleaded. What was it like? What was I like?

"I can't remember. I can't remember, Mother," she would say. When Laura was moved into a nursing home, she had begun calling Sophie "Mother," which only underlined how completely they had now traded places. Where Laura had once drilled Sophie on the catechism, Sophie now pressed her for information Laura could no longer retrieve, or had no desire to. Still, Sophie tried. But she could see that the past was disappearing forever, like a tarnished heirloom dropped overboard, descending slowly into the depths.

Every weekend she'd collect her mother from the nursing home and bring her to her house. One day Laura sat swaddled in a blanket in her wheelchair in Sophie's backyard in Great Neck. Sophie, sitting next to her, tried one last time.

"Do you think Herr Leming ever suspected?" she asked her.

"No, Mother."

"When we walked out of the ghetto in 1942, did no one stop us and ask us for our papers or where we were going?"

"No, Mother," Laura said. "No more. I don't want to do this anymore."

Laura was crying suddenly. It was heartbreaking. Sophie had never, ever, not once, seen her mother cry.

In 2007 Sophie's husband, David, died after a long battle with Parkinson's disease. He had taught her how to show her love, just as she thought he would. The marriage had lasted thirty-seven years and provided Sophie with a big Jewish family to be part of forever, and David had lived long enough to sing to his two-year-old granddaughter, Emily. Three years later two events exposed yet another layer of the onion that was Sophie's emotional memory. In quick succession, Sophie's daughter-in-law Andrea lost her father, a survivor who had left Austria after Kristallnacht, and at the same time her granddaughter Emily (now the sister of a younger brother, Jack) turned five, the age Sophie had been when her father was murdered and she escaped the ghetto with her mother. If she thought she had mourned all she was ever going to mourn, she was wrong. Out of the blue, Sophie was bombarded by some of the memories she had tried to pry out of her mother. For the first time she was able to see herself at that age, and give flesh and feeling to what had been only skeletal recollections. Watching her five-year-old granddaughter, Sophie was overcome with compassion and grief for Selma Schwarzwald and Zofia Tymejko and their impossible journey. She had a hard emotional time with it, but she felt she was saying good-bye at last to the little girl she had been.

And through it all Refugee, the bear, had survived. It was the one toy, the souvenir of the childhood Sophie did not want to remember, yet it defied all her efforts to discard it. When her other memorabilia went into storage, Refugee stayed behind. Sophie never lost track of it as she moved from apartment to apartment in Manhattan, then to Neponsit, Queens, then to Great Neck, Long Island. Refugee sat on a shelf, then on her dresser, then *in* her dresser drawer, landing finally in a walnut armoire in Great Neck that Sophie had received as a gift from Flora Hogman.

Had she kept it as exhibit A of the past she suppressed and otherwise protected her children from? Or had she held on to it as most of us hold on forever to some emblem of our innocence? Sophie's sons may not have known many details of their mother's past in Poland, but they knew Refugee, the bear that had followed their mother since 1944.

The stripes on the little coat Putzi had made for him had faded from blue to pale gray, almost invisible, and Refugee's plush coat was worn bare in spots, but he and his movable limbs were otherwise in surprisingly good shape. Sophie had once come close to throwing Refugee out in the late 1990s. Her grown sons were helping her do some housecleaning when she came across Refugee in the armoire. She decided it was time to let go of him.

"Absolutely not," Jeffrey said.

"I've had him sixty years," she said. "Enough's enough."

"Leave him alone," Daniel chimed in.

"What am I going to do with him?"

"The same thing you've always done with him," Jeffrey said. "Find a place for him."

"But he looks so down and out." Indeed he did—more than ever. "And some of the plush has worn off."

"Whose hasn't?" Jeffrey said. "He's brought you luck so far, right?"

Of course it wasn't the bear that brought her luck, but her mother. In addition to being smart, resourceful, and beautiful, Laura Schwarzwald Turner had been lucky, and her luck had been Sophie's luck. The mothers were the real heroes, Sophie thought. The more she attended meetings at the U.N.'s Commission on the Status of Women, the more she understood that when conditions were overcome, it was the mothers who overcame them. When the mothers were strong, the daughters were strong too. When the mothers live, the daughters live. When women are educated, the world is a better place. And no one knew this better than Sophie.

Sophie had succeeded in not imposing her childhood on her sons, and the little she'd told them had been burnished into anecdotes about close calls and burned gooses, the stuff of any family's folklore. But they knew a little, and the bear, she realized, would remind them that she was there, and that she survived it, and that was why they were here, and the grandchildren too. When they would hold Refugee in the future, they would be holding what their mother held as *her* mother had led her slowly out of hell.

But the new United States Holocaust Memorial Museum had other plans for the bear. The museum was in the process of collecting more than 16,000 objects from survivors of the Holocaust, and in 2002 Sophie donated her crucifix, her catechism, some childhood drawings, and Refugee to the museum.

Then, in 2006, space shuttle *Discovery*'s commander Mark Polansky, who is half-Jewish, chose a Refugee replica as one of two objects he carried with him on his December 22 mission. Refugee traveled 5,330,398 miles on the almost thirteen-day journey. Facsimiles of Refugee soon became one of the better-selling items in the museum's gift store, a favorite purchase for the parents of little girls from Wyoming or Delaware or Alabama. The copies are eight inches tall, not three, and the replica's off-white coat doesn't bear even the faint marks of the Putzi blouse's blue stripes. Nor is the bear a Steiff, but an inexpensive, mass-produced version with longer, softer hair. But the eyes— the eyes are uneven, just like Refugee's.

Fastened to each bear's paw is a folded tag that reads "My Name Is Refugee" on the outside, and on the inside reads:

I got my name from another bear owned by a Jewish girl named

Selma. As a child in Poland, Selma lived during the Holocaust. Her father died during World War II. Selma and her mother had to hide from people who wanted to harm them. She even had to change her name.

It's not a lot to go on, but there is only so much a child of five or six or seven can understand.

BIBLIOGRAPHY

I am indebted to many books, memoirs, articles, movies, and documentaries for enriching my understanding of the Holocaust. The following list contains some of the most helpful and memorable sources and background materials.

Appleman-Jurman, Alicia. *Alicia: My Story*. New York: Bantam Books, 1988.

Arendt, Hannah. *Eichmann in Jerusalem: A Report on the Banality of Evil*. New York: Viking Press, 1963.

Borowski, Tadeusz. *This Way for the Gas, Ladies and Gentlemen*. New York: Viking Penguin, 1967.

Breznitz, Shlomo. *Memory Fields: The Legacy of a Wartime Childhood in Czechoslovakia*. New York: Alfred A. Knopf, 1993.

Browning, Christopher R. *Ordinary Men: Reserve Battalion 101 and the Final Solution in Poland*. New York: HarperCollins, 1992.

Cahill, Thomas. *The Gift of the Jews: How a Tribe of Desert Nomads Changed the Way Everyone Thinks and Feels*. New York: Nan A. Talese/Anchor Books, 1999.

Carroll, James. "Shoah in the News: Patterns and Meanings of News Coverage of the Holocaust." Cambridge, Mass.: Joan Shorenstein Center on the Press, Politics and Public Policy, John F. Kennedy School of Government, Harvard University, 1997.

Cohen, Roger. "For a Priest and for Poland, a Tangled Identity." *New York Times*, October 10, 1999.

Coleman, Fred. *The Marcel Network: How One French Couple Saved 527 Children from the Holocaust*. Washington, D.C.: Potomac Books, 2013.

Friedländer, Saul. *When Memory Comes*. New York: Farrar, Straus and Giroux, 1979.

Gruener, Ruth. *Destined to Live: A True Story of a Child in the Holocaust*. New York: Scholastic, 2007.

Gutenbaum, Jakub, and Agnieszka Latala, eds. *The Last Witness: Children of the Holocaust Speak*, vol. 2. Translated from the Polish by Julian Bussgang, Fay Bussgang, and Simon Cygielski. Evanston, Ill.: Northwestern University Press, 2005.

Hallie, Philip. *Lest Innocent Blood Be Shed*. New York: Harper and Row, 1979.

The Hidden Child. Various issues of a newsletter published by Hidden Child Foundation/ADL, New York.

Hogman, Flora. "Adaptive Mechanisms of Displaced Jewish Children During World War II and Their Later Adult Adjustment." A paper presented at the Second International Conference on Psychological Stress and Adjustment in Time of War and Peace, Jerusalem, 1977.

———. "Displaced Jewish Children During World War II: How They Coped." *Journal of Humanistic Psychology* 23 (1983).

———. "Role of Memories in Lives of World War II Orphans." *Journal of the American Academy of Child Psychiatry* 24 (1985).

———. "The Press and the Hidden Children of the Holocaust—Reflections on Resilience." New York State Psychological Association, 1991.

———. "The South of France—Summer of 1988." *Jewish Currents*, a publication of Congregation Emunath Israel (April 1994).

———. "Memory of the Holocaust." In *Echoes of the Holocaust*. N.p., Israel: 1995.

———. "The Double Edged Sword of Memory: Issues and Conflicts Faced by Survivors Remembering Their Holocaust Experiences." *Hidden Child Foundation/ADL Newsletter* (2007).

Holocaust Chronicle: A History in Words and Pictures. Lincolnwood, Ill.: Legacy Publishing, 2009.

Kaufman, Lola Rein, and Lois Metzger. *The Hidden Girl: A True Story of the Holocaust*. New York: Scholastic, 2008.

Kestenberg, Judith S., M.D., and Ira Brenner, M.D. *The Last Witness: The Child Survivor of the Holocaust*. Washington and London: American Psychiatric Press, 1996.

Klukowski, Zygmunt. *Diary from the Years of Occupation*. Urbana and Chicago: University of Illinois Press, 1993.

Konner, Melvin. *Unsettled: An Anthropology of the Jews*. New York: Viking Compass, 2003.

Lanzmann, Claude. *Shoah: An Oral History of the Holocaust*. New York: Pantheon, 1985.

Lessing, Carla. "The Vanished Communal Heritage of Holocaust Survivors: Its Impact on Survivors and Their Children." *Journal of Jewish Communal Service* (1999).

———. "Aging Child Holocaust Survivors of Sexual Abuse." In *Kavod: Honoring Aging Survivors*, an online publication of the Claims Conference, 2012.

Lev-Wiesel, Rachel, and Marianne Amir. "Posttraumatic Stress Disorder Symptoms, Psychological Distress, Personal Resources and Quality of Life in Four Groups of Holocaust Child Survivors." *Family Process* 39 (2000).

———. "Holocaust Child Survivors and Child Sexual Abuse." *Journal of Child Sexual Abuse* 14 (2) (2005).

Lipstadt, Deborah E. *Beyond Belief: The American Press and the Coming of the Holocaust 1933–1945*. New York: The Free Press, 1986.

Marks, Jane. *The Hidden Children: The Secret Survivors of the Holocaust*. New York: Fawcett Columbine, 1993.

Millen, Rochelle L., ed. *New Perspectives on the Holocaust*. New York: New York University Press, 1996.

Mogilanski, Roman. *The Ghetto Anthology*. Los Angeles: American Congress of Jews from Poland and Survivors of Concentration Camps, 1985.

Moskowitz, Sarah, and Robert Krell. "Child Survivors of the Holocaust: Psychological Adaptations to Survival." *Israeli Journal of Psychiatry and Related Sciences* 27 (1990): 81–91.

Muller-Paisner, Vera. *Broken Chain: Catholics Uncover the Holocaust's Hidden Legacy and Discover Their Jewish Roots*. Charlottesville, Va.: Pitchstone Publisher, 1995.

Prose, Francine. *Anne Frank: The Book, the Life, the Afterlife*. New York: HarperCollins, 2009.

Rosenbaum, Ron. *Explaining Hitler*. New York: Random House, 1998.

Rosenberg, Maxine B. *Hiding to Survive: Stories of Jewish Children Rescued from the Holocaust*. New York: Clarion Books, 1994.

Sherman, Judith. *Say the Name: A Survivor's Tale in Prose and Poetry*. Albuquerque: University of New Mexico Press, 2005.

Sliwowska, Wiktoria, ed. *The Last Witness: Children of the Holocaust Speak*, vol. 1. Translated from the Polish and annotated by Julian and Fay Bussgang. Evanston, Ill.: Northwestern University Press, 1993.

Spiegelman, Art. *Maus I: A Survivor's Tale: My Father Bleeds History*. New York: Pantheon, 1986.

———. *Maus II: A Survivor's Tale: And Here My Troubles Began*. New York: Pantheon, 1992.

Traverso, Enzo. *The Origins of Nazi Violence*. New York: The New Press, 2003.

Valent, Paul. "Early Abuse and Its Effects: Anne, a Holocaust and Sexual Abuse Survivor." Presentation at the Victorian Association of Psychotherapists Annual General Meeting, Melbourne, Australia, 1995.

———. "Resilience in Child Survivors of the Holocaust." *Psychoanalytic Review* (August 1998).

Van Gelder, Fredrik. "Anne Frank Was Not Alone: The Hidden Child Congress in Amsterdam." A paper delivered in 1999.

Wiesel, Elie. *Night*. Translated by Marion Wiesel. New York: Hill & Wang, 1972.

Wolf, Arnold Jacob. *Unfinished Rabbi: Selected Writings*. Chicago: Ivan R. Dee, 1993.

LIST OF DOCUMENTARIES
AND FEATURE FILMS

Documentaries

All My Loved Ones, directed by Matej Minac, 1999.

As If It Were Yesterday, directed by Myriam Abramowicz and Esther Hoffenberg, 1980.

The Flat, directed by Arnon Goldfinger, 2012.

Four Seasons Lodge, directed by Andrew Jacobs, 2008.

Generation War (Our Mothers, Our Fathers in the original German), directed by Philipp Kadelbach, 2013.

Hidden Children, directed by John Walker, 1994.

Hitler's Children, directed by Chanoch Ze'evi, 2011.

Image Before My Eyes, directed by Josh Waletzky, 1981.

Imaginary Witness, directed by Daniel Anker, 2004.

Inheritance, directed by James Moll, 2006.

A Life Apart: Hasidism in America, directed by Menachem Daum and Oren Rudavsky, 1997.

The Nazi Officer's Wife, directed by Liz Garbus, 2003.

Torn, directed by Ronit Krown Kertsner, 2011.

Triumph of the Will, directed by Leni Riefenstahl, 1935.

Features

Defiance, directed by Edward Zwick, 2008.

In Darkness, directed by Agnieszka Holland, 2011.

Inside Hana's Suitcase, directed by Larry Weinstein, 2002.

The Pianist, directed by Roman Polanski, 2002.

Sarah's Key, directed by Gilles Paquet-Brenner, 2010.

Schindler's List, directed by Steven Spielberg, 1993.

A Year of the Quiet Sun, directed by Krzysztof Zanussi, 1984.

ACKNOWLEDGMENTS

My greatest debts of gratitude are to Sophie Turner Zaretsky, Flora Hogman, and Carla and Ed Lessing for letting me explore the world of the Holocaust's youngest survivors through their narratives. Obviously, the existence of this book depended entirely on their courage in entrusting their stories to me, as well as their patience in humoring my ignorance and correcting various drafts of this book. I treasured their cooperation and now I cherish their friendship.

At a fairly early stage in the writing of this book, my wonderful agent, Victoria Skurnick—who combines publishing and literary savvy with a love of diners and a beautiful singing voice—made a suggestion that set this book on a far better course. As if that were not enough, when the time came she found it the perfect home.

Editor David Hirshey of HarperCollins was that home. With a degree of attention, brilliance, and diplomacy that is increasingly associated with a forgotten era of book publishing, David pushed me to revise and rethink a manuscript whose flaws I could no longer see. A few years ago, I edited one of David's books and he much more than returned the favor. He has given fresh meaning to the adage that there's no such thing as writing, only rewriting.

In addition, Susan Squire could not have been more generous with her time, or intelligence, in improving this book. *Merci.*

Many thanks to Teresa Pollin of the United States Holocaust Memorial Museum for her explanations, translations, and scrutiny of my manuscript. I'd also like to thank Myriam Abramowicz, Abba Lessing, Dr. Vera Muller-Paisner, Henry Rozycki, Susan Sanders, Judith Sherman, Dr. Paul Valent, and Daniel and Jeffrey Zaretsky for sharing their stories and insights with me. Alice Herb, thank you for your help, for your interview with your cousin Sophie back in the 1970s, and for finding a place for me at your seder in 2010; and thanks to Gary Hoenig and Betsy Carter for sharing that seder, and so much else.

"Grateful" doesn't begin to describe my feelings about the late Laura Turner, formerly Schwarzwald, née Litwak, without whose unbelievable bravery and resourcefulness in surviving the Second World War this book would not have been possible. Her seventeen-page memoir, which she delivered at college in New York City in the 1970s, helped immeasurably in anchoring the book in reality.

I am indebted to Flora Hogman for her beautifully written essay about her memories of the convent that hid her and her visit there in 1988 (in addition to several other papers of hers); to Carla Lessing for her essay on sexual abuse of hidden child survivors; to Ed Lessing for his essay on the First International Gathering in 1991; and Sarah Rozycki's interview with her grandmother, Putzi Rozycki. Numerous personal accounts in *The Hidden Child*, the Hidden Child Foundation's newsletter, edited by Rachelle Goldstein, as well as interviews conducted by Jane Marks for her book *The Hidden Children*, were very valuable.

Among my friends, no one helped me more with this book than Charles Dawe, who's known me since kindergarten and has been a most thoughtful and generous sounding board and informal editor for many years. My sister Joyce Friedman, who's known me exactly as long, was an extremely helpful early responder and supporter, as were old, dear friends David Bloom and Stephen Molton. To Sydney

Pierce at HarperCollins, thank you for all your excellent curatorial help.

As always, I'm grateful to my late parents, Carolyn and Sol Rosen, for supporting my destiny and for setting so many examples of how to live, the wisdom of which impress me more and more each day.

I wish they were here to read the book that, in so many ways, they inspired.

About the Author

R. D. Rosen has written numerous books, ranging from narrative nonfiction, including *A Buffalo in the House: The Extraordinary Story of Charlie and His Family* and *Psychobabble: Fast Talk and Quick Cure in the Era of Feeling* to mystery novels, including Edgar Award–winning *Strike Three You're Dead*. He has worked as a book editor, television producer, and humorist and satirist on PBS, HBO, and NPR's All Things Considered. For more, visit rdrosen.com.